AMERICAN DEFENSE

AND

NATIONAL SECURITY

American Defense

and

National Security

TIMOTHY W. STANLEY

Foreword by Robert Cutler

*Former Special Assistant to the President of the
United States for National Security Affairs*

Public Affairs Press, Washington, D. C.

TO MY PARENTS
AND TO N. T. AND A. M.

2162 Florida Avenue, Washington 8, D. C.
Printed in the United States of America

Library of Congress Catalog Card No. 56-12472
Copyright, 1956, by Public Affairs Press

FOREWORD

The forthcoming tenth anniversary of the unification of the armed forces highlights the subject matter of Mr. Stanley's book. In effect, he tells the story of the most significant developments in the national security structure during the past ten years.

The National Security Act of 1947 grew out of two convictions forced upon this country's leaders by the events of World War II and the emergence of the United States as the military bulwark of the free world: (1) better integration of foreign, economic and military power was essential if these factors were to have maximum effectiveness; (2) a degree of unification of the Army, Navy, Air Force was a basic requirement of effective national security at acceptable cost. Mr. Stanley's book is especially valuable because it traces the developments leading up to the National Security Act of 1947 and continuing on through its various amendments. It carefully analyzes the policies and operations of the National Security Council and the role of the Department of Defense as the instrument of unification of the services. Since the author presents his material with clarity and discernment his book should furnish the specialist and layman alike with a comprehensive background in this vital area of national affairs.

The interested citizen is daily confronted by events, issues, and personalities involving American defense. One who wishes to keep abreast of our national security policies will need to understand the decision making processes dealt with in this book. He will find food for thought in the compromises and adjustments out of which the present structure has emerged, and will doubtless further evolve.

Additionally, the specialist will find that the comparative material on Britain and the key documents in the Appendices provide a resource not otherwise easily available.

ROBERT CUTLER

INTRODUCTION

As the country approaches the tenth anniversary of the National Security Act of 1947, it is an appropriate time to appraise our defense and national security structure. The purpose of this book is to indicate where we may be going by showing where we have been and where we are at present. In these pages I endeavor to objectively trace the evolutionary pattern and describe the present structure, processes and people—and the inter-relationships between them—as factually and concisely as possible.

Although this book is concerned to a considerable degree with substantive problems, I have not undertaken to add to the many excellent studies on particular topics such as intelligence, the budget, manpower, and strategic doctrine; on these subjects references can be found in the footnotes and bibliography. My former colleagues in the Harvard Defense Studies Program are now engaged in preparing a basic text which will survey the major problem areas in the field of defense and it is hoped that the present book will supplement this and other needed efforts by treating in some detail the framework within which solutions must be sought. I have described this framework in terms of practice rather than as a theory of organization or of civil-military relations in order to avoid introducing purely subjective criteria.

In effect, this book is designed to fill a gap. Most existing literature is frankly partisan, largely historical, highly personalized, or quite technical in its treatment. Although there are a number of good studies on such specific areas as the Presidency or the National Security Council, to my knowledge these are nowhere combined into a single book in which the defense ingredient is adequately described. If it be argued that defense and national security constitute too broad a subject to permit meaningful examination in a relatively short book, I must disagree. As Robert Cutler indicates in his foreword, the lessons of recent years show a need to look at the whole rather than at particular fragments, although the latter certainly need continued investigation. Accordingly I have divided the book into two parts having the same headings as the two major titles of the National Security Act: "Coordination for National Security" and "The Department of Defense." These are closely connected not only in the basic legislation, but also as a matter of practical politics, for the National

Security Council was created as compromise between the Army and Navy views of unification into a single department, rather than as an end in itself.

In summary, it is my hope that this small book will do three things: first, serve as a useful reference for scholars and students with a general interest in this important field; second, provide a convenient summary for civilian and military officials; and third—perhaps most important of all—be a useful guide for the average citizen who wishes to be fully informed about national affairs.

ACKNOWLEDGMENTS

Complete objectivity on unification matters is of course difficult to obtain. I have been fortunate in having available advice from persons with extensive backgrounds in the various services. I have not always acepted this advice for quite often it has been inconsistent. If any bias remains it must be my own and I assume complete responsibility for what the book contains and for any errors of omission or commission. However, since publication deadlines have not permitted as careful a check on secondary materials and citations as I would have desired, I hope that the meticulous reader who finds an error will not therefore condemn the book in its entirety.

Since this book is in a sense a product of the Harvard Defense Studies Program in which parts of it were used as mimeographed readings, I am very much indebted to my colleagues there. First and foremost, many thanks are due to W. Barton Leach, Professor of Law and first Director of the Program. He found time to criticize drafts of this book not once but twice, and his knowledge of personalities and events proved invaluable in interpreting published information. Dr. Edward L. Katzenbach, Jr., Associate Director, has made many incisive suggestions particularly on Part One. Other members of the staff have rendered helpful assistance on particular aspects: Dr. Harry H. Ransom on coverage of the Presidency, John A. Ballard on Reorganization Plan No. 6, and Maury D. Feld on the bibliography. Laurence W. Levine deserves full credit for the valuable comparative description on British defense in Appendix I. I wish to thank Mrs. Ruth Shepard and Mrs. Ann Hernstadt for typing the manuscript under the pressure of deadlines and Mrs. Marian Feld for preparing many of the charts. For helpful editorial suggestions I am indebted to Ephraim Kahn of the Bureau of National Affairs, and for the preparation of the index, to Mrs. Virginia Terris of New York. Robert

W. Berry has given most generously of his time and experience both on matters of substance throughout the book and in correcting the proofs.

Jerome A. Gross of the University of Chicago permitted me to make use of his unpublished case study on the organizational background of international security affairs which proved very helpful in writing Chapter V. I am also indebted to Randal H. Deasy for making available his own studies while he was at Harvard in 1954-1955 on leave from the Australian Ministry of Defense.

Portions of the manuscript were read by the following persons whose advice on practical defense department matters was invaluable: Frank C. Nash, former Assistant Secretary of Defense (International Security Affairs), and Burton B. Moyer, Jr., Raymond Albright, and Richard Cornell all of the Office of the Secretary of Defense. However, I hasten to absolve them of any responsibility for errors.

This book owes a very large debt to General Robert Cutler, not only because his articles and lectures on the National Security Council were a most valuable source material, but also because it is in part due to his work as Special Assistant to the President that there now exists a sturdy national security structure about which to write a book.

Finally, I must acknowledge the contribution of my wife and children who suffered, if not silently, at least with reasonable good humor while this book was in preparation.

TIMOTHY W. STANLEY

Washington, D. C.

TABLE OF CONTENTS

PART ONE

COORDINATION FOR NATIONAL SECURITY

CHAPTER I

POLITICAL-MILITARY RELATIONS

Contrary to the views of some theorists and to the practice of a few states, power is not generally sought for its own sake. On the international scene, power is a relative concept—sought as a means to attain both general and specific national objectives. In a successful national policy some kind of a balance between means and ends must be maintained. Generally it is the function of foreign policy to define the ends toward which power is to be directed and to consider means before international commitments are made. When it fails to do so or when the military establishment fails to provide and properly use the means, national security suffers. Thus national security results from the equilibrium of means and ends. The inter-relationship between political and military factors and between foreign and defense policies has therefore become almost inextricable. Although military strength is perhaps the most basic element in the power equation, there are others, such as skillful diplomacy, to be considered.

One of the criticisms of American policy during World War II is that "it was preoccupied with gaining quick and complete military victory and thus gave less consideration than was wise to political problems and objectives of longer range."[1] But it has also been said by some military leaders during the Korean war that "political considerations were permitted to overrule military necessities."[2]

Confusion between political and military factors has existed in every period in history and on a variety of subjects, ranging from blockade and embargo to armistice and truce negotiations. Winston Churchill's six volumes on World War II provide numerous examples of the politico-military nature of most major wartime decisions. Often cited are Churchill's penchant for the allegedly "soft underbelly" and his view that even troop movements in Germany had "acquired a political significance that demanded the intervention of political leaders."[3] "Political" is, of course, a word with many different meanings and connotations. It may pertain to partisan politics or to elected representatives; it can apply merely to non-military matters, or it can be used to distinguish professional from non-career personnel. More often than not, it is a catch-all characterization, as when the Supreme

3

Court tells us that "political questions" are not justiciable. Although it must remain such a catch-all word for the purposes of this book, it is worthwhile to suggest that a clear-cut and universal definition may be an illusory goal.

The Korean war is a useful laboratory for examining politico-military problems. It was a very real war waged in at least one sense for purely military objectives. Yet there were a number of built-in limitations. The United States was not technically at war with Communist China. Korea was a multilateral "police action" waged in the name of the United Nations. It was a limited war in the sense that virtually no one is on record as urging that it be expanded into World War III. The same issues were raised over and over again—the probability that Russia would enter the war if the United Nations attacked enemy bases beyond the Yalu; the possibility that there were leaks to the enemy regarding our intentions toward their "sanctuary"; the denial of permission to use Chinese Nationalist troops; and the considerations that should or should not have been relevant to the truce negotiations. During the hearings which resulted from the recall of General Douglas MacArthur, many more questions were asked on these points than were answered. Senator Bourke K. Hickenlooper had a colloquy with General George C. Marshall on "policy" decisions which generated confusion rather than clarity. The Senator finally concluded: "Well, I understand. Apparently I haven't made myself clear. I am attempting to get clear in my mind what seems to me to be the fact that the failure to use the power we have . . . deep in the enemy's territory . . . must in the last analysis be a political decision, that is it must be in the field of politics."[4] During the Korean war itself a Joint Chiefs of Staff paper is reported to have observed that "from a purely military standpoint," the 38th Parallel is of "purely political significance."

More recently, the Senate Internal Security Subcommittee headed by Senator William E. Jenner attempted to get further answers. The hearings, labelled "Interlocking Subversion in Government Departments," attempted unsuccessfully to put the finger on the "mysterious 'they'" who may have "subverted" American policies. Although the only testimony was that of five military commanders in the Korean war—Generals Mark W. Clark, James A. Van Fleet, and Edward M. Almond (Army); General George E. Stratemeyer (Air Force), and Admiral Charles Turner Joy (Navy)—Senator Hendrickson informed General Almond that the subcommittee was "not concerned with either foreign policy or military policy per se" but rather "with the national security of this great country of ours."[5] Senator

Jenner subsequently declared: "If our military are not permitted to develop a defense or to fight a war . . . but their strategy is diluted by political considerations of the State Department, what chance . . . do we have to defend this country . . .?"[6] It was in the same vein that Senator Olin D. Johnston summed up General Van Fleet's testimony as evidence that "this was a war fought by the military but guided by the State Department."[7] Finally, Admiral Joy expressed the view that "An armistice agreement is simply an agreement between two opposing commanders to stop the fighting. It is not concerned, nor should it be, with political questions."[8]

In the recommendations concluding its report the Subcommittee stated "that the proper sphere for political decisions in the conduct of war should be outlined and the area of military operations to be conducted by professionals should be defined," and urged "that methods should be explored to eliminate political interference in the conduct of hostilities and the negotiation of a military armistice."[9] Interestingly enough, the National Security Council was nowhere even mentioned in the report, although that body is charged by statute with advising the President "with respect to the integration of domestic, foreign and military policies relating to the national security." Nor is there any suggestion of how, by whom, and on what criteria the "proper sphere" should be defined. Indeed, the subcommittee seemed to imply that the mysterious "they" was to be found somewhere between its two favorite whipping boys—the State Department and the United Nations—and that this "they" was responsible for the intrusion of political factors. The answer may lie in the fact that there was no intrusion at all but merely a situation in which both military and political factors were inherent. Or, in General MacArthur's words, that there were certain "vital decisions . . . yet to be made, decisions far beyond the authority vested in me as the military commander, which are neither solely political nor solely military . . ."[10]

One need not look far to find any number of other examples of joint political-military ventures. Establishment of the North Atlantic Treaty Organization (NATO) became necessary to meet an essentially military threat posed by the Soviet Union. Russian capability in turn had been made possible partly because our preoccupation with military victory led us to ignore the political situation which might follow the conclusion of World War II. For example, the Western Allies voluntarily withdrew from the Balkans and failed to advance into Czechoslovakia. NATO still has substantial political, economic, and psychological implications, and the political problems involved in such military decisions as rearming Germany are too well known to require detailed discussion here. Significantly enough, General Dwight D. Eisenhower was chosen as the first Supreme Commander in NATO at least partly because of his proven capacity for political leadership in international alliances. Even a "routine" military matter such as the NATO air maneuvers in June 1955 raised serious "political" obstacles. The German newspaper accounts of this exercise—code-named "Carte Blanche"—stressed that 1.7 million Germans were "killed" and another 3.5 million "wounded" by atomic bombs that were supposedly dropped. These press reports cast some doubt on the validity of NATO's atomic strategy at the very time the bill to recruit a new German army was before the Bundestag and almost certainly did no good to the cause of defending Western Europe.[11]

The end of a war offers an even more treacherous mixing ground for military and political ingredients. Confusion has occurred not only in armistice negotiations, as during the Korean war, but also in military government. Problems in civil-military relations during planning for the occupation of Germany led indirectly to the creation of a predecessor body to the National Security Council. In Japan the situation was somewhat better because General MacArthur was given an unequivocal position as Supreme Commander. The General answered with a firm "I did" to the statement: "So that you operated not only as a military commander in military operations but you operated in a political capacity?"[12]

The inevitable conclusion is that the terms military policy, foreign policy, and economic policy are no longer self-defining—if indeed they ever were. They are part of an interdependent complex which, for want of a better phrase, may be called "national security policy." Although these terms were once thought to represent separable elements, they never were—any more than the atmosphere was ever anything different from what it is now. Just as the ancients thought that air was ether or oxygen, so until recently Americans have tended to think of national security in terms of geographical isolation in time of peace and unconditional surrender during war. Now the quantum jump in technical progress and the magnitude of the current threat have sharpened our awareness that national security, like the air we breathe, is a fragile compound which must be dealt with as such. Many believe that an era of "nuclear stalemate" has arrived—that the atomic destruction which each side is capable of delivering makes a major war unlikely. Even if this is true, it does not follow that the American air-atomic power needed to maintain an effective deterrent can sustain itself without great national effort. Nor does it follow that the Communist bloc has changed or will change its basic objectives. Conflict—whether limited, brushfire, local, or cold war variety —is if anything more likely under these conditions. It follows that the application of military force is a delicate matter with definite limits. Apply too much in the wrong place and we may slip into the major war which neither side desires, but which neither can avoid without giving the other the upper hand. Fail to apply it in the right place at the right time, and creeping gains by the Soviet bloc may turn the tide against us. A premium is thus placed on correct judgments of place, time, and degree and on balancing military and non-military techniques. Included in the latter are foreign economic aid and technical assistance, informational and intelligence activities, economic defense measures (the strategic embargo), foreign trade and investment, and last, but by no means least, the traditional role of diplomacy: negotiation, interpretation and persuasion—with particular reference to alliances and to the challenge of disarmament.

But it is not only foreign relations which have become vital. Fiscal, agricultural, economic, and even social and educational policies—all once thought to be exclusively domestic—now have a distinct impact on national security. Clearly, the free world cannot sacrifice its democratic ideals for a garrison state; national security policies which produced this as a by-product would be self-defeating. In short, the inescapable fact is that the prospect of "nuclear stalemate" demands *integrated national security policies*. The parts need to be cut to fit the pattern of *total* national policy; too often in the past the pattern has been loosely shaped from separately formed pieces. The organization for national security which makes and carries out these policies may very well be the key to survival. That organization must include to some extent Congress and the public. But the judgments of place, time and degree require so much specialized knowledge that the initial formulation of policy and its implementation must be the responsibility of the executive branch. Thus when the word organization is used in this book, it refers only to that of the executive arm.

The failure of organization will in all probability mean that policies will fail; this in turn may well mean defeat for the West. In other words, the "vital decisions . . . neither solely political nor solely military" which, as General MacArthur stated, were *not* made during the Korean war, *must* be made. Success in this connection means not only avoiding failure, but also moving forward into an era where national security need not be the primary concern of government.

WORLD WAR II EXPERIENCE

Development of the supra-departmental structure for coordination of policy in Washington is recent history. Before U.S. participation in World War I, a Joint State and Navy Neutrality Board dealt with the difficult questions of international law and neutrality brought about by embargo, blockade, and enemy submarine activities. But the basic politico-military issue of war or peace was never effectively considered by this body. During the war itself, a Council of National Defense was created to handle mobilization planning, especially its impact on civilian economy. Although the Council is still on the statute books, it ceased operations at the end of the war and, except for a short period at the beginning of World War II, has remained inactive.

In 1919 Franklin D. Roosevelt, as Assistant Secretary of the Navy, proposed a joint civilian-military planning organization. But nothing came of the suggestion which was apparently never even considered by the Secretary of State.[13] Two years later, the Navy—this time with the Army—tried again. When they proposed State Department representation on the Joint Board of the Army and Navy,[14] Secretary of State Charles Evans Hughes replied: "The only officials of the State Department who can speak for it with authority on matters of national policy are the Secretary and Undersecretary of State, and it is impossible, in the existing circumstances, for either of them to undertake this additional responsibility." Mr. Hughes would have been somewhat shocked by the number of such "additional" duties his present day counterpart must perform. Subsequent relations between the military and the State Department were not improved by the lightness with which Hughes treated the military viewpoint during the 1922 Washington Conference on the Limitation of Naval Armament. However, by the time Secretary of State Cordell Hull was called to attend the 1935 London Naval Conference, Navy opinions were given more consideration.

But there was little top level contact, other than on a purely *ad hoc* basis, between military and political planners from 1919 to 1939. This is not surprising, for the decade of the 1930s was the era in which wars were supposed to be caused by the "merchants of death" —the munitions makers and shipbuilders. Congress investigated not the adequacy of national defense but the munitions industry; it held hearings on such matters as neutrality, peace and foreign intervention.[15] The military and the State Department went completely separate ways; even a Standing Liaison Committee of the Undersecretary of State and the two military chiefs failed to reach a joint appreciation

of national security needs.[16]   But, as George Kennan points out,[17] the
State Department during this period devoted much of its energies to
developing arbitration agreements and other legal devices, all predi-
cated upon an international harmony of interests which did not exist.

As World War II approached, an informal war council was organized as an *ad hoc* Cabinet committee of the Secretaries of War, Navy,
and State.   But it had no secretariat, agenda, or machinery for lower
level coordination.   After Pearl Harbor, Secretary of War Henry L.
Stimson often regretted that we did not have a War Cabinet similar
to Churchill's.[18]   American separation of powers had hindered the
development of such an organization in peacetime, and when war came
the Commander-in-Chief relied more on improvisation and personal
advisers than on institutions.   The German invasion of Poland did,
however, convince President Roosevelt of the need to establish the
Executive Office of the President as an administrative staff agency
as had been proposed previously by a committee headed by Louis
Brownlow.   However, the relationship between means and ends, between military victory and postwar political objectives, was not
clearly seen, nor were the consequences of inadequate civil-military
relations yet apparent.   The prevalent theory was that policy could
and should be separated from administration and the organization
for policy formulation was thought to be relatively unimportant.

The executive branch under FDR was totally unprepared to make
postwar plans and objectives, especially in regard to Germany.
Roosevelt had enunciated the "unconditional surrender" doctrine at
the Casablanca Conference without consulting the military and psychological warfare advisers most directly concerned.[19]   The Morgen-
thau Plan for a pastoral Germany, for a brief time official United
States policy, was formulated at the Quebec Conference without either
the Secretary of War or the Secretary of State being present.[20]   Even
when finally disavowed by the President, its influence, exercised
mainly through the Treasury, was strong enough to reverse all the
planning that had been done in Washington and in overseas military
government headquarters.[21]   When authority for a full study was
assigned, it was given to the Foreign Economic Administration rather
than to either the State or War Departments.[22]   On the international
level, various federal agencies often opposed each other in such groups
as the Combined Chiefs of Staff and the European Advisory Commission.   A working security committee set up to advise the U.S. member
of the latter body did not even attempt to coordinate military and
civilian views on such an important matter as the occupation zones
of Germany and access to Berlin.[23]

As to American occupation of Germany, General Lucius D. Clay reports that upon his appointment as Eisenhower's Deputy for Military Government no one advised him of the role of the State Department in military government and that he had not talked to anyone in that agency.[24] In effect, American military government responsibilities in Germany were split between the Office of Military Government in Berlin and the civil affairs officers at Frankfurt. Although the command channel was through the War Department, the advice received through it sometimes differed from that received via the political adviser directly from State. This complicated the already confused relationship of military government to the military commanders.

In attempting to clarify the situation the State Department succeeded only in disguising the very real problems of practical application: "The formulation of United States policy toward Germany has been assigned primarily to the Department of State. But because of the military character of the occupation and the security issues . . . the Joint Chiefs of Staff have shared largely in policy making . . . inter-departmental committees have advised . . . the War Department, as the agency charged with immediate responsibility for the occupation and control of Germany has exerted considerable influence in shaping policy in Washington and in its application in the field." [25]

According to General Mark Clark, a similar confusion confounded the occupation of Austria. Some of the points raised in his book *From the Danube to the Yalu*[26]—especially as to the Soviet Union being granted certain rights on the Danube—were considered by the Senate Judiciary Subcommittee in 1954. After considering State Department documents pertaining to the agreement on Austrian zones of occupation and to the Americans who had worked at the Council of Foreign Ministers and European Advisory Commission in London, the subcommittee concluded that at the very least there were serious difficulties in coordinating political and military views.[27]

In fact, throughout 1943 and 1944 the State Department was in constant need of military advice. Although there were various *ad hoc* committees in existence from time to time, it was not until December 1944 that a standing inter-departmental body known as the State-War-Navy Coordinating Committee (SWNCC) was formed.[28] This Committee soon evolved into a device for exchanging political and military advice, but it operated at too low a level to be much more than a clearing house for information. However, SWNCC, together with an Informal Policy Committee on Germany, under the direction

of State, did participate in the drafting of the occupation directives
for Germany, Austria, and Japan. But it was not until after the end
of the war, in October 1945, that SWNCC was designated by the
Secretaries of State, War and Navy as "the agency to reconcile and
coordinate action to be taken by . . . the departments on matters of
common interest . . . and establish policies on politico-military questions . . . Action taken by SWNCC is construed as action taken in
the names of the three Secretaries, and decisions of the committee
establish the approved policy of the three departments . . ." [29] It is
perhaps to be regretted that such authority was not granted while
the acute problems of 1944-1945 were being decided.

After the 1947 "unification" of the military services, SWNCC be-
came the State, Army, Navy, Air Force Coordinating Committee
(SANACC) and—despite the establishment of the National Security
Council—continued functioning until it was abolished in 1949.[30]

Unification of the military services had been a controversial subject
for many years. Altogether some 55 bills or resolutions on the topic
had been introduced into Congress, and more than a dozen studies of
the problem were made between 1924 and 1945. After World War II
the failures of inter-service coordination at Pearl Harbor and the
success of a unified command system in the field led to a new group
of proposals for unification. The Army urged a strong, centralized
Department of the Armed Forces with an integrated top command
structure. The Navy felt that if unification was necessary at all, it
should be as loose and flexible as possible. The Air Force generally
sided with the Army and helped to promote its plans.[31]

On May 15, 1945, Senator David I. Walsh, Chairman of the Senate
Naval Affairs Committee, wrote to Secretary of the Navy Forrestal
that the Navy could not take merely a "negative position" but must
propose a "constructive alternative" to the merger envisaged by the
Army. Forrestal accordingly called on a former partner, Ferdinand
Eberstadt, to make a thorough study of the subject. The work done
by Eberstadt with the help of a staff of Navy officers resulted in a
report submitted to Forrestal on September 25.[32] One volume was
composed of recommendations; the other two of detailed staff studies.
Besides being mindful of the Navy's desire for coordination among,
rather than integration of, the services, the Eberstadt report drew on
British experience with the Committee of Imperial Defense (now the
Defense Committee) under Lord Hankey. Also discussed were some
of the shortcomings of politico-military coordination in the United
States, especially experience with the State-War-Navy Coordinating
Committee.

The basic plan of the Eberstadt report called for three separate and equal military departments tied together at the top through interlocking boards and committees. Among these were to be Joint Chiefs of Staff, a Munitions Board, and a Research and Development Agency operating within a loose federation of the military establishment. The major supra-departmental features were a National Security Council (NSC), a Central Intelligence Agency (CIA), and a National Security Resources Board (NSRB).

Hearings on various unification bills, from October 1945 until the spring of 1947, were often marked by acrimonious exchanges. The services had reached a substantial measure of agreement by 1946, but they were still sharply divided on such questions as the existence and authority of the Secretary of Defense and the organization and control of air power. Finally, in the spring of 1946, President Truman took the initiative in urging agreement on a single plan of organization. In January, 1947, after further hearings and negotiations, the President transmitted to Congress a compromise proposal.

Although there was considerable testimony and controversy on the authority of the Secretary of Defense and the status of the Air Force, Naval Air Arm, and the Marines, the proposals dealing with the National Security Council and the top-level coordination machinery urged by Eberstadt were accepted with little discussion. However, further compromise and adjustment were necessary because of differences in the House and Senate legislative measures. The final version was passed by the Senate on July 24, 1947, and signed by the President two days later as the National Security Act of 1947.[8] For the first time in its history, the United States had the nucleus of an adequate organization to coordinate the various elements of national security.

---

[1] Burton M. Sapin and Richard M. Snyder, *The Role of the Military in American Foreign Policy*, Doubleday Short Studies, New York, 1954, p. 9.

[2] *The Korean War and Related Matters*, Report of the Internal Security Subcommittee of the Senate Judiciary Committee, 84th Congress, 1st Session, Washington, 1955, p. 24.

[3] See Dwight D. Eisenhower, *Crusade in Europe*, Doubleday, New York, 1948, p. 399.

[4] *Military Situation in the Far East*, Hearings before the Senate Armed Services and Foreign Relations Committees, 82nd Congress, 1st Session, 1951, Part 1, pp. 502-3.

[5] *Interlocking Subversion in Government Departments*, Hearings before the Internal Security Subcommittee of the Senate Judiciary Committee, 83rd Congress, 2nd Session, 1954, Part 25, p. 2048.   [6] *Ibid.*, Part 21, p. 1704. *Report*, p. 7.

[7] *Ibid.*, Part 24, p. 2029.   [8] *Ibid.*, Part 26, p. 2143.

[10] *Military Situation in the Far East*, pp. 511-12.   [9] *Report, op. cit. supra*, p. 25.

[11] For a well documented account of the effects of Carte Blanche see Gordon Craig,

NATO and the New German Army, Center of International Studies, Princeton University, 1955, pp. 25-29.   [12] *Military Situation in the Far East,* p. 54.

[13] Indeed, according to one historian, the organizational blueprint attached to the plan had apparently never been unstapled until he opened it in the State Department Archives. See Ernest R. May, "The Development of Political-Military Consultation in the United States," *Political Science Quarterly,* Vol. LXX, June 1955, p. 167.

[14] For a discussion of the Joint Board see Chapter VI *infra.*

[15] *Cf.* The Senate Special Committee to Investigate the Munitions Industry under Senator Nye established by Sen. Res. 179 and 206, 73d Congress, 2d Session, 1934. The Committee held lengthy hearings which were influential in the passage of the Neutrality Act of 1934. Even as late as 1939, when "Neutrality and Peace Legislation" hearings were held, a majority of witnesses still clung to the theory of arms restrictions as the basis for national security.

[16] See William L. Langer and S. Everett Gleason, *The Challenge to Isolation, 1937-1940,* New York, 1952, pp. 596-7 *passim.*

[17] George F. Kennan: *Realities of American Foreign Policy,* Princeton University Press, 1954, pp. 17-23.

[18] Henry L. Stimson and McGeorge Bundy, *On Active Service in Peace and War,* Harper and Brothers, New York, 1947, p. 262. The Chiefs of Staff also met with the three Secretaries, but by the time of the Quebec Conference, the War Council was merely a name for a group of Presidential advisers; the membership and use of the group varied with the whims of FDR. See May, *op. cit.,* pp. 173-174.

[19] See Harry C. Butcher, *My Three Years with Eisenhower,* Simon and Schuster, New York, 1946, p. 518; Robert E. Sherwood, *Roosevelt and Hopkins,* Harper and Brothers, New York, 1948, p. 782; James P. Warburg, *Germany: Bridge or Battleground?,* Harcourt Brace, New York, 1946, p. 262.

[20] Cordell Hull, *Memoirs,* Macmillan, New York, 1948, Volume II, p. 1110; Stimson and Bundy, *op. cit.,* pp. 568-582.

[21] Marshall Knappen, *And Call It Peace,* University of Chicago Press, 1947, p. 43.

[22] James Byrnes, *Speaking Frankly,* Harper and Brothers, New York, 1947, p. 185. U.S. Congress, House Select Committee on Foreign Aid, Subcommittee on Germany, *Report on Germany, Washington,* 1948, Appendix II, p. 31.

[23] Albert L. Warner, "Our Secret Deal Over Germany," *Saturday Evening Post,* August 2, 1952, p. 30.

[24] General Lucius D. Clay, *Decision in Germany,* Doubleday, New York, 1950, p. 6.

[25] U. S. Department of State, *Occupation of Germany, Policy and Progress 1945-1946,* Washington, GPO, 1947 (State Department Publication 2783), p. 13.

[26] Harper and Brothers, New York, 1954.

[27] *Interlocking Subversion in Government Departments,* Part 21, pp. 1658-1689.

[28] *Department of State Bulletin,* Vol. XIII, 1945, No. 333 p. 745.   [29] *Ibid.*

[30] Commission on Organization of the Executive Branch, *Task Force Report on National Security Organization,* 1949, p. 75.

[31] See Chapters VI and VII for a more detailed treatment of the unification proposals.

[32] *Unification of the War and Navy Departments and Postwar Organization for National Security,* Report to the Honorable James Forrestal, Senate Committee on Naval Affairs, Washington, 1945. The correspondence between Walsh, Forrestal, and Eberstadt is printed on pp. iv, v, and vi of the Report. This document is cited hereafter as the Eberstadt Report.

[33] P. L. 253, 80th Congress, 61 Stat. 495, 50 U. S. C. 401, Appendix II *infra.*

CHAPTER II

THE PRESIDENT AND THE EXECUTIVE OFFICE

That the Chief Executive of the United States is the focal point of national security policy was aptly pointed up by President Eisenhower when he was questioned about the controversy resulting from General Matthew B. Ridgway's opposition to reductions in Army manpower. The President said that his operating subordinates and advisers, including the Army Chief of Staff, have a special or "parochial" responsibility for national defense[1] and "their advice is often expressing their own deeply felt, but, let us say, narrow fears."[2]   The President then neatly summed up the responsibility of his office.   "They are entitled to their opinions, but I have to make the decisions."[3]

Some aspects of the Presidency are shrouded in myth, legend, and dark isolation.   Former President Truman has written: "No one who has not had the responsibility can really understand what it is like to be President, not even his closest aides or members of his immediate family.   There is no end to the chain of responsibility that binds him, and he is never allowed to forget he is President."[4]   Yet any student of defense and national security must undertake to understand the American Presidency, for here lies the heart of the nation's decision-making machinery.

No two Presidents are ever alike.   The very nature of the Presidency can change every four years under our system of government.   The powers and policies of the office vary according to the personality and ideology of the White House occupant and are necessarily influenced by the temper of the times.   Moreover, the circumstances of war and peace and of international tensions sharply condition the nature of the Presidency.

Ours is a Constitutional government—a government of limited power.   Although Article II of the Constitution defines the powers and duties of the President, it does so ambiguously.   For the Constitution grants separate but related powers to the President and the Congress.   By interpreting the laws of the land the Supreme Court has assumed a portion of this divided power.

The Constitution gives to the President the "executive Power" of national government; it charges him with the faithful execution of the laws and it bestows upon him the rank of Commander-in-Chief of the nation's military forces. Just what does this mean? What can the President execute but the laws passed by Congress? What armed forces may he command but those raised and supported by the national legislature? What war can he make against an enemy of the United States, except that declared by Congress? There can be only complex answers to these simple questions. Not only the Congress but the Supreme Court add and subtract Presidential powers from time to time. Moreover, the Presidency is in effect an office of unwritten, inherent powers. In today's world the Commander-in-Chiefship is in itself a source of vast potential power.

Since the President is constitutionally obliged to see to it that laws are faithfully executed, does this mean that he may order seizure of the nation's privately-owned steel mills to prevent a work stoppage in the production of goods vital to war needs? President Truman, during the Korean war, believed this to be his power and duty. Three members of the Supreme Court agreed with him, but six others—a decisive majority—said No, not under the circumstances. It has been said that the Constitution is what the Supreme Court says it is. It might also be said that the Presidency is what any given President says it is —at least until Congress or the Supreme Court effectively revises his interpretation.

Any new occupant of the White House, regardless of his views of what the office *should* be, is to a certain extent bound by precedent, tradition, and the organization-in-being—the vast colossus on the Potomac. Thus the development of the Executive Office under President Truman—dictated by the needs of the time, by Congressional action, and by Truman's personality—predetermined at least the outlines of what the Office became under President Eisenhower. Yet Eisenhower has used its machinery—particularly the Cabinet and the National Security Council—in a manner significantly different from that of his predecessor.

The nature, powers, duties, and multiple roles of the President can hardly be summarized in a few pages. Article II of the Constitution establishes the framework for the executive branch and its chief in a little over 1,000 words, but a leading authority on the Presidency, Professor Edward S. Corwin, needs well over 100,000 words to summarize is nature in his book *The President, Office and Powers*.[5] In considering the President and national security policy, it would be a mistake to stress only his role as the nation's chief administrator and as Commander-in-Chief of the military forces. The President must also be Chief of State, Chief of Foreign Policy, Chief Legislator, and Chief of the Political Party to which he belongs. Although his powers as leader of foreign policy are to some extent shared with Congress, few would disagree with John Marshall's statement that the President is the "sole organ of foreign relations." And as top political leader, his election is the major point at which *national,* as distinguished from *local,* issues are presented to the electorate. A chief of department, agency, bureau, or military organization may take a "parochial" view of national necessities; not so the President, for his is the most powerful and important office of government today.

In order that a President may perform his tremendously complicated and sometimes conflicting roles, the Presidency has become highly institutionalized in recent years. Today the Executive Office of the President is a major bureaucracy in its own right, with over 1,200 employees and a total cost of about $8,000,000 annually; nevertheless, many experts on national administration are not yet satisfied with the organization and staffing of the Presidency,⁶ even though much progress has been made in the past twenty years.

Much of the growth in the Presidential *institution* has been the result of national security needs—domestic and international. Coordination of political, economic, diplomatic, military and overall foreign policy is a major undertaking today, and this responsibility is in the President's lap. President Truman reportedly kept on his White House desk a placard with the slogan, "The buck stops here."

The Presidential office is the peak of the vast pyramid of our national defense organization. Referring to important foreign-military policy decisions in 1953-55, Secretary of State Dulles has said of the tremendous decision-making responsibility of a President: "We walked to the brink [of war] and we looked it in the face. We took strong action. It took a lot more courage for the President than for me. His was the ultimate decision. I did not have to make the decision myself, only to recommend it."⁷ With this remark, Mr. Dulles stuck his head into a political hornet's nest; regardless of the issues raised, it well describes Presidential responsibility.

The President is the chief organ in the nation's foreign relations, but quite obviously his advisors in the State and Defense Departments, National Security Council and Central Intelligence Agency play a major role in shaping White House policies. Yet *his* must be the final decision. This is illustrated by the now threadbare story of President Lincoln, who ended a discussion with his Cabinet—all of whom had opposed him on an issue—with the remark: "Seven nays, one aye, the ayes have it."

The President directly commands all elements of the national security organization. The Secretaries of Defense and State, the Joint

Chiefs of Staff, members of the National Security Council (in which statutory membership is ex-officio), and the heads of the Central Intelligence Agency, Office of Defense Mobilization and Bureau of the Budget are all Presidential appointees. Theoretically the second lieutenant in the field is at the bottom of a chain of command which starts with the President as Commander-in-Chief, just as a junior vice-consul of the U. S. Foreign Service, or Central Intelligence Agency secret agent, is at the bottom of the hierarchy over which the Chief Executive presides. But quite obviously the complex machinery of the Defense Department or the Department of State is a significant buffer between Presidential legal authority and actual policy-making in Washington and operations in the field.

A number of functions—especially in foreign aid—have been performed by special agencies created by Congress. Even within the Departments of State and Defense, tenure, classification, and duties of career employees are determined in considerable degree by Congress or the Civil Service Commission. Moreover, the addition of agencies which perform quasi legislative and judicial functions has limited the President's power to dismiss civil servants,[8] although of course he can still fire members of his Cabinet and other officials whom he appoints.

The President's 1937 Committee on Administrative Management and extensive studies by the Hoover Commissions of 1949 and 1955 have contributed much to the theory of what the Presidency should be in today's world. And their advice has largely shaped the administrative structure now surrounding the White House. Of primary importance is the Cabinet. This body, composed of the heads of the ten executive departments, has no constitutional or statutory basis, but it has become institutionalized through custom although its prestige and actual use have varied widely with different Presidents. Under President Eisenhower, the Cabinet has held a more prominent place than under his immediate predecessors. It meets regularly, has a specific agenda, and a small secretariat. There is a "reasonable accommodation" and tacit division of functions between the National Security Council and the Cabinet, the latter tending to concentrate on such domestic areas as agriculture, labor, or commerce.[9]

THE EXECUTIVE OFFICE

If it is true that the organization for national security cannot be understood without reference to the Presidency, it is also true that the Presidency cannot be understood without some knowledge of the vast machinery by which the Executive Office works. This Office—established in 1939 by a Reorganization Plan—is in effect a type of holding company for the President's staff agencies. As of June, 1956, it has the following divisions: The White House Office, the Bureau of the Budget, the Council of Economic Advisers, the National Security Council, the Central Intelligence Agency, the Operations Coordinating Board, the Office of Defense Mobilization, and the Committee on Government Organization.[10]

THE WHITE HOUSE OFFICE

In the measured words of the *Government Organization Manual,* the White House Office "serves the President in the performance of the many detailed activities incident to his immediate office." More realistic perhaps is the statement that "The White House Office takes precedence over the other units in the Executive Office. This relationship is not shown on any of the organization charts, but it is nevertheless real." [11]

A recent issue of *Time* magazine devoted a feature article to this Office, and particularly to Sherman Adams, who runs it as the Assistant to the President. "The men who work under Sherman Adams are no mere spear-carrying extras; they include some of the key men in government," *Time* reported.[12] This fact has given pause to some students of political science. What happens, they ask, to the responsibility of the Cabinet when some of the functions of its members are duplicated by a Presidential staff agency or by special assistants to the President? A recent study on "The Executive Branch and Disarmament Policy" [13] questions "how a 'minister without portfolio' fits into the American system" and specifically whether Mr. Stassen's position as Special Assistant to the President for Disarmament supplements or disrupts the responsibilities of the Defense and State Departments. But whatever opinions may be held about it, the White House Office, headed by the President, is in a very real sense the top of the pyramid, for which the operating levels of the executive branch provide the base.

COUNCIL OF ECONOMIC ADVISERS

For so young an organization the Council of Economic Advisers has had a fairly stormy career.[14] Congress created it by statute in 1946 and significantly made it part of the Executive Office rather than an independent body.[15] Its primary duty is to analyze the national economy and advise the President on the impact of economic policies. But controversy was inevitable in an organization born in the so-called "full employment" act and which dealt with matters as close to American pocketbooks as deficit financing and the "butter" portion of guns vs. butter questions. Although some jurisdictional rivalry has existed with the Bureau of the Budget and the Office of Defense Mobilization, the Council has on the whole maintained good working relations with other staff agencies.

The Council of Economic Advisers works with an interdepartmental Advisory Board (representing Agriculture, Commerce, Labor, State, Treasury, Bureau of the Budget and Federal Reserve Board) and it has on many occasions consulted with advisory committees from private life representing business, labor, consumers and farmers. After a slow start with the new administration in 1953, the council, under the chairmanship of Arthur Burns, has gained considerably in importance. Whatever its shortcomings, it has proved its worth in acting as a "shield for the President . . . against conflicting economic viewpoints"—i.e., in focusing upon the *national* economy rather than segments of it as seen from the often parochial viewpoints of various departments.[16]

THE PRESIDENT'S ADVISORY COMMITTEE ON GOVERNMENT ORGANIZATION

Created by one of President Eisenhower's first executive orders [17] to work with and broaden the efforts of the Budget Bureau's Office of Management and Organization, the President's Advisory Committee on Government Organization has played a leading part in the wholesale changes brought about by the nine Reorganization Plans of 1953. The success of the Committee—sometimes called the President's "personal Hoover Commission"—can in part be traced to Nelson Rockefeller, who served as its chairman until his resignation from government late in 1955. In view of the President's power under the Reorganization Acts [18] (which let reorganization plans submitted to Congress by the President become effective unless disapproved by concurrent resolution within sixty days), it is clearly desirable that he have a mechanism to advise him on its use.

THE BUREAU OF THE BUDGET

Antedating the Executive Office by some eighteen years is the Bureau of the Budget. Although the idea of a "budget" as distinguished from "estimates of public expenditure" developed soon after the turn of the century, it was not until the Budget and Accounting Act of 1921 [19] was passed that the Bureau came into existence. It was transferred from the Treasury to the Executive Office in 1939. Some critics —for example, the Fiscal, Budgeting, and Accounting Activities Task Force of the 1949 Hoover Commission—have maintained that duplication can be avoided by returning the Bureau to the Treasury. But the multitude of non-budgetary duties which the Bureau has assumed seem likely to justify its being retained as a Presidential staff agency.

The Bureau of the Budget has for the most part commanded the respect of Congress—and of the executive branch as well, perhaps because the holder of the purse strings is always respected. Since Charles G. Dawes first assumed the office, the Directors of the Bureau have been men of strong character and outstanding ability. They have often risen high in other parts of the Federal government. Harold Smith, James E. Webb and Frank Pace, for example, achieved further prominence respectively in the International Bank, the State Department, and the Army; Joseph Dodge is today serving as Special Assistant to the President. It is indicative of the greatly increased emphasis on "cost accounting of policy"—the "performance budget" —and tight fiscal controls that Rowland Hughes, predecessor of the present Director,[20] Secretary of the Treasury Humphrey, and Defense Comptroller McNeil, have been called the "three strong men" of the Eisenhower administration.

The Bureau has a staggering number of functions—few of them suggested by the title. In addition to coordinating and holding hearings on budget requests and preparing the budget itself, it reviews requests for apportionment after funds have been appropriated. Moreover it is responsible for drawing up regulations on such diverse matters as government travel allowances and the printing of forms, for control of government statistics, and for "improving government-wide management and organization." During World War II, the Bureau undertook such varied jobs as writing a history of wartime administration and investigating defense construction. Indeed, it has been referred to as the President's "own private Gestapo."[21]

The most important of the Bureau's non-budgetary roles is coordinating and "clearing" *all* legislative programs from the executive branch, whether or not they involve appropriations. It is thus the focal point for legislative programming, and since almost everything involved in national security requires money, legislation, or both, the Bureau of the Budget is an important part of the organization which determines and administers national security policies.[22]

THE CENTRAL INTELLIGENCE AGENCY

Although responsible and advisory to the National Security Council, the Central Intelligence Agency is for all practical purposes an independent agency and is only nominally within the Executive Office. Created by Title 102 of the National Security Act of 1947, it succeeded the wartime Office of Strategic Services and the National Intelligence Authority, the organization that replaced the OSS at the end of the war. The Central Intelligence Agency Act of 1949,[23] like the National Security Act Amendments of 1949, resulted in part from the recommendations of the first Hoover Commission. While no basic structural changes were made a number of important powers and exemptions were given to the Agency to protect its confidential nature and to permit overseas operations. CIA, for example, is not required to publish personnel data in the *Federal Register,* is exempt from furnishing certain reports to Congress and to the Bureau of the Budget, and may bring up to 100 aliens a year into the country without normal immigration procedures.

The CIA budget is concealed within the budgets of other agencies; not more than a few key officials know the total amount of its expenditures. Its secretive nature—generally admitted to be necessary—has resulted in a number of Congressional proposals for a joint watchdog committee on intelligence similar to the Joint Committee on Atomic Energy. The 1955 Hoover Commission Task Force on Intelligence Activities, headed by General Mark W. Clark, recommended a mixed Congressional-citizens committee as a watchdog, but the Commission itself recommended that the committtee be composed exclusively of "experienced private citizens." The Task Force concluded that the national intelligence program was on the whole sound and well run, although a number of defects were noted, particularly the lack of adequate information from behind the Iron Curtain. On January 3, 1956, President Eisenhower acting on the Hoover Commission recommendation, appointed an eight-man citizens' committee to monitor CIA activities. Dr. James R. Killian, Jr., president of Massachusetts Institute of Technology, was named chairman.

The five major functions assigned to CIA by the National Security Act of 1947 can be broken down into three general types:

(1) The Agency is required to provide the National Security Council with up-to-date, evaluated intelligence. CIA prepares, through a Board of National Estimates, the "National Intelligence Estimates"— the heart of strategic intelligence upon which policy decisions are made. However, CIA is also a program operator; it performs such functions as the National Security Council determines can be more efficiently accomplished centrally or otherwise assigns it. (2) CIA advises the National Security Council with respect to intelligence organization and procedures throughout the "intelligence community". However, the Agency has no right to inspect the organization and operations— as distinguished from the product—of other intelligence agencies. This limitation has been criticized by some observers as a serious defect. By "intelligence community" is meant the Central Intelligence Agency, the National Security Council, the National Se-

curity Agency,[24] the Federal Bureau of Investigation, and intelligence sections of the Department of State, the Army, the Navy, the Air Force, and the Atomic Energy Commission.[25] (3) CIA correlates, evaluates, and circulates the data produced by other members of the "intelligence community."

This inter-agency coordination necessarily involves numerous committees—such as the Intelligence Advisory Committee under the National Security Council—and working groups and specialized subcommittees representing anywhere from three to ten different departments and agencies. Intelligence is fed into top level policy-making only after constant checking, cross-checking, and ironing out of differences. However, if a clear-cut opinion split does in fact exist, it is given as such. Much of the coordination takes place within the Intelligence Advisory Committee and other interdepartmental committees (or their subcommittees and working groups) although there is similar correlation and evaluation within the Joint Intelligence Committee of the Joint Chiefs of Staff. But the main link between intelligence as information and policy decisions is provided not by CIA but by the National Security Council Planning Board to be discussed in Chapter III.

Two theories about intelligence have affected the over-all pattern: (1), that intelligence can and should be separated from decision-making except at the highest level; and (2), that a "federal" type of organization with decentralization among the various members of the community—that is, with coordination rather than centralized direction—is most appropriate. It remains to be seen whether the trend toward centralization which exists in the Defense Department will be followed in the intelligence field.[26]

THE OFFICE OF DEFENSE MOBILIZATION

Of all the staff agencies, the Office of Defense Mobilization has had the most irregular pattern of development. To trace this pattern properly would require beginning with World War II experiences with the Office of War Mobilization and Reconversion.[27] Space precludes such an account here, but it is necessary to go back at least to 1947.

The National Security Resources Board (NSRB), created by the National Security Act of 1947, followed very closely the blueprint of the Eberstadt Report. The Board's central purpose was to advise the President with respect to coordination of civilian and military mobilization. Almost at once the Board had difficulty in organizing its work and assigning priorities to various projects. Prof. Edward H. Hobbs quotes a speech to the Industrial College of the Armed Forces

in which a speaker states, "Most of you know that government may
be somewhat cumbersome, but it usually takes about a hundred years
to get that way. We [the NSRB staff] got that way in two short
years." [28] It is impossible to list the many functions assigned by
statute and executive orders between 1947 and 1950, but the number
was such that it was necessary to reorganize the Board—usually with
a change of Chairman—at least once each year. It was transferred to
the Executive Office in 1949 and in December 1950, President Truman
declared a state of national emergency and created the Office of Defense Mobilization (ODM) to direct mobilization activities necessi-
tated by the Korean war. This required that a division of labor be
worked out among ODM, NSRB, and the National Production Authority (which had also been created to meet problems brought about
by Korea.) Although during the war it worked closely with the Munitions Board of the Department of Defense, NSRB was inevitably limited more and more to long-range mobilization and resources planning.
In 1950 Reorganization Plan 25 vested the functions of NSRB in its
Chairman and the Board became advisory. Reduced in size, the staff
continued to work on planning and programming and maintained a
close relationship with the Office of Defense Mobilization. Under Reorganization Plan 3 of 1953, President Eisenhower merged the two
entities into a new Office of Defense Mobilization within the Executive Office. This agency succeeded to all the functions previously assigned or delegated to the Director of the old ODM, to the NSRB, or
to its Chairman. Additional responsibilities have since been added
by other executive orders, a list of which occupies several paragraphs
in the U. S. Government Organization Manual.

The present duties of the Office of Defense Mobilization are suggested by the fact that it has assistant directors for manpower, materials, production, stabilization, and telecommunications. The degree
to which ODM must work with and through other agencies is illustrated by the membership of the advisory Defense Mobilization
Board which includes the Secretaries of State, Defense, Treasury, Interior, Agriculture, Commerce and Labor as well as the heads of the
Federal Reserve System, the Foreign Operations Administration (now
the International Cooperation Administration) and the Federal Civil
Defense Administration. ODM cooperates with these agencies through
appropriate task forces or working groups. In the manpower field
for example, the Armed Forces Reserve Act of 1955 can be said to
have germinated in a study made by ODM in 1953. It was constantly
associated with the Department of Defense in estimating manpower

resources and in plans for screening essential skills in recalling military reservists.

Credit must be given to the Eberstadt Report for recognizing that mobilization of national resources was too important a matter to be left to improvisation. Although the National Security Resources Board proved unwieldy, it set a precedent for such an organization in peacetime. In its present stage of evolution the Office of Defense Mobilization seems to provide a good blend of long-range planning and day-to-day coordination. The Director of ODM sits on the National Security Council and is represented on the Council's Planning Board. Interdepartmental contact is maintained through the Defense Mobilization Board and myriad working relationships at the staff level. ODM also focuses the advice of civilian experts through advisory committees concerned with such subjects as health resources, science, labor-management manpower, and numerous consultants, especially in the fields of transportation and industrial defense and mobilization.

OTHER DEPARTMENTS AND AGENCIES

Although this chapter has been concerned with the President's immediate family—as represented by the Executive Office—a number of other organizations play a significant role in national security. As pointed out in Chapter I, national security now embraces much of the entire executive branch. In addition to State and Defense, which are discussed elsewhere, the Treasury and the Department of Commerce are of particular importance among the ten Cabinet Departments. The Secretary of the Treasury has a strong influence on the proportion of the country's wealth to be devoted to national security, and this in turn tends to predetermine the ceilings under which foreign and military policies must operate.[29] In addition to this financial leadership, the Treasury is responsible for one of the nation's five armed services. Except in time of war when it becomes part of the Navy, the Coast Guard operates as a service in the Treasury rather than under the Defense Department. Efforts to transfer this service to Defense have thus far made little headway. The Department of Commerce also has many contacts with national security matters. There is an Assistant Secretary for International Affairs with important responsibilities for export controls. The Business and Defense Services Administration (which succeeded the National Production Authority and carries out industrial mobilization and defense production programs under the guidance of the Office of Defense Mobilization) is also located within the Department of Commerce. In addition, Commerce, through its Maritime Administration, is responsible for the merchant marine and maintains the important national defense reserve fleet.

Among the independent agencies, the Atomic Energy Commission has an increasingly central role in view of the development of atomic weapons and atomic powered ships. The AEC will be mentioned again in Part Two. The Federal Civil Defense Agency, although primarily an advisory and coordinating body in peace time, has been delegated vast authority in major disasters. The Administrator, by order of the President, may direct any Federal agency—including the Armed Forces—to make available personnel and equipment, a power of no small concern to defense officials planning for an enemy attack.

Although research and development will be further discussed in Chapter X, mention should be made here of the National Science Foundation established in 1950 which—in addition to other tasks—initiates and supports basic scientific research at the request of the Secretary of Defense. There is also an Interdepartmental Committee on Scientific Research and Development which makes studies and reports on federal research activities. Another body, listed as a "quasi-official" agency, is also active in this area. This is the National Academy of Sciences dating from Lincoln's administration which, together with its National Research Council, makes investigations and research studies on request of government agencies. Turning from science to the manpower field, the Selective Service system administers the draft and thus provides the basic raw material of national defense. The National Security Training Commission, although universal military training never became effective, has supervisory responsibility over the 6 month reserve training program established by the Reserve Forces Act of 1955. Finally, the General Services Administration, mainly concerned with the housekeeping arrangements of the Federal government—which includes managing the vast Pentagon—is mentioned from time to time in connection with proposals for a fourth military service for supply or other devices to reduce duplication in military supplies and installations. Significantly, it is now headed by Franklin G. Floete, formerly Assistant Secretary of Defense for Properties and Installations.

It is of course impossible to list all the organizations having a relationship to national security without virtually duplicating the *Government Organization Manual*. But the reader should be aware that there are others. Some, such as the Small Business Administration (and the small business offices in Defense and Commerce) affect only one aspect—in this case, defense procurement. Others, such as the Federal Bureau of Investigation (under the Department of Justice) or the Subversive Activities Control Board and other groups concerned with loyalty and subversion have a paramount position in domestic security matters. But since this book is concerned with security from *external* threats, space precludes discussion despite their obvious importance.

[1] *N.Y. Times,* February 3, 1955.

[2] *N.Y. Times,* January 20, 1956.

[3] *N.Y. Times,* February 3, 1955.

[4] *Years of Trial and Hope,* Vol. II of the Truman *Memoirs,* Doubleday, New York, 1956. This excerpt is from *N.Y. Times,* January 22, 1956.

[5] Third edition, New York University Press, New York, 1948. For other descriptions of the Presidency see the works listed in Appendix IV.

[6] See, for example, *Administrative Vice President,* Hearings and Report, Senate Government Operations Subcommittee, 84th Congress, 2nd Session, 1956.

[7] *Life,* January 16, 1956, p. 78.

[8] This trend is indicated by comparing the earlier decisions such as *Myers v. U.S.,* 272 U. S. 52 (1926) which sustained the removal power with the later ones such as *Humphrey v. U.S.,* 295 U. S. 602 (1935) which restricted it. The latter case, however, was concerned with regulatory agencies such as the Federal Trade Commission.

[9] For a discussion of the Cabinet and the extent to which it has copied the procedures of the National Security Council, see Robert Cutler. "The Development of the National Security Council," *Foreign Affairs,* April 1956, pp. 446-7.

[10] *United States Government Organization Manual, 1956-1957,* Washington, Federal Register Division, National Archives and Records Service, General Services Administration, 1955. This manual lists not only the top officials, but also the creation, authority, functions and organization of all executive agencies. The Legislative and Judicial Branches are also covered in considerable detail. The manual is a very useful tool for the student of government. For a graphic picture of the Executive Office in relation to the executive branch as a whole, see the chart in Appendix V *infra.*

[11] Edward H. Hobbs, *Behind the President: A Study of Executive Office Agencies,* Public Affairs Press, Washington, 1954, p. 86.

[12] *Time,* January 9, 1956, pp. 18-22.

[13] *Staff Study No. 1,* Subcommittee on Disarmament of the Senate Committee on Foreign Relations, 84th Congress, 2d Session, Washington, February 20, 1956. See pp. 18-19.

[14] The CEA should not be confused with the National Advisory Council on International Monetary and Financial Problems created in 1945 as a result of the Bretton Woods Agreement and which is a statutory (59 *Stat.* 512, 22 U. S. C. 286b) interdepartmental committee chaired by the Secretary of the Treasury. The CEA must also be distinguished from the Council on Foreign Economic Policy created by the President in December 1954, to improve the organization for coordination of foreign economic policy. As of July, 1956 it was chaired by Special Assistant to the President Joseph M. Dodge, but it is a Cabinet level interdepartmental committee rather than an organizational entity.

[15] By the Employment Act of 1946, 60 *Stat.* 24, 15 U. S. C. 1023. It was reorganized by Reorganization Plan No. 9, 1953.

[16] For a thorough discussion of the Council see Hobbs, *op. cit.,* Chapter V.

[17] Executive Order 10532, January 24, 1953.

[18] Similar enactments, although with different jurisdictional scope, were passed in 1939, 1945, and 1949. The Reorganization Act of 1949 was extended in January, 1953, to cover plans submitted prior to April 1, 1955. See: H.Rep. 6, 83d Congress, 1st Session, 1953 and 99 *Congressional Record*, 759-786 (1953). In March 1956, the President's reorganization powers were extended to June 1, 1958 by PL 16, 84th Congress, 69 *Stat.* 14.

[19] The Act also established the General Accounting Office, which post-audits executive expenditures for Congress. 42 *Stat.* 20, 31 U. S. C., 11-16.

[20] Mr. Hughes retired during the spring of 1956 and was succeeded by Percival F. Brundage.

[21] *Cf.* Robert E. Sherwood, *Roosevelt and Hopkins,* Harper and Brothers, New York, 1948, p. 210.

[22] Hobbs, *op. cit.* has provided a good analysis of the Bureau and its development in Chapter II.

[23] P. L. 110, 81st Congress, 1949. 50 U. S. C. 403 a-j, 63 *Stat,* 208.

[24] The National Security Agency is a semi-autonomous agency of the Department of Defense. It includes the Army Security Agency and similar organizations in the Navy and Air Force. Its main responsibility is communications security and intelligence. Details of its organization and function are as highly classified as those of CIA.

[25] *Cf.* Commission on Organization of the Executive Branch, *Intelligence Activities,* A Report to the Congress, June, 1955, p. 13.

[26] In addition to those listed in the bibliography (Appendix IV) the following references are useful on intelligence: Snyder and Furniss, *American Foreign Policy,* Rinehart & Co., New York, 1954, pp. 224-238, Roger Hilsman, Jr., "Intelligence and Policy Making in Foreign Affairs", *World Politics,* October, 1952, Vol. V, pp. 1-45, and the Hoover Commission Report on *Intelligence Activities,* 1955.

[27] This history can be found in full in the Bureau of the Budget's *The United States at War,* and in summary form in Hobbs, *op. cit.,* Chapter VIII.

[28] Hobbs, *op. cit.,* p. 165.

[29] For an interesting analysis of budget ceilings and their effect on strategic concepts see Samuel P. Huntington, "Radicalism and Conservatism in National Defense Policy," *Journal of International Affairs,* Columbia University, Vol. VIII, No. 2, 1954, p. 206.

CHAPTER III

THE NATIONAL SECURITY COUNCIL

The steps which led to the creation of the National Security Council by the National Security Act of 1947 have been discussed in Chapter I. As defined by the Act—in language very similar to that of the Eberstadt Report—the Council functions are: to "advise the President with respect to the integration of domestic, foreign and military policies relating to the national security so as to enable the military services and other departments and agencies of the government to cooperate more effectively in matters involving the national security . . ."; to "assess and appraise the objectives, commitments and risks of the United States in relation to our actual and potential military power, in the interest of national security, for the purpose of making recommendations to the president in connection therewith, and . . . to consider policies on matters of common interest to the departments and agencies of the government concerned with national security and to make recommendations in connection therewith."[1]

Membership in the Council was initially prescribed to include the President, the Secretary of State, the Secretary of Defense, the secretaries of the three military services, and the Chairman of the National Security Resources Board. The President was authorized to appoint the Chairman of the Munitions Board and the Research and Development Board, but other appointments required the advice and consent of the Senate.[2] The Act also provided for a National Security Council staff headed by a civilian Executive Secretary with power to appoint other personnel. This remedied one of the major shortcomings of earlier interdepartmental committees and gave the Council an institutional basis.

Almost simultaneously with the establishment of the fledgling Council, the first Hoover Commission was established by the 80th Congress. The Task Force on National Security Organization, appropriately headed by Ferdinand Eberstadt, had 14 members and a staff of 25—of which three had served on the original (1945) Eberstadt Committee. The Task Force began its investigations in June, 1948 and completed its report in November.[3] The report's main findings and recommendations may be summarized as follows: Although the

National Security Organization was too new to be fully appraised, it appeared to be basically sound because it met a fundamental and continuing need. This much is hardly surprising in view of Eberstadt's natural preference for the organizational pattern which he had blueprinted. However, the Task Force went on to pinpoint a number of critical areas in which the machinery was not working smoothly and in which improvement was needed: Liaison on foreign policy was weak; the "bitter lesson" of winning two wars only to lose the peace both times "does not yet seem to have been fully learned." National security was "still thought of too much in terms of military strength alone" and ignored the contributions that can and should be made by political, economic, human, and spiritual resources.' The Task Force report recommended: "integration of domestic, foreign, and military policies" through recognition that the "National Security Organization is an instrument of higher authority" as focused upon the President and urged that "policy—based on adequate intelligence"—should originate at the highest level of civilian authority, "pass down through the National Military Establishment for translation into strategic plans . . ." and return upward as specific programs. The report also proposed that more adequate working-level relations be established between the various committees of the Joint Chiefs and Joint Staff and their counterparts in the Council, Central Intelligence Agency, and National Security Resources Board, as well as the Munitions Board and the Research and Development Board. Most significant of all was the recommendation that the Secretary of Defense be the sole representative of the National Military Establishment on the Council and that the Joint Chiefs be invited to attend meetings without actual membership. This proposal was aimed not only at redressing the military over-balance but also at increasing the authority and prestige of the Secretary of Defense.

The evaluation of the Task Force led to a number of the changes in the National Security Council made by the National Security Act Amendments of 1949.⁵ Membership in the Council was revised to make the Secretary of Defense the only representative of the newly established Department of Defense. The President was authorized to appoint to membership the Secretaries and Under-Secretaries of other executive departments, including the three armed services, subject to the advice and consent of the Senate. Finally, the Council was given authority to appoint, through its Executive Secretary, advisory committees and to employ part-time consultants—authority similar to that already possessed by the Secretary of Defense, the Chairman of NSRB, and the Director of CIA. From 1949 until 1955, the Council slowly began to evolve towards the "instrument of higher authority" which the Task Force had called it. There were minor changes under President Truman, but the next major reorganization did not come until after President Eisenhower's inauguration.

Several weeks before his election Eisenhower made a campaign speech at Baltimore in which one of the key points was the need for "revitalization" of the National Security Council. The initial draft of this part of the speech was written by General Robert Cutler, who was later to undertake this job as Special Assistant to the President for National Security Council Affairs.[6] Soon after Eisenhower's election, the Council became less of a meeting of top level department representatives and more of a war cabinet style body of Presidential advisers. Smaller meetings furthered the shift away from particular departmental positions, encouraged free discussion, and forced the Secretaries, who could no longer rely on aides, to do their homework. With participation by the Secretary of the Treasury and the Director of the Bureau of the Budget and the requirement that all Council papers have a "financial appendix", the cost factor in policy received much more emphasis. Finally, the old "senior staff" of the Council was reorganized as the National Security Council Planning Board and designated "the principal body for formulation and transmission of policy recommendations to the Council."[7]

The effects of Eisenhower's revitalization can be seen in the fact that during 1953 the Council met 51 times and considered 305 items; the highest previous number of meetings in a year was 34 with 192 items considered.[8]

DEVELOPMENTS SINCE 1953

The National Security Council includes several different types of membership. Statutory members are the President, as Chairman, the Vice President—added in 1949 and signifying recognition of his role as the President's alter ego, the Secretaries of State and Defense, and the Director of the Office of Defense Mobilization. The Secretary of the Treasury is a "standing request" member, a status fully equal to that of a statutory member. "Participant members" may be either on a "standing request" or an *ad hoc* basis. The Director of the Bureau of the Budget, the Special Assistant to the President for Disarmament,[9] and the Chairman of the Atomic Energy Commission[10] usually attend in this status. The so-called "special request" members at present include the Attorney General, the Director of the United States Information Agency, and the Chairman of the Council of Economic Advisers.

Observers are usually invited for a particular session and take no part in the discussion. However, the Chairman of the Joint Chiefs of Staff, the Director of CIA and certain Special Assistants attend and participate as advisers to the President. The membership of any particular meeting is flexible; it may include the Ambassador to the United Nations, the three Chiefs of Staff, the Secretary of Commerce or Civil Defense officials, according to the nature of the business to be discussed.

Before 1950, the Council's preliminary planning was done mainly through consultants. Although civilian consultants are still used and occasionally give reports on particuar studies at meetings, this arrangement gave way to the so-called senior staff, which in turn became the Planning Board. The Special Assistant to the President for National Security Affairs—originally Robert Cutler, who was succeeded in 1955 by Dillon Anderson [11]—is a key figure at the meetings of the Council and is the chief liaison between the Council and the Planning Board of which he is Chairman. Although the President is Chairman of the Council, the Special Assistant often outlines the problem and keeps the discussion on the track. He has, moreover, the very important duty of regularly briefing the President on national security matters.

THE STAFF

The Executive Secretary and his Deputy—who are career officials—are also present at meetings and keep a record of actions taken, although no detailed transcript of the discussion is made. Although the Special Assistant is nominally the executive officer of the Council, the Executive Secretary runs the staff, which acts as the Secretariat for the Council. He also aids the Special Assistant, especially in matters regarding the Planning Board and briefs the Vice President. The Deputy heads the special staff, which is to be distinguished from the Council's staff proper. The special staff independently analyzes and reviews all Planning Board reports before they are submitted to the Council and undertakes a "continuous examination of the totality of national security policies." It also acts as a secretariat for various *ad hoc* civilian committees. One of its important jobs is to insure that the language used in a report says exactly what it means—no more and no less.

The role of the National Security Council's staff has remained the same despite the changes made during the Eisenhower Administration. This is in part because the views of the first Executive Secretary, Admiral Sidney W. Souers, have apparently been shared by James S. Lay and S. Everett Gleason, who hold the top staff positions. One description of the job is that, "Like the clutch in an automobile, he [Lay] undertakes to transmit ideas—smoothly and with a minimum of friction. He doesn't try to be the engine . . . but to see that all views are fairly presented." [12] The NSC career staff has remained small, with less than 30 members of which almost half are secretarial—a phenomenon in Washington—and a "passion for anonymity"; it has resisted efforts to expand its scope from what it conceives to be its main duty: to service the Council.

THE PLANNING BOARD

The Planning Board, composed of a representative (usually at the Assistant Secretary level) of each member of the National Security Council, is headed by the Special Assistant to the President for National Security Affairs. It is advised by representatives of the Joint Chiefs of Staff, the Central Intelligence Agency, the Bureau of the Budget, and the Operations Coordinating Board. The staff work is directed by the Executive Secretary, aided by his Deputy, but the Board relies primarily upon Board Assistants representing the members, with a Coordinator from the NSC staff. It is significant that the State Department representative is the Director of the Policy Planning Staff in that Department, since this in itself assures a certain amount of coordination.

It can be seen that the National Security Council has three levels: Member, Planning Board, and Staff. Of these, the Planning Board has the key role in making policy recommendations. The "traffic of ideas . . . may be . . . from the Council downward for study and report . . . from any agency . . . or from any member or advisor of the Planning Board." [13] Moreover, established NSC policies are constantly reviewed and a "forward agenda" of items for review and of new ideas to be considered is maintained by the Special Assistant. Sometimes, of course, both the Planning Board and the NSC must operate on a crash basis, as during the Indo-China crisis in 1954.

Usually a departmental staff paper on a problem is circulated to the Board, discussed, revised—usually by the Board Assistants—and finally reduced to either an agreed Planning Board paper or a split paper. It is circulated to Council members a week before the scheduled meeting and is discussed by each member with his Planning Board representative. After being placed on the agenda by the Special Assistant, it is discussed by the Council. Finally "the sense of the meeting"—agreement or defined issues for decision by the President—is reached, and the President may or may not accept the NSC's advice. The Council acts only in an advisory capacity and thus does not "make" policy, but once a policy paper is signed by the President, it becomes official national policy.

Suggestions for changing the National Security Council have been offered almost constantly since it was created in 1947. Students of government, observing the need for legislative-executive coordination in national security matters, have sometimes fastened on the NSC the likeliest body for the job. Indeed the original Eberstadt Report included this concept in the suggestion that Council reports be made available to Congress. Others have urged that the membership include selected Congressmen and Senators.[14] It has been suggested that the NSC add "a group of 100 top flight specialists,"[15] or that the NSC should become a "national staff"[16] for national security policy similar to the Army general staff. Sometimes a group studying a special aspect of national policy will recommend changes in the Council mechanism in order to improve consideration given to that particular problem.[17]

But just as there are limits in terms of controllable size, which would prevent a "super department for national security" in which the Departments of State and Defense would be joined, so there are limits to the possible expansion of the National Security Council. Capable department heads are unwilling to be "layered" by having another official between them and the President. Congress would almost certainly object to a national staff which might tend to create a "monolithic" executive branch. And finally, the addition of further consultants or specialists would create major difficulties of coordination and administration. The Council is designed to make available to the President the advice—not just of experts—but of the men with primary *operating* responsibility in national security matters. The advice can thus be based on the known capabilities and limitations of the agencies that will execute the policies. It seems unlikely, therefore, that there will be a major change in the NSC during the Eisenhower administration.[18]

THE OPERATIONS COORDINATING BOARD

The Committee on International Information Activities, headed by William Jackson, reported to the President in June, 1953 that "a significant gap existed at the interdepartmental level" between policymaking by the National Security Council and the detailed actions required to execute the policies. Accordingly, on September 3, 1953, President Eisenhower by executive order established the Operations Coordinating Board.[19] President Truman had established a Psychological Strategy Board in April 1951[20] to deal with this particular aspect of national security operations. Significantly the temptation to expand the responsibilities of the Council itself was resisted—perhaps partly because it was felt the already heavily burdened members should not receive still more duties. Probably the main reason was that the problem of psychological warfare was thought to be distinctive because it involved *operations* rather than broad policies.

One criticism made of the old Psychological Strategy Board was that it met resistance in obtaining compliance with its recommendations, especially from the State Department and in its relations with the Joint Chiefs of Staff.[21] More significant perhaps was the question raised by the Jackson Committee as to whether "psychological strategy" can be separated from overall politico-military strategy.[22] At all events, when the Operations Coordinating Board succeeded to the functions of the Psychological Strategy Board, its responsibility was broadened to provide for the "integrated implementation of national security policies" by the various agencies concerned. As General Robert Cutler puts it, "The OCB arose like a phoenix out of the ashes of the old Psychological Strategy Board."[23]

The membership is composed of the Under Secretary of State as Chairman, the Deputy Secretary of Defense, the Directors of the International Cooperation Administration (which replaced the Foreign Operations Administration), the Central Intelligence Agency, and the U.S. Information Agency. A Special Assistant to the President[24] usually sits regularly with the Board. Other *ad hoc* members, such as the Chairman of the Atomic Energy Commission, attend from time to time. It should be noted that the Joint Chiefs of Staff is not represented on the Board. OCB's staff, headed by an executive officer[25], is supplemented by working groups from member agencies and by OCB Board Assistants, who perform a similar function to that of their counterparts on the NSC Planning Board. But the Board has no authority as such, it cannot order anyone to act. However, its members usually follow the integrated courses of action agreed upon by the Board.

In addition to the staffing of papers pertaining to operations of interdepartmental concern, the Operations Coordinating Board performs an important service in monitoring the progress of coordination, checking up, noting deficiencies, and reporting to the President through the National Security Council. If the National Security Council as a corporate body is a kind of national chief of staff, then the Operations Coordinating Board is his G-3 (Operations) officer. When the Council completes a policy paper pertaining to a certain country, the document is in very broad terms and general language. The Board's country plan, on the other hand, is specific enough to be used by the program operators in executing broad NSC policies.

In view of its comparative newness on the Washington scene, it is difficult to evaluate the Board's success. It has helped to eliminate the huge complex of lower level coordinating committees, but many of these, like old soldiers, never seem to die. Both the State Department and the Central Intelligence Agency have been successful in by-passing the Board on occasion. The Board, however, represents an important step forward in interdepartmental coordination, and it has already achieved much of the prestige necessary to act as the "strong right arm" of the NSC.

Each member organization of the Board has a small "backstopping staff" to help get action. The Deputy Secretary for example represents the Defense Department on the OCB. Until recently the Office of Special Operations, headed by a special Assistant to the Secretary, maintained an operations section to coordinate the views of the Military Departments, the Joint Chiefs of Staff, and the Office of the Secretary of Defense. In December 1955, a reorganization of the International Security Affairs area established an Office of OCB Affairs within the Office of the Assistant Secretary of Defense (International Security Affairs) to parallel the existing Office of NSC Affairs.[26] This action has thus left the Office of Special Operations free to specialize in intelligence and National Security Agency matters. As of June 1956, however, the Deputy Secretary of Defense, Reuben B. Robertson, Jr., is still the Defense representative on the Operations Coordinating Board.

---

[1] The National Security Act of 1947, P.L. 253, 80th Congress, 61 *Stat.* 495. 50 U. S. C. 401, Section 101 (a). See Appendix II for the full text as amended.

[2] This provision was interpreted to mean that the President could appoint the existing Secretary of a Department, but that if a new one took office, the Senate's advice and consent must be obtained. See Senate Report No. 239, to accompany S 758 (on the National Security Act) 80th Congress, 1947.

[3] Commission on the Organization of the Executive Branch, Committee on National Security Organization, *Task Force Report on National Security Organization,* January 1949, (Printed separately as Appendix G of the Commission Report).

[4] *Report.* p. 4. A detailed list of the findings and conclusions which are scattered through the report appears on p. 23.

[5] P. L. 216, 81st Congress, 63 *Stat.* 578, 50 U. S. C. 401.

[6] There is a considerable amount of periodical literature dealing with the NSC under Cutler. See bibliography.

[7] "The National Security Council," memorandum on organization and operation prepared by the NSC Special Staff in January, 1954.

[8] George A. Wyeth, Jr., "The National Security Council," *Journal of International Affairs*, Columbia University, Vol. VIII, No. 2, 1954, p. 192.

[9] Harold Stassen who attended Council meetings on a "standing request" basis as Director of the Foreign Operations Administration continues his participation as a Special Assistant. However, John B. Hollister, Director of the International Cooperation Administration, is not a member of the Council. The Secretary of State represents ICA as well as the State Department.

[10] There have been bills introduced in Congress to make the Chairman of the AEC a statutory member, but none have gotten beyond the Committee stage. The fact that Congress controls the membership either by statute or the advice and consent required for new appointments is indicative of the concern the legislature feels regarding those who advise the President in national security matters.

[11] Mr. Anderson— assisted by General Cutler—has written an article on "The President and National Security" in the January, 1956, *Atlantic Monthly*, which indicates that few changes have been made in the administrative operation of the Council since he assumed office. However, an article by James Reston in the *N.Y. Times*, March 9, 1955, suggests that the transition from Cutler to Anderson is illustrative of a "fundamental change," but Mr. Reston does not spell out the direction of the alleged change. For General Cutler's views, see "The Development of the National Security Council," *Foreign Affairs*, April 1956. In September 1956, Anderson was replaced by William H. Jackson who in 1953 was influential in establishing the OCB.

[12] John Fischer, *Master Plan U.S.A.*, Harper and Brothers, New York, 1951, p. 41. Chapter II on "Mr. Truman's Politburo" is a good account of the Council as it functioned prior to the Eisenhower administration.

[13] Wyeth, *op. cit.*, p. 189.

[14] Edward H. Hobbs, *op. cit.*, p. 227.

[15] General Wedemeyer, quoted in Fischer, *op. cit.*, p. 40. Bernard Baruch has also long advocated expanding the NSC. See, for example, *N.Y. Times*, November 17, 1954.

[16] "White House Strategy Making Machinery, 1952, 1954", by Col. Wendell E. Little, USAR, Air University, Maxwell Air Force Base, Alabama, p. 34. This study is an excellent analysis of the NSC in transition from the administration of President Truman to that of President Eisenhower.

[17] Thus a staff paper prepared for the 1955 Hoover Commission Task Force on Procurement recommended a stronger national security staff to assist the President and Council in balancing national security requirements with national resources. This would also aid the Council in recommending priorities among major national programs. See "Defense Procurement: The Vital Roles of the National Security Council and the Joint Chiefs of Staff," Volume I, Hoover Commission staff paper, June, 1955, pp. A-11 to A-24.

[18] A convincing argument against enlarging either the Council or the Staff is made in General Cutler's article *op. cit. supra*, note 11. From time to time, however, rumors circulate that a new study of the Council is pending and that changes may be forthcoming. These have thus far proved unfounded.

[19] Executive Order 10483, September 1953. This was amended by Executive Order No. 10598 of 28 February 1955.

[20] Executive Directive of 4 April 1951. The PSB became operative in July of that year.

[21] An excellent critical analysis of the PSB may be found in the Air War College Study, *op. cit.*, pp. 20-22.

[22] *Cf.* Snyder and Furniss, *American Foreign Policy*, Rinehart, New York, 1954, p. 261.

[23] *Foreign Affairs*, April 1956, p. 448.

[24] Initially this post was filled by Mr. C. D. Jackson (not to be confused with William Jackson of the Jackson Committee) as Special Assistant to the President "For the Cold War". He resigned in March, 1954, and his place was taken in December by Mr. Nelson Rockefeller, who dropped the designation "for the Cold War". When Mr. Rockefeller left the government in December, 1955, no successor was appointed. However, the Special Assistant to the President for National Security Affairs, Dillon Anderson, works closely with the OCB.

[25] Elmer Staats, formerly with the Bureau of the Budget, holds this position at the present time.

[26] Directive No. 5132.6, May 1, 1956, "Department of Defense Support for the Operations Coordinating Board."

CHAPTER IV

FOREIGN AFFAIRS

In the past 11 years the State Department has undoubtedly been subjected to more reorganization than any other major unit of the Executive Branch. At the end of World War II the Department was not prepared to cope with the responsibilities which were transferred to it in wholesale lots. Such agencies as the Foreign Economic Administration, the Office of War Information, and the Board of Economic Warfare were abolished and their functions—and many of their employees—were assigned to the State Department. Since State was itself readjusting to post war responsibilities, these added burdens proved difficult to handle.

The State Department, under Secretary James F. Byrnes, resisted assuming operational responsibility for the occupation of Germany and Japan, since this "tail" would in effect be wagging the departmental "dog". In the Secretary's own words, he "opposed the efforts of the War Department to transfer to the State Department control of our occupational organizations in Europe . . . [for which] the State Department is not adapted and cannot recruit high caliber personnel for a temporary position; if all the myriad duties were transferred to State, its capacity to wisely define foreign policy would be hampered . . ." [1] Here was just one of the many manifestations of the perennial question of whether the Department of State should be a program operator as well as a policy maker. The 1949 Commission on Organization of the Executive Branch, while unable to agree unanimously on this point, stated that as a general rule, the Department "should not be given responsibility for the operation of specific programs, whether overseas or at home". [2] However, in June 1951 the Brookings Institution prepared a report for the Bureau of the Budget on *The Administration of Foreign Affairs and Overseas Operations*, which dissented strongly from this statement. [3] The most recent study, by the Hoover Commission in 1955, reverted to the earlier view and stated that the basic responsibility of the Department of State "is policy, not operations". It was recognized, however, that with the transfer to State of certain Foreign Operations Administration functions the Secretary would be responsible for operations. [4]

Another important controversy developed as the newer functional areas such as economic affairs and relationships with international organizations like the United Nations were superimposed on State's traditional geographic setup. The question of functional versus geographical organization was eventually compromised through creation of Assistant Secretaries for Economic Affairs and International Organization Affairs, plus Assistant Secretaries for Administrative, Public and Congressional Affairs. The major regional bureaus remained "responsible for applying over-all political, security, economic, public affairs, social, consular, administrative and other policies and practices" within their respective areas.[5] The 1955-56 organization of the Department—excluding the International Cooperation Administration—is shown by the chart on page 40.

In addition to its internal problems, the State Department has also had difficulties in its relations with Congress. Part of the trouble may be the "irrational prejudice" of some Congressmen who seem to view the Department as somehow representing foreign interests against those of the United States [6] or as "riddled with security risks." Concerning the problem of Congressional investigations, a high official of the Department declared in his testimony before the House Foreign Affairs Committee: "You gentlemen know as well as anyone that the Department of State has been under tremendous criticism. It has lost prestige in the minds of the American people . . . Also it appears that the State Department is going to be the most carefully investigated department in the history of the United States, because at the present time the Committee on Government Operations of the House is carrying on an investigation of an aspect of the Department's work, the Committee on Government Operations of the Senate is carrying on a separate investigation; the Internal Security Committee is carrying on an investigation, and the Foreign Relations Committee of the Senate is creating a loyalty subcommittee." [7]

Congress has traditionally been reluctant to increase the responsibility of the State Department, although it has recognized its leadership in the making of foreign policy. This attitude has been particularly evident in foreign aid programs where responsibility has often been given to new agencies which Congress could more easily control.[8] For example, in 1943 the job of administering foreign economic aid was assigned to the Foreign Economic Administration, moved to State, Commerce, Agriculture, and the Reconstruction Finance Corporation in 1945, assigned to the Economic Cooperation Administration in 1948 when the Marshall Plan got underway, and transferred to the Mutual Security Agency in 1951. The Point Four programs of the Technical

DEPARTMENT OF STATE

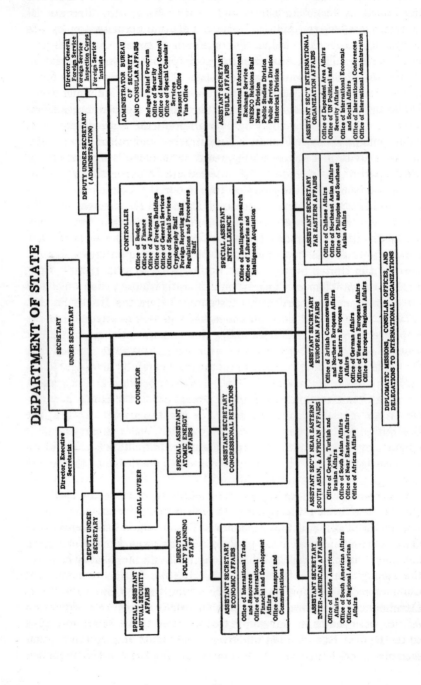

Cooperation Administration were likewise transferred from State to the Mutual Security Agency in June, 1953. Then, with Reorganization Plan 7, effective August 1, 1953, the Mutual Security Agency was abolished and its place taken by the Foreign Operations Administration (FOA). The Mutual Security Act of 1954, however, provided that FOA should cease to exist as of June 30, 1955; accordingly Executive Order 10610 of May 9, 1955, transferred FOA's functions to the Department of Defense and to the International Cooperation Administration (ICA), which was established within the State Department on a "semi-autonomous" basis. The Hoover Commission Task Force on Overseas Economic Operations had recommended two alternatives: assignment of full responsibility to the State Department, or, for the President to appoint an official acting under the Council on Foreign Economic Policy to complete the liquidation and reassignment of FOA functions, and for the *Council* to assume responsibility for "coordinating all continuing functions in the foreign aid program." The Task Force report was submitted in March 1955 and was presumably considered by the President in drafting his Message to Congress on April 20 in which he outlined the plan which was eventually followed. The Commission Report to Congress, submitted June 6, 1955, urged that the Secretary of State maintain strong control over policies, objectives, and programs through the Director of the ICA—who is responsible directly to him. The complexity of foreign aid organization makes it impossible to offer more than cursory treatment here.

Most aspects of national security policy for which the State Department has primary responsibility are interdepartmental. The line between domestic and foreign affairs has become so obscured that the 1947 Hoover Commission noted that over half the executive departments and agencies had foreign affairs responsibilities. The 1955 Hoover Report on Overseas Economic Operations discusses the role of the following bodies in the Executive Office of the President which are concerned with foreign aid: the National Security Council, the Operations Coordinating Board, the National Advisory Council on International Monetary and Financial Problems, the Economic Defense Advisory Committee, the Council on Foreign Economic Policy, and the Council of Economic Advisers. Outside the Executive Office the Departments of State, Treasury, Defense, Agriculture, Interior, Commerce, and Labor, the Export-Import Bank, the International Development Advisory Board, and the Institute of Inter-American Affairs have major foreign aid responsibilities. The total, according to the Hoover Report, is 34 different departments and agencies. This seemingly endless list points up the reason for the complex structure of interdepartmental committees—many of them chaired by State—which work out the day-to-day problems of coordinating foreign programs.[9]

Almost equally complex is the problem of representation overseas. Relationships with such regional organizations as the North Atlantic Treaty Organization, Organization for European Economic Cooperation, and the European Coal and Steel Community further complicate matters. Agencies maintaining field offices overseas frequently resist State Department control of personnel and policies and seek to maintain independent communication with the home office. On the other hand, it is now generally recognized that the Chief Diplomatic Officer, as the ranking U. S. representative, is responsible for all activities conducted by American agencies in the particular country. But in practice, there have been difficulties with technical missions from other Departments, military representatives (such as Military Aid Advisory Groups) and intelligence agencies. A unique solution to this problem, the creation of a special representative in Europe, was devised by the framers of the Mutual Security Act. But in general, the current trend is to stress the primary coordinating role of the Ambassador, who reports directly to the State Department. This is consistent with the increased emphasis on State Department leadership, particularly since primary responsibility for overseas programs was shifted from the independent Foreign Operations Administration to a "semi-autonomous" agency within the Department. Except for military aid, the lines of responsibility now run directly to the Secretary of State.

The State Department is thus represented at all four levels of the national security structure: the National Security Council, the Planning Board—where its representative heads the State Department's Planning Staff—the Operations Coordinating Board and numerous interdepartmental committees and working groups. The Department's Executive Secretariat reviews and coordinates work done within the Department and furnishes the secretariat for several of the more important interdepartmental committees. The Brookings Institution study stated that the main role of the State Department should be leadership in "securing voluntary coordination", backed up by the Executive Office,[10] and advising the President in the determination of overall foreign policies. As presently organized, the Department seems to be fulfilling this role.

The fate of informational activities has followed a pattern similar to that of foreign aid. Primary responsibility has been shifted from the Office of War Information, to the State Department, to an International Information Administration within the State Department, and finally, by Reorganization Plan No. 8, 1953, to the United States Information Agency. The importance of this work has been heightened by the cold war. Explaining our policies to allies, neutrals, and potential enemies has become a major phase of national security. According to the National Security Council, the mission consists of "explaining . . . the objectives and policies of the U.S. . . . depicting . . . the correlation between U.S. policies and the legitimate aspirations of other peoples . . . unmasking and countering hostile attempts to . . . frustrate the policies of the U.S., and . . . delineating those important aspects of the life which facilitate understanding of the policies and objectives of the . . . U.S." [11] The importance attached to such matters is illustrated by the many investigations and studies made of information programs by both Congress and the Executive, totaling more than half a dozen in 1952-1953 alone.

The United States Information Agency—an independent body in the executive branch—seeks to carry out the objectives of the National Security Council directive through all available media, including overseas information centers, cultural projects, and educational exchange programs. The agency has assistant directors for five major regions plus offices for each major media. The Office of Policy and Programs, headed by an assistant director, is an important coordination center for activities inside and outside the Agency. Although the United States Information Agency is responsible to the National Security Council, from which it receives instructions under the policy guidance of the Secretary of State, the Director is not a statutory member. Originally, he was only an adviser to the Operations Coordinating Board. Now, however, he is a full member of the Board as well as the National Security Council—a vital relationship in view of the importance of information to all other overseas operations.

---

[1] James F. Byrnes, *Speaking Frankly*, Harper and Brothers, New York, 1947, p. 224.

[2] *Report to the Congress*, 1949, Foreign Affairs Recommendation No. 7. The Report of the Foreign Affairs Task Force is printed separately as Appendix H.

[3] U. S. GPO, Washington, 1951, pp. 239-40. This report, a valuable analysis of the problem, covers the entire executive organization concerned in foreign affairs including the Defense Department and the Executive Office of the President.

[4] Commission on Organization of the Executive Branch of the Government, "Overseas Economic Operations", *Report to the Congress*, June, 1955, p. 41.

[5] *U.S. Government Organization Manual*, 1955-56, p. 82.

[6] For comments on this attitude, see Daniel S. Cheever and Field Haviland, *American Foreign Policy and the Separation of Powers*, Harvard University Press, Cambridge, 1952, p. 107; William Y. Elliott, *United States Foreign Policy*, Columbia University Press, New York, 1952, p. 99.

[7] Testimony of Mr. Humelsine *Hearings* before the Committee on Foreign Affairs, House of Representatives, 83rd Congress, on S. 243 and H.R. 1377, "To Provide for an Under-Secretary of State for Administration", p. 5.

[8] The Mutual Security Agency as well as the Technical Cooperation Administration soon came under Congressional fire. Reports urging "centralization and unification of major economic activities—the double themes of unity and autonomy" were made as early as 1950. For a good summary of the history and development of U. S. foreign aid structure, see Arthur MacMahon, *Administration in Foreign Affairs*, University of Alabama Press, Tuscaloosa, 1953, Chapter 3, especially pp. 125-127, 129-130. A comprehensive treatment of foreign aid will be found in W. A. Brown and Redvers Opie, *American Foreign Assistance*, Brookings Institution, Washington, 1953.

[9] The Commission *Report on Overseas Economic Operations* is a brief and readable summary of the organizations, programs, and terminology of foreign aid. The Task Force report contains over 20 staff papers and ten country studies.

[10] Brookings Institution, *op. cit.*, pp. 240-242. The study further recommended a Vice Chairman of the NSC to insure coordination at the highest level.

[11] See *U.S. Government Organization Manual 1955-56*, p. 505 for the full NSC Directive.

CHAPTER V

INTERNATIONAL SECURITY AFFAIRS

Military policies are both a means to and a limitation upon the objectives of the United States; the Department of Defense is the backbone of the organization for national security as well as its largest —and most expensive—element. The organization, roles, and missions of the Defense Department and its component military services are topics in themselves and since they are treated at length in Part Two, they will not be discussed in detail here. The present chapter is primarily concerned with the international security affairs responsibilities of the Secretary of Defense. Of all the units under him, the Office of the Assistant Secretary of Defense for International Security Affairs is the one most directly related to the overall organization for national security. As such it provides a convenient point of reference for discussing the roles of the military services and the Joint Chiefs of Staff and the relationships of the State and Defense Departments.

Formulation of national security policy can be likened to a triangle with the President at the apex, the Secretary of State at one angle, and the Secretary of Defense at the other. The National Security Council might well occupy the center. The two Secretaries, however, are themselves the peaks of their own vast organizational pyramids. Each and each alone is charged with the primary responsibility for his area. It is the office and the person of the Secretary, rather than the department itself, which is assigned responsibilities and must give advice to the President. Although he cannot dodge the ultimate responsibility, the Secretary must delegate some of it. It is important, therefore, to bear in mind that in the case of International Security Affairs it is the powers and the duties of the *Secretary of Defense* which have been delegated to an Assistant Secretary and his staff.

Since its inception in 1950, International Security Affairs has had three major responsibilities: military aid, the politico-military-economic aspects of foreign military matters, and National Security Council affairs. These three offices, plus a fourth, a comptroller, have until recently been the main elements of what has sometimes been called the "Pentagon's State Department." As the scope and nature of U.S. commitments overseas have changed, so has this body's organization. ISA has not only kept pace with but sometimes exceeded the rest of the Defense Department in being organized and reorganized. On January 1, 1956, a complete revision was made by the new Assistant Secretary of Defense (International Security Affairs), Gordon Gray.

HISTORICAL DEVELOPMENTS

It is useful to examine briefly the development of the four major components of the International Security Affairs organization.

Before the Korean war the Office of the Secretary of Defense was relatively small. In addition to the Joint Chiefs of Staff, the Munitions Board, and the Research and Development Board, there was only the War Council—now called the Armed Forces Policy Council.[1] The Secretary had a small staff with three civilian special assistants. Although the 1949 Hoover Task Force on National Security Organization referred to them as "trouble shooters" who should be free for special assignments,[2] it noted that work demanded that they double as staff assistants. As Wilfred J. McNeil, now Defense Comptroller, inevitably specialized in fiscal and budget matters, so John Ohly specialized in military aid matters and worked with the armed services in coordinating the Defense Department's responsibilities. During this period, the War Council advised the Secretary of Defense on both civilian and military matters. In 1949 Secretary Louis A. Johnson made it the major intra-departmental body to consider problems before they were submitted to the National Security Council. But the War Council proved ineffective as a "policy formulating instrument for politico-military affairs", partly because meetings were too large and partly because it overlapped the role of the Joint Chiefs of Staff as the "principal military advisers" to the President and the National Security Council. Furthermore the State-Army-Navy-Air Force Coordinating Committee (SANACC) which was still functioning, tended to short circuit the War Council's work.

After passage of the Mutual Defense Assistance Act of 1949 the Secretary of Defense established an Office of Military Assistance (OMA) to work with State and the Economic Cooperation Administration in administering the program. The Army, however, did much of the work since it had been designated by the Joint Chiefs of Staff as their executive agent for Mutual Defense Assistance.

The Korean war and the defense build up which followed brought about a great expansion in the international security affairs area. U.S. military aid was greatly increased, NATO was strengthened, plans were made to rearm Germany, and a Japanese peace treaty was signed. The embryo International Security Affairs organization, which then consisted of the War Council, the Office of Military Assistance, and the "specialized" Special Assistant, proved inadequate to handle all of the politico-military problems that arose. Some, such as the strategy reevaluation contained in one of the basic National Security Council policy papers and the instructions to the United States delegate at the Panmunjom armistice negotiations, were apparently handled by special ad hoc groups composed of State Department and Joint Chiefs of Staff representatives. On others, a representative of International Security Affairs was included, as with the proposal to rearm Germany. Interestingly enough, according to one participant in the State-JCS-ISA conferences on the subject, the National Security Council never formally discussed this decision, although it was cleared with each member individually.

On December 19, 1950, President Truman established the position of Special Assistant to the Secretary of Defense for International Security Affairs.[3] During the next two years the responsibilities of this office and of the staff which accumulated around it were increased. By 1952, these responsibilities included general politico-military matters, NATO and the Mutual Defense Assistance Program, and coordination of all National Security Council matters (the last having been assigned because of the shortcomings of the War Council).

Meanwhile a "memorandum of agreement" between the heads of Defense, State, the Economic Cooperation Administration, and the Treasury and approved by the President had established the International Security Affairs Committee (ISAC) in 1950. The Office of the Director of International Security Affairs, although in the State Department, was almost "supra-departmental" since the Director, in his capacity as Chairman of ISAC, exercised responsibility for the government as a whole.

The complex relationships during 1951 and 1952 among the various departments, the Director for Mutual Security[4] and that unique creation, the President's Special Representative in Europe, is too involved for detailed discussion. Briefly, the Special Representative (initially William H. Draper) was to act "for the President as the senior U.S. civilian representative" and to speak "for the U.S. Government as a whole." In effect, he possessed a merger of the authority of the Secretaries of Defense, State, and Treasury and the Director for Mutual Security.[5] The Defense Department's focal point for coordinating foreign aid was the Assistant to the Secretary for International Security Affairs, Frank Nash. Defense was represented—usually by someone from the ISA staff—on such interdepartmental groups as the Foreign Military Assistance Coordinating Committee, and the Economic Defense Advisory Committee as well as the International Security Affairs Committee.[6] Although the Department of the Army handled most of the actual operations, International Security Affairs played an important role, coordinating materiel procurement through an Office of International Programs within the structure of the Munitions Board and also working closely with the Joint Chiefs of Staff.

The complicated accounting and budgetary arrangements involved (in the Mutual Defense Assistance Program) had required the addition of a budget adviser and a statistical adviser to the International Security Affairs staff. They specialized in international programs but were responsible to the Defense Comptroller. This was the first step toward creation of an ISA comptroller.

In February 1953 the Assistant to the Secretary for International Security Affairs was promoted to the rank of Assistant Secretary of Defense, and his office underwent still further reorganization. Later in 1953, Reorganization Plan No. 6 abolished the unwieldy structure of Boards and Committees within the Office of the Secretary of Defense and added six additional assistant secretaries. The Munitions Board's Office of International Programs was transferred to ISA and became the Office of Foreign Economic Defense Affairs[7] under the Office of Foreign Military Affairs. This latter office developed area branches which were assigned to work closely with the country experts at the State Department. During Frank Nash's administration of ISA he particularly stressed the importance of this direct liaison to insure that the Defense officials were kept abreast of the current thinking and developments at State.

Other changes were brought about when H. Struve Hensel succeeded Frank Nash as Assistant Secretary in March 1954. An agreement worked out between Hensel and Wilfred J. McNeil, the Defense Comptroller, set up an ISA comptroller. On the surface this seems an insignificant matter, but it was important because it involved not only the division of authority between two strong personalities but also a departure from the usual organization—a set-up still unique in the Office of the Secretary of Defense. Significantly, while the personnel affected were "employees and representatives" of the Defense Comptroller, they were paid from ISA funds and constituted a part of the latter organization. Moreover, a Director of National Security Council Affairs was created to improve coordination with the NSC.[8] In effect this official wears three hats: As Director, he is responsible for a synthesis of Defense Department recommendations on matters to be considered by the Council—or on policies and actions of the Council—and his office coordinates them. He is also a Special Assistant to the Secretary of Defense for National Security Council Affairs and is responsible for briefing the Secretary. And he is the Defense representative on the National Security Council Planning Board. The merger of these functions in one office has been a marked improvement in integrating the Defense Department into the larger national security structure.

Another innovation during Mr. Hensel's administration was the International Security Plan, which brings together by country various directives, policies, and programs concerned with mutual defense assistance. National Security Council guidance was so broad that different agencies interpreted policy in different ways. There was too little coordination between the Joint Chiefs of Staff and the State Department. The plan is designed to overcome jurisdictional disputes and insure coordination; this might have been done by the Operations Coordinating Board, but since the problem concerned only State, Defense, the International Cooperation Administration and the Joint Chiefs of Staff—the latter not being formally represented on the OCB —it was decided to keep the plan at the departmental level. It has been continued with some revisions under Gordon Gray.

To summarize briefly: before the 1956 reorganization the major units in the Office of the Assistant Secretary for International Security Affairs were: (1) The Office of National Security Council Affairs; (2) The Office of Foreign Military Affairs, (including a Plans Division, a Policy Division with area branches, a Foreign Economic Defense Division, and the Permanent Joint Board on Defense (U.S. and Canada)); (3) A Comptroller; (4) The Office of Military Assistance Programs. The last named was divided into a control division, which directly supervised the Military Aid Advisory Groups in foreign countries; the Operations Division, which coordinated and processed military aid requirements requested by our allies and approved by the Joint Chiefs; and the Procurement and Production Division, which was concerned with such matters as off-shore procurement.°

At present the "legal advisor" for International Security Affairs is an assistant general counsel of the Department. These assistants work for one or more of the assistant secretaries while assigned to the Office of the General Counsel. Although some of ISA's work is done by the legal staffs of the three armed services, its legal advisor has tremendously complex and diverse problems ranging from the Saint Lawrence Seaway to NATO "status of forces" questions. It remains to be seen whether there will be an ISA counsel as there is now an ISA comptroller, or whether the present arrangement will continue.

The functions discussed have been reassigned within ISA by Mr.

Gray's reorganization. One major addition (or more accurately, a transfer from the Office of Special Operations), an Office of Operations Coordinating Board Affairs, performs for OCB what the Office of National Security Council Affairs does for the NSC. A complete separation of the International Security Affairs Comptroller from the Defense Department Comptroller was also brought about by the 1956 reorganization. This far-reaching internal shakeup has produced these major changes:

Regional Directors now handle liaison with Military Aid Advisory Groups. Their establishment as independent units suggests an increased parallel with International Cooperation Administration and State Department organization. The Plans Division of the old Office of Foreign Military Affairs has become the Office of Planning—one of the six major units of International Security Affairs, not counting the Regional Directors. Foreign Economic Defense responsibilities have been transferred to the new Office of Special International Affairs, which prepares Department of Defense policies on international organizations such as NATO and SEATO, on disarmament, and for international conferences. Preparing for and arranging defense representation at these conferences is one of ISA's most important tasks, since the large number of collective security pacts requires that defense participate equally with the State Department. U.S. support of NATO military activities is furnished by the military departments as "Administrative Agents" for the various headquarters. Internationally budgeted support is, however, provided directly by the Secretary of Defense from military assistance appropriations. The Office of Military Aid Programs has been abolished, its functions transferred to a new Office of Programming and Control. The revised organization of the Office of the International Security Affairs is shown by a chart in Appendix V.

The role of the Assistant Secretary of Defense for International Security Affairs is going to become increasingly important. Creation of an additional Deputy Assistant Secretary indicates the increased responsibility assigned to the ISA "Vice-President". For example, the Assistant Secretary is personally assuming a more active part in directing National Security Council affairs—particularly in Planning Board meetings. It is important, however, to recognize that the operations of International Security Affairs, even more than most other organizations, vary widely under different officials. The office was different under Mr. Nash from what it became under Mr. Hensel and subsequently under Mr. Gray. In the same way, personal civilian-military relationships within the organization are also significant factors.

THE MILITARY DEPARTMENTS

Most of the functions so far discussed as international security affairs are routine operations or logistics matters within the military services. The Army's role in military aid or support of NATO, for example, will be handled within the regular command channels by the Staff sections for operations (G-3) and logistics (G-4). Although there is a Chief of Civil Affairs and Military Government on the Army Special Staff, he deals mostly with problems of U. S. troops stationed abroad. Supervision of Army responsibilities in Military Aid Advisory Groups comes under the Deputy Chief of Staff for Operations, who has a deputy for international security matters. The Navy and the Air Force have the same set-up within their regular command and staff organization.

At the *Secretariat* level, however, there is an Assistant Secretary who advises the Secretary of the Army on international security matters. Responsibilities of this Assistant Secretary of the Army (Civil-Military Affairs) are described below. This long list is quoted in full to give at least a rough idea of the magnitude of the job, even though no detailed discussion is possible within the scope of this book. ". . . international security affairs, other than Mutual Defense Assistance Program; foreign relations affecting the mission of the Army, economic defense, base rights negotiations, and international monetary affairs; National Security Council and Operations Coordinating Board matters; United Nations, North Atlantic Treaty Organization, and similar international organization matters; unified and specified commands; special operations, psychological warfare, unconventional warfare, and international information activities; intelligence, counter-intelligence, and foreign liaison; politico-military policy of the Army; and civil affairs and military government. He is responsible for continental defense and civil defense, and for evacuation of non-combatant United States Nationals from sensitive areas; for staff support of the Army Policy Council, and of secretarial participation in the Armed Forces Policy Council and the Joint Secretaries; and for coordination of secretarial contributions to the preparation of agenda for Cabinet meetings. The Assistant Secretary of the Army (Civil-Military Affairs) is also responsible for the civil functions of the Department of the Army; the Alaska Communications System; and for direction and supervision of the business aspects of the Panama Canal, including the Canal Zone Government and the Panama Canal Company. He serves as the Army member of the Air Coordinating Committee." [10]

The Assistant Secretary of the Army (Logistics and Research and Development) has an executive assistant who coordinates Army activity under the Mutual Defense Assistance Program. The Assistant Secretary of the Air Force (Materiel) also has a Deputy for Mutual Security Assistance Affairs. This arrangement is paralleled in the Office of the Deputy Chief of Staff (Materiel). There is a similar staff arrangement under the Assistant Secretary (Research and Development).

Although Navy organization charts do not show any particular office charged mainly with mutual security or international affairs, there are staffs concerned with this in both the Office of the Chief of Naval Operations (or the Deputies for Plans and Policy and for Logistics) and the Office of the Undersecretary of the Navy.

As noted earlier, international security affairs is a dynamic, not a static function. The organizational relationships are constantly in flux, changing to meet the needs of particular programs and responsibilities assigned by Congress. Consequently, generalizations are even more dangerous than usual. But in discussing the over-all pattern of relationships between International Security Affairs in the Office of the Secretary of Defense and the military services—who are nearly always backed up by their Secretaries—one generalization at least is quite safe. This is that from the very beginning there has been a constant struggle between them over foreign military aid.

In 1949, the Army, as executive agent for the Joint Chiefs in Mutual Defense Assistance matters proposed that it present "consolidated recommendations" and "coordinate action by the three services." The Director of the Office of Military Aid in ISA wrote to Secretary of Defense Louis A. Johnson that the contact between his office and State was "so continuous that a consolidated view of the three services alone may be incomplete and premature if this relationship is not taken into account from the beginning." The Secretary upheld the Director as prime coordinator. When International Security Affairs was reorganized in 1951, the issue was raised again. In commenting on the scope of ISA's "Charter" both the Army and the Air Force proposed that "operating functions *will* be delegated" to the services and that ISA "will *not* undertake extensive operating functions." These amendments were rejected—with brevity unusual in a government memorandum—by a one-word notation: "No!"

Late in 1954, still another reorganization of International Security Affairs was planned, negotiations continued until July 1955. Mr. Hensel was forced to substitute "Secretary of Defense" for Assistant Secretary of Defense (International Security Affairs) in the draft of the Directive to make it clear that ISA was acting only in the Secretary's name, but the fact that the Secretary could delegate his authority made this of no practical effect. As little as two days before the Directive was issued the service secretaries were still protesting the trend towards loss of their authority to the Assistant Secretary of Defense (International Security Affairs). But the Directive—backed by Secretary Wilson, the Deputy Secretary (then Robert Anderson) and the incoming Assistant Secretary (Gordon Gray)—was issued as written, and the indications are that the trend is continuing. However, there is something to be said for the service viewpoint. For the most part they, rather than the Office of the Secretary of Defense, actually operate the programs through their regular organizations. They are closer to the problems, and, they argue, should have full operational authority.

This controversy is part of the pattern of unification, and is by no means limited to international security affairs. But the trend seems to be to put more and more authority in the hands of the assistant secretaries, even though they are technically staff advisors and outside the command line. In any event, there are certain aspects peculiar to ISA.

First of all, the Mutual Security Act of 1955 assigns certain functions to the Secretary of Defense and to the Department of Defense, not to the services. Others have been transferred to Defense upon termination of the Foreign Operations Administration. Most important, the funds provided by Congress are appropriated to the Secretary of Defense, rather than to the Army, Navy, or Air Force. Second, foreign military aid is considered separately by Congress from military appropriations and is subject to scrutiny based on considerations other than those usually involved in the military budget. The relationship with the Department of State is such that requests for Mutual Security are prepared jointly. This highlights the fact that close coordination with the entire executive branch is necessary, and the Office of International Security Affairs, rather than military departments, is best equipped to sustain this contact. Finally, foreign aid—both its grant and its withholding—is a sensitive matter to foreign governments. The figures by country are labelled "not to be released to foreign nationals," although not otherwise classified information. This fact also argues for a specialized treatment in one office, rather than three.

In fact, ISA directly engages in operations, both in connection with trade controls (economic defense activities) and military assistance. The new Office of Programming and Control issues shipping instructions and program orders, and justifies Mutual Security activities of the Department before Congress. The nature of these activities makes it even more difficult than usual to achieve a proper "staff-line" relationship between International Security Affairs and the military services.

THE JOINT CHIEFS OF STAFF

The Joint Chiefs of Staff are designated by law as the principal military advisers to the President, the National Security Council, and the Secretary of Defense. This gives them a unique position in the organization for national security. As the main source of professional military estimates upon which judgments on national security matters depend, they are both a part of and yet separate from the Office of the Secretary of Defense in which they are administratively and geographically located. By statute the Joint Chiefs include (1) the Chairman—who, like the other members, is appointed by the President; (2) the Army Chief of Staff; (3) the Chief of Naval Operations; (4) the Air Force Chief of Staff; and (5)—on matters affecting the Marines—the Commandant of the Marine Corps.

Hereafter Joint Chiefs of Staff will mean the institution rather than the group of individuals. In addition to the service Chiefs, the organization includes the Joint Staff, an integrated staff with a Director, which has a statutory limit of 210 members. They are assigned full time to the Joint Staff and are to be distinguished from the service *representatives* on the various Joint Committees of the Joint Chiefs. These representatives serve in addition to their other duties, usually *ex officio*. This distinction can be illustrated by the Joint Intelligence Committee composed of the Army G-2, the Chief of the Office of Naval Intelligence, the Air Force A-2, and a Deputy Director of the Joint Staff for Intelligence. Under this Committee is the Joint Intelligence *Group*—a unit of the Joint Staff—which makes the detailed studies (drawing where necessary upon the service intelligence organizations) upon which the *Committee* makes its recommendations to the Joint *Chiefs*—and to the other members of the intelligence community.

The relationships involved are shown in detail in the Joint Chiefs organization chart in Appendix V.

The criticisms that have been made of the Joint Chiefs have more often been concerned with its external relationships rather than with its internal workings. In part these criticisms have involved such esoteric factors as the "military mind" and have stressed the need for effective civilian control. But one group, which, in their own words, does not "share the frequently expressed suspicion of the 'military mind'" has stated the problem more realistically as follows: "It is important to emphasize the special policy-making function of the Secretary of Defense . . . Only when the Secretary of Defense is himself a man of policy, and an effective deputy to the President, will it be possible for the counsels of the *State* Department to receive their due weight. A line of decision and counsel which goes from the Secretary of State to the Secretary of Defense to the Joint Chiefs of Staff is proper and practicable; a direct line to the Joint Chiefs from the Department of State cannot do the job." [11]

In theory, the line does go from the Joint Chiefs through the Secretary of Defense (via the ISA Assistant Secretary) to the National Security Council or State. But in practice there exists a tendency for a "direct line" between the Joint Chiefs and State. In spite of the designation of International Security Affairs as the principal contact point between all elements of the Defense Department and the rest of the executive branch, the State Department is still given weekly briefings by the Joint Chiefs.

Although the situation is of course considerably different since International Security Affairs was established, the basic problem is best illustrated with reference to the pre-Department of Defense period in 1946 when President Truman, faced with a serious problem in Palestine, desired to have a full appraisal of the military factors involved and asked his Secretary of State to get an opinion from the Joint Chiefs of Staff. "The Joint Chiefs of Staff urged that no United States armed forces be involved . . . They believed that the *political* shock attending the reappearance of United States Armed Forces in the Middle East would unnecessarily risk serious disturbances . . . They were primarily concerned about Middle East oil and in long range terms about the danger that the Arabs, antagonized by Western action in Palestine, would make common cause with Russia . . ." [12]

This quotation illustrates still another dimension of the problem: the relationship of political and military factors which was discussed in Chapter I. It is extremely difficult to frame a military appraisal which is not given a political frame of reference. Conversely, it is difficult to make a political judgment without some assumptions about military capabilities. If these assumptions are not clearly stated—or are implicit in the context of the question—the answer may be misleading. And this tendency is increased when the military advice that reaches the level of the National Security Council is based upon unstated assumptions furnished by State to the Joint Chiefs through direct contact since advice coming from the Joint Chiefs is invariably stated to be "from a purely military" standpoint.

But inevitably the two poles of military and foreign policy—the Joint Chiefs and the State Department—attract each other. Such an urgent matter as the instructions to the Senior U. N. delegate at the Panmunjom Armistice Conference tended to by-pass the Secretary of Defense. These instructions were reportedly "drafted by a high powered group from State and the Joint Chiefs of Staff." [18]

One possible solution would be to incorporate representatives of all the agencies concerned with national security into the Joint Chiefs' structure. But such a "junior National Security Council" would nullify the major lines of responsibility within the executive branch as well as the American tradition of civilian control. At the opposite extreme, might be complete separation of the Chiefs and all other bodies below the level of the National Security Council. But this would prove unworkable; there would be none of the working level contact which is so essential to policy-making.

The present arrangement is a compromise between the two extremes. The Secretary of Defense—through his organization for international security affairs—has been inserted between the two poles, and has been designated their primary contact point. Where civilian leadership is lacking, the military tend to fill the vacuum—not from a desire to run things their own way, but because the job must be done. This need for civilian leadership has been a prime factor in the growth of the International Security Affairs organization. This may well be the best and only solution. But it is clear that it has some built-in problems. The State Department, jealous of its prerogatives, tends to keep a firm hold on its working papers. It sometimes seeks advice directly from the Joint Chiefs if necessary, and then submits them to ISA as *faits accomplis*. On the other hand, no one but the Chiefs themselves can speak for them. Their representative on certain interdepartmental groups has been called the "Russian delegate" because he can only report to his principals but never commit them. However, in view of the tendency to claim JCS support for papers advancing a departmental position, this conservatism may be wise. Another difficulty is the need to take into account known service disagreements in requesting advice from the Chiefs. Since the Chiefs are usually unwilling to send back a paper showing divided opinion, advice on a matter of inter-service dispute may represent their lowest common denominator and be valueless.

But the major problem is that, in the words of a 1955 Hoover Commission Task Force, "decisions and information do not flow freely from the Joint Chiefs of Staff to the Assistant Secretaries of Defense."[14] Similar criticisms have been made by the 1947 Hoover Task Force on National Security Organization, by the Rockefeller Committee in 1953, and by other groups. Although the Joint Chiefs use some civilian consultants the organization is entirely military. It has been suggested that the gap could be bridged by having a liaison representative from the appropriate ISA staff section work with the country and functional "teams" which do the basic study of issues presented to the Joint Chiefs. Against this it can be argued that the injection of non-military considerations at the level of purely "military" planning would only confuse the issue.

In defense of the JCS it should be stated that a majority of its critics admit that, internally, it functions efficiently.[15] The number of requests for opinions from the Joint Chiefs of Staff is staggering. Their processing is often time-consuming, but they are handled comparatively smoothly. Progress is being made in preparation of realistic war plans. These furnish guidance for requirements and force level planning of concern to all elements of the national security structure.

To go back and look at the defense structure from the vantage point of the Secretary of Defense, it is clear that advice may reach him through a number of different channels: First, the Joint Chiefs of Staff may provide him directly with "military advice and recommendations on international security affairs, including the continuous correlation of the Mutual Defense Assistance Programs."[16] Second, the Assistant Secretary of Defense (International Security Affairs) represents and advises the Secretary (and by delegation exercises his authority) in this area. This official, through his staff, also serves as the defense contact point for the National Security Council and its related organs, the Department of State, and other agencies outside the Defense Department.[17] Third, the combined advice of the Office of the Secretary of Defense, the Service Secretaries and the Joint Chiefs may reach the Secretary through such bodies as the Mutual Defense Assistance Management Council.[18] Similarly, the Secretary may receive advice through the Armed Forces Policy Council—composed of the Secretary and Deputy Secretary of Defense, the three Service Secretaries and Chiefs of Staff—or through the Joint Secretaries. The last two bodies will be discussed in Chapter X, but it is worth noting here that, of all the Assistant Secretaries of Defense, the Assistant Secretary for International Security Affairs is the only one who is a regular member of the Joint Secretaries—who otherwise comprise the top two civilian officials of the Secretary's office and of each military department.

Although this flexibility may complicate organizational relationships, it permits adjustment to new developments. As the cold war with Russia shifts its emphasis from purely military to economic-political-psychological techniques—and perhaps back again to military—it should be possible to adjust the emphasis in defense policies accordingly. In any case, whether the best approach is to separate the channels for military and political advice or to merge them, the personal relations between key individuals in the Office of the Secretary of Defense, particularly in ISA, the Joint Chiefs, and in the State Department are the key factor.

A HYPOTHETICAL EXAMPLE OF THE PROCESSING OF A POLITICO-MILITARY DECISION

Unfortunately, the organization for national security cannot be presented in simple terms and still be meaningful. The complexity of this book illustrates the complexity of the organization itself. It seems desirable therefore to review the whole organization with a hypothetical case history of the decision-making process. The reader should be cautioned that this is not only hypothetical but also oversimplified and generalized for illustrative purposes.

1. The problem—in this case, the danger of an internal Communist threat to Country X which for diplomatic reasons cannot be met by direct military aid—is reported by the chief of the U. S. diplomatic mission. He may consult on the spot with military and intelligence agents in the area. His report goes to Washington, probably by courier and in code. At the State Department it is decoded and routed to the Country X desk in the XYZ Regional Bureau. Information copies go to the Pentagon where they are sent to the Joint Chiefs and to the appropriate International Security Affairs Regional Director. (Any other reports submitted—as by a military attache—are processed for preliminary staff work in the Defense Department.)

2. A State Department staff paper—proposing certain types of economic and indirect military aid to strengthen the internal security forces of Country X—is drawn up at State. It may be given a final check by the Executive Secretariat, and cleared with the Policy Planning Staff. This is transmitted to the National Security Council Staff which recirculates it to the Defense Department and other agencies concerned as an *NSC staff* paper.

3. Once arrived within the Office of National Security Council Affairs in International Security Affairs, the proposal will be sent around for preliminary comment to the services, the Joint Chiefs, and other groups in the Office of the Secretary of Defense. Informal dis-

cussions are held under the auspices of the Office of National Security Council Affairs in which the comments are compared and discussed. A Defense Department "position paper" is then prepared.

4. This position paper is processed by the NSC Planning Board's Board Assistants and is discussed in detail by the Planning Board. Its recommendation—which may or may not be unanimous—is circulated back through State and Defense, this time called an "NSC Buff" paper (because of the color of the cover sheet.) The same distribution for comments within the Defense Department will occur, the end result being a "briefing paper" for the Secretary of Defense.

5. Thus briefed, the Secretary of Defense attends a National Security Council meeting, at which the problem has been placed on the agenda by the Special Assistant to the President for National Security Affairs. The proposed NSC policy paper (with its "financial appendix" giving an estimate of the cost) is discussed by the members, and the "sense of the meeting" is determined. When this is written up as a record of the Council's action, it becomes a recommendation to the President. If he rejects the recommendation, the matter must be reopened. If he accepts it—usually with an "O.K., DDE"—the paper becomes official U. S. Policy. Designated by a number such as NSC/1234/5 it is transmitted to the Secretaries concerned and to the Operations Coordination Board.

6. The document approved by the President is usually couched in very general terms. It may refer only to the principle of aid for internal security purposes in the XYZ area. The Operations Coordinating Board working initially through Board Assistants, will draft a "Country X Plan." This is circulated for comment in a fashion similar to the original NSC drafts. Based on these comments the members of the Board—who are at the Deputy Secretary level—agree on an integrated plan for carrying it out. Defense, State, International Cooperation Administration, Central Intelligence, and the U.S. Information Agency may have activities in the area which must be coordinated. Within the Defense Department, the Army may be designated to carry out the defense mission—for example, to supply small arms and instructors—under the guidance of the appropriate regional director in International Security Affairs. Each member usually undertakes his agreed assignment, even though the Board does not have authority to order him to do so.

7. The Operations Coordinating Board Country X Plan will be distributed—in Defense through the Office of OCB Affairs in ISA— and the necessary actions taken.

8. The Board oversees the progress of the program, and reports on

it to the National Security Council. Unforseen obstacles may arise that require revision of the Country X Plan, or perhaps of the basic NSC policy paper. In that case, the Special Assistant to the President for National Security Affairs and the NSC staff see that the item is placed on the Council's forward agenda for reconsideration.

This process takes anywhere from one to three weeks. Some long-term programs such as the 1955 reserve bill (which came before the NSC several times within a year) take much longer. Other matters such as the Dienbienphu crisis or the President's statement following Stalin's death, may have to be handled almost overnight.[19] Indeed some crucial decisions—on the Berlin Blockade[20] and German rearmament[21]—were not formally processed through the Council.

---

[1] It was redesignated by the National Security Act Amendments of 1949.

[2] *Task Force Report on National Security Organization,* 1949, op. cit., p. 61.

[3] MacMahon, *op. cit.,* p. 180.

[4] This position was filled by Averell Harriman. While nominally the head of the Mutual Security Agency, which replaced the Economic Cooperation Administration (ECA) in 1951, he actually operated it through a deputy and acted as a "coordinator" in the Executive Office of the President.

[5] For a more detailed discussion see MacMahon, *op. cit.,* pp. 125-163.

[6] For a comprehensive examination of interdepartmental committees from the foreign affairs standpoint, see the Commission on the Organization of the Executive Branch, Task Force on Foreign Affairs, mimeographed staff studies, Appendix V, A to E, Washington, 1949. A more general treatment will be found in James L. McCamy, *The Administration of American Foreign Affairs,* Knopf, New York, 1950.

[7] This office dealt with trade agreements, intergovernmental mobilization planning, economic intelligence, and the strategic embargo and export controls.

[8] DOD Directive 5132.4, April 26, 1954. Until very recently Army Brigadier General Charles H. Bonesteel III, has held the position, even though it is officially a civilian post. Part of the credit for the success of the office must go to General Bonesteel who has had wide experience in working with State and other agencies.

[9] For further detail on the organization for mutual security see the diagram in Appendix V.

[11] *U.S. Government Organization Manual,* 1956-57, p. 141.

[11] *United States Foreign Policy,* Report of a Study Group for the Woodrow Wilson Foundation, William Y. Elliott, Chairman, New York, Columbia University Press, 1952, p. 109.

[19] Harry S. Truman, *The Truman Memoirs,* Vol. II, *Years of Trial and Hope,* Doubleday, New York, 1956. This excerpt was taken from the *N.Y. Times,* January 30, 1956, p. 16.

[13] Testimony of Admiral Joy, "Interlocking Subversion in Government Departments," *Hearings* before the Internal Security Subcommittee of the Senate Committee on the Judiciary, 83rd Congress, 2nd Session, 1954, Part 26, p. 2138.

[14] Report on *The Business Organization of the Department of Defense,* 1955, p. 16.

[15] This is, however, by no means unanimous. One group which studied the JSC as recently as 1955 stated, "The problem is to find a way to convert the Joint Chiefs of

Staff organization from a trading post to an objective group in which the national interest is paramount and which will facilitate the reaching of decisions." Staff paper prepared for the 1955 Hoover Commission Task Force on Procurement, "Defense Procurement; The Vital Roles of the National Security Council and the Joint Chiefs of Staff." p. A-31. The paper recommends that the Secretary of Defense direct that a thorough study of the entire JCS organization be made. See also the *N.Y. Herald Tribune*, May 25, 1956.

[16] DOD Directive 5132.3, July 14, 1955, "Policy, Organization, and Responsibilities in the Department of Defense Relating to the Conduct of International Security Affairs."

[17] *Ibid.*

[18] See paragraph III G of DOD Directive 5132.3.

[19] See Robert J. Donovan, *Eisenhower: The Inside Story*, Harper and Brothers, New York, 1956, pp. 261-4 and 40-41.

[20] *The Forrestal Diaries*, Walter Millis, ed., Viking Press, New York, 1951, p. 454.

[21] See p. 47 *supra*.

PART TWO

THE DEPARTMENT OF DEFENSE

CHAPTER VI

THE PROBLEM OF DEFENSE ORGANIZATION

Almost everyone coming from civilian life to the Pentagon, whether as a politically appointed official, an efficiency expert, or a member of one of the many commissions studying defense, faces an organization so vast that it defies comprehension. The Defense Department currently spends about 61 cents out of each tax dollar. It employs more than twice the combined manpower of the ten largest corporations. Its assets equal in value all privately owned land in the U. S., and it conducts activities in some 16,000 locations in all 48 states and some 52 foreign countries. But its mere size is not all. Its task in defending the U. S. (and much of the free world) has no civilian counterpart. It cannot be judged in terms of profit and loss. Its organization embodies relationships and nuances that can only be described as metaphysical. The relationship of the Department of Defense to its three military departments is not that of a holding company to subsidiaries, nor of a head office to branches; it can be understood only in the light of the evolution of unification and the nature of the military missions assigned to various components.

In Great Britain the chiefs of the armed services advise, but the Cabinet determines what military policy is and its decision is final. In this country, however, there is an alternative authority. Department of Defense decisions—in fact, any decisions of the Executive Branch—can be appealed to Congress. Our doctrine and practice of the separation of powers make possible a military "end run" to Congress in an attempt to force a change in policy.[1]

Few government bodies can—by both action and inaction—step on so many politically sensitive toes as the Defense Department. Every man in the armed forces (except, some say, the Marines) has a mother who votes. About one out of three male citizens between 18 and 50 is a veteran. The veterans' organizations, together with the National Guard Association, are among the most powerful lobbies in the country. The vast defense procurement operation is hedged about with Congressional injunctions and restrictions. The procurement officer must Buy America, ship 50 per cent in U. S. bottoms, aid small business, relieve distressed industries, and purchase in distressed areas. He must also buy from the lowest bidder in competitive bidding. If logic and efficiency dictate the elimination of a duplicated function in State X, the harassed official will hear from the Senator from X if he eliminates it. If he yields to pressure and eliminates Y installation instead, the Senator from Y is on his phone. If he does nothing, the Chairman of the appropriations subcommittee can make his life miserable. All of these currents swirl about Defense, pushing here and pulling there and adding to the difficulty of understanding its already complex organization and operation.[2] Yet some understanding of how the defense establishment evolved is essential to grasp the major problems of defense policy and administration.

Part Two of this book attempts to outline the major aspects of unification in terms of its impact on the defense structure, to present in abbreviated form the important characteristics and problems of the present organization in terms of the Department of Defense rather than of the services themselves. First, however, a word of caution. This is only a summary. It can merely give the reader an increased awareness of the problems, not an understanding of all their ramifications. Moreover, the Department of Defense does not exist in a vacuum. It must be set in context in its relationship not only to the President and the rest of the Executive Branch but also to Congress and the general public. That context cannot be provided here, but its existence must be borne in mind. And of course, the American doctrine of civilian control of the military is an integral part of the problem.

"Unification", nominally legislated in 1947, continues to raise problems which are a subject of disagreement in the judgment of thoughtful military officers. Armed service loyalties and ambitions have been and continue to be factors to be reckoned with. But even if all the officers in the armed services could be 'brainwashed' of all other considerations except that of providing the best possible defense for the United States, there would still be serious differences of opinion concerning the defense organization and the roles and missions of the various services. "Unification" (a word used by those who believe in it) or "triplification" (a word used by those who do not) is not something settled by the National Security Act of 1947. Indeed the 1947 Act has been patched and repatched and will be again. And old ideas will be and are coming up over and over again. For example, the second Hoover Commission, albeit with several dissents, proposed a separate fourth service for supply and procurement. It was forcefully advocated in 1944, again in 1945, and by several groups since 1947. Furthermore, such a set-up was tried under the World War II Army Service Forces. Current questions such as Navy participation in strategic bombing, Army aviation, and control of guided missile programs all are rooted in World War II and the controversies of the post-war years, if not in even earlier history.

In the earliest days of the Republic the Army and Navy were in a single government department. The job of directing the two services proved too much for a single individual—or at least, there was dissatisfaction with the handling of naval matters. Consequently, in 1798, a separate Navy Department was established by Congress. The two services remained administratively separate for a century and a half, and it was only after a third had been born and the military establishment had grown many thousandfold that they were once again combined in a single department. For most of this time of divorced administration there was little awareness of a need for unification. It was only in 1898, with the acquisition of overseas possessions such as the Philippines and Hawaii, and the end of Indian fighting as the Army's main peacetime role, that joint defense problems became important. In wartime, inter-service conflict may have made the task of fighting just that much more difficult. Certainly the argument that because the U. S. has been successful in all but one of its wars, the separation of War and Navy has worked out for the best, is scarcely a tenable one. Success depended on cooperation, which was sometimes present as at Lake Champlain in 1814 and sometimes absent as during the Spanish-American War at Santiago.

In 1903, the Joint Board (Army and Navy), was established by agreement between the services. It had four officers from each service, and who advised the two Secretaries. Although it published such general command guides as "Joint Action of the Army and the Navy" (in 1927, 1935, and 1938), it had no permanent staff and was not adapted to the demands of wartime. Indeed, it was suspended by President Wilson during the period of American neutrality in World War I on the surprising ground that it might encourage preparation for war before the United States was involved! In 1939, the Joint Board was placed under the direction of the President, and although it became inactive after 1942, it was not formally abolished until September, 1947. "Joint Action" was based on "mutual cooperation" and "paramount interest" which concepts failed dramatically at Pearl Harbor.

By the end of World War I the advent of aviation had produced a new area for jurisdictional rivalry. General "Billy" Mitchell's attacks on both the Army and Navy for allegedly neglecting the new weapon did not, however, draw "old line" elements of Army and Navy any closer together. Instead the two-way split became a three-cornered rivalry with dissension within, as well as between, the services.

In 1925 unification was suggested by a Congressional resolution proposing a single department with under-secretaries for Army, Navy, and Air. But as with other similar bills and resolutions—over fifty were introduced in Congress between 1924 and 1945—the effort failed. In the 1930s the issue was one of real consequence. There were many in Congress who urged it, but both the Army and the Navy—and their civilian secretaries as well—were against it. So Congress, which generally takes the advice of the military seriously in such matters, did not force service unification.

It is reasonable to suppose that the Cabinet might have coordinated military policy. After all, the service secretaries, being political appointees, should have been above interservice rivalry and misunderstanding; but the civilian secretaries have often been as partisan as th men in uniform. Usually during time of war the Secretaries of Army and Navy have taken critical views of each other. This was as true of the relations between Secretary Stimson and Secretary Knox during World War II as it was between other secretaries in other wars and in peacetime as well. There has been as little unity on large issues at the top as there has been on the lesser issues at lower levels.

UNIFICATION IN A NUTSHELL

The treatment of unification which follows is chronological in order to show the continuity of problems. But it is possible to separate main issues that have come up over and over again; some of them are still current in Washington. These issues are stated in the ten questions listed below. By noting the service views on the points mentioned the reader can easily get a grasp of the controversy as it has developed during the past decade.

1. Should there be a *single department* of the armed services? If not, should there be two, or three? And if more than one, what should be the relationship between them?

2. Should there be a *single secretary* as the responsible Cabinet officer? It the job, as Secretary Forrestal testified in 1944, too big for any one man? And if there is to be a single secretary, what should be the extent of his authority over the military services and what should be the *size* and *function* of his *staff*?

3. Should there be a *single chief of staff*? And if so, should he have any command functions? What should be the relationship between the military chiefs of the services? If the *Joint Chiefs of Staff* are to exist as a corporate body, should they be divorced from the actual operation of their services?

4. Should there be a *separate service for supply* and procurement?

Would this result in elimination of duplicated functions and increase efficiency? Or would such an arrangement violate the military axiom that the commander must control his logistics?

5. Should there be a *separate air force?* If so, what should be the extent of its control over all elements of air power with reference to the following: carrier-based air for control of the sea and for operations against land targets? land-based air for anti-submarine warfare operations? short and long range air logistics for support of surface operations? tactical support of ground operations?

6. Should there be land combat elements in another service than the Army, specifically in the *Marines?*

7. To what degree, and based on what criteria, should a service have organic to it *all elements*—ground, sea, or air—*necessary to perform its mission* even though primary responsibility for that element is assigned to another service? (Obviously, this question is closely related to the two next above, and to the two which follow.)

8. What should be the *roles and missions* of the services? To what degree should these be *legislated* by Congress instead of *decided* by Executive Order of the President or by Directive of the Secretary of Defense or by agreement by the Joint Chiefs of Staff?

9. What criteria should determine the assignments of responsibilities to the three services in *joint command* arrangements? Should there be "cooperation" based on "paramount interest" of one or another service, or "unity of command"?

10. To what extent is it desirable—and possible—to create *one military service* with allegiance to the armed forces as a whole rather than a particular branch, having, for example, a common uniform and a common service academy and training schools?

[1] A good analysis of this problem is contained in "Should Our Military Leaders Speak Up?" by Edward L. Katzenbach, Jr., *N.Y. Times*, Magazine Section, April 15, 1956, p. 17.

[2] Although not concerned specifically with defense, an interesting study of the interaction of pressure groups, Congressional Committees and Executive agencies will be found in J. L. Freeman, *The Political Process: Executive Bureau-Legislative Committee Relations*, Doubleday Short Studies, New York, 1955.

CHAPTER VII

UNIFICATION OF THE MILITARY SERVICES

With the approach of World War II, the Army began to look favorably at unification. Surprisingly enough, in view of the Navy's subsequent opposition, the first move came from the Navy Department. On June 20, 1941, the Navy General Board[1] unanimously recommended that "unification" take place—a single department, with a Joint Chiefs of Staff composed of two officers, including one air officer, from each Department. The recommendations were forwarded to Secretary of the Navy Frank Knox, who sent them on to Secretary of War Henry L. Stimson. They went first to the Joint Board and then to the Joint War Plans Committee. This Committee, composed of a representative of each department, was unable to agree: the Navy member, Rear Admiral Richmond Kelly Turner, opposed the plan, the Army member, Brigadier General Dwight D. Eisenhower, strongly endorsed it. Pearl Harbor intervened before further action could be taken. The matter remained in abeyance until September 1943, when a proposal for unification by General Marshall was placed before the Joint Chiefs of Staff and referred to the Special Committee of which more will be heard later.

In considering progress in practical unification during World War II, it is necessary to distinguish between command of forces in the field and strategic direction from Washington. The former was generally recognized as a necessity under the conditions of 1941 to 1945. General Eisenhower, a particularly strong advocate of this view, mentions it a number of times in his book.[2] The British had already had unified command before America entered the war, and at a very early period, the U. S. was brought into a combined command arrangement through the appointment of General Wavell as Supreme Commander of all Allied forces (American, British, Dutch, Australian) in the short-lived ABDA Command in the Far East.

Still, there were lapses—chiefly in the Pacific. General MacArthur's command arrangement for the initial invasion of the Philippines was not firm enough with reference to Admiral Halsey's Third Fleet to protect the vast carrier task forces against foreseeable efforts by the Japanese Navy to crush the invading forces.[3] As a result the outcome of the battle of Leyte Gulf was jeopardized by the successful decoy operation that drew the Seventh fleet into the Second Battle of the Philippine Sea (unofficially dubbed the "Battle of Bull's Run"). Again, when the Japanese surrendered, U.S. plans called for the invasion of the home islands within a matter of weeks. But unified command arrangements for this hazardous operation had not been made; the double command arrangements that had persisted in the two thrusts at Japan, from the Southwest Pacific and from the Central Pacific, were still in effect. In general, however, unified control in the field was attained by U. S. forces in World War II.

In Washington, the Joint Chiefs of Staff had their origin in the need to provide American counterparts of the British Chiefs of Staff Committee, who accompanied Churchill to Washington for the conference (code named ARCADIA) in December, 1941. The two groups merged as the Combined Chiefs of Staff to provide Anglo-American strategic advice to Roosevelt and Churchill. A by-product of this was the inclusion of the Commanding General, Army Air Forces (General H. H. Arnold) as a co-equal with his nominal superior, Army Chief of Staff, General George C. Marshall. This, it is worth noting, was proposed not by the military, but by Harry Hopkins on the ground that "our organization must parallel their [the British] organization,"[4] though there is no record that General Arnold, or any of his airmen objected to this de facto creation of a status they had sought for decades. On the civilian side of the military departments in Washington no change occurred during the war, except that Assistant Secretary of War for Air, Robert A. Lovett, enjoyed a practical degree of autonomy roughly parallel to that of General Arnold. The Army and Navy Departments remained organizationally, as well as physically, separated.

In post-war discussions, unified command in the field, which was accepted in principle, engendered relatively little dispute as to detail. But organization in the capital was the subject of controversy, debate, and hearings, from General Marshall's revival of the unification issue in 1943 to the passage of the National Security Act of 1947—and the end is not yet in sight. Early in this public debate, division along service lines was not clear, but as time passed, pressure for unification came from the War Department—particularly from the Air Force—and resistance came from the Navy.

Any short account runs the risk of over-simplification. Public records, memoirs (such as the *Forrestal Diaries*), and private memoranda do not contain the full story. Except for an unpublished thesis,[5] there is no single account that attempts to present the whole picture. Nor it is likely that any "official" history will be prepared. The subject is so enmeshed in personalities and controversy that historians in the various services and the Department of Defense have avoided it except to document some particular viewpoint.⁶ Besides, the matter is inherently complex. To speak of the *Army view* or the *Navy plan* is merely a necessary bit of shorthand. Within each department there were many shades of view. Even names attached to various specific proposals merely identify the official sponsors before Congress; in some cases the officers involved had little or no part in drafting the proposals.

THE WOODRUM COMMITTEE AND THE McNARNEY PLAN

A select committee of the House of Representatives, chaired by Representative Clifton A. Woodrum, began hearings in 1944 on post-war military policy and organization. The first version of the Army plan was presented by Air Force General Joseph T. McNarney, who, incidentally, had been in charge of the War Department reorganization in 1942. The main points—a single Department with Under Secretaries for each service and for common supply are illustrated by the chart on page 79. Army and Air Force officers backed the plan in broad terms, but mostly they emphasized the need for an integrated structure, rather than any particular blueprint.⁷ The Navy was generally noncommittal at the hearings, which adjourned with a report urging further study, but not recommending legislation.

THE RICHARDSON COMMITTEE

While the Woodrum Committee was holding its hearings, the Joint Chiefs of Staff in May 1944, created a Special Committee for Reorganization of National Defense. The "Richardson Committee"⁸ interviewed some 800 officers from all services—including Generals Eisenhower and MacArthur and Admirals Nimitz and Halsey—and visited the major overseas theaters. Questions were asked on the relative merits of a one-, two-, or three-department organization. The officers interviewed were fresh from actual operations in the field, and since they were still overseas, they had not been "briefed" on the attitudes of their colleagues in Washington. Fleet Admiral Chester W. Nimitz testified before Congress in 1945 that a merger "into a single department cannot help and may hinder the . . . efficient use of our seapower." Yet in his earlier statement to the Richardson Committee, the Admiral favored "the single-department organization." He explained the change in opinion as due to his wartime view that a single commander could reach decisions more speedily. Other Navy witnesses also changed their minds. John J. McCloy, Assistant Secretary of War, commented, "Mr. Forrestal who transmitted the [Richardson] Committee's directive . . . now finds that the study based on the directive deals with but a fragment of the problem. Admiral King, who selected half of the committee, finds that the members lacked objectivity . . . Mr. Hensel has the following to say about the field commanders whose testimony Mr. Forrestal so urgently called for at the Woodrum Hearings: '. . . few if any of them, have had experience in the operation of the governmental department during this war.' In a word, the top echelon of the Navy does not approve the report. . . ." [9]

The Committee submitted its report to the Joint Chiefs of Staff on April 11, 1945.[10] Its recommendations for a single armed forces department went as far as any official group had gone in urging complete service merger and integration. (The proposed organization should be compared with the other plans in the comparative charts on pages 79 and 80. Admiral Richardson, the Chairman, presented a dissenting opinion, in which Admiral King concurred when the Report came before the Joint Chiefs of Staff. Even the Committee members themselves showed signs of apprehension lest a single military commander of the Armed Forces such as they had proposed become a Frankenstein. They expressed the hope that the U.S. Chiefs of Staff would restrain him from becoming all-powerful. Since the Joint Chiefs could not agree, the Report was forwarded without further action to the President in October 1945.

Meanwhile, President Franklin D. Roosevelt had died. This change in the Commander-in-Chief probably had some effect on the thinking of those who later testified on unification proposals. President Roosevelt was a former Assistant Secretary of the Navy, who had chosen Admiral William D. Leahy as his personal chief of staff. President Truman, a former Captain of Artillery in World War I, had already favored unification in an article in *Colliers* magazine. Some who might have accepted some form of unification under President Roosevelt could well have been more hesitant after the change in the Presidency.

In May, 1945, President Truman started action by requesting Congress to pass legislation similar to the Reorganization Act of 1939[11] in order to facilitate the transition of government from war to peace. This streamlining objective was again mentioned in another message to Congress following the Japanese surrender in September, 1945.

THE SENATE MILITARY AFFAIRS COMMITTEE HEARINGS

The Senate Military Affairs Committee began hearings on two bills[12] proposing a single Department of the Armed Forces. Army spokesmen supported the Collins Plan (named for Lieutenant General J. Lawton Collins), which followed the general outline of previous Army proposals. The most important modification was a single *chief of staff* instead of a single commander. Other main points are illustrated graphically on page 80. Secretary of War Robert Patterson and Army Air Force Generals Arnold, Kenney, Doolittle and Spaatz testified strongly in favor of the Collins Plan, but General Marshall was less enthusiastic. Navy Department witnesses—among whom were Secretary James V. Forrestal, Assistant Secretary H. Struve Hensel, and Admirals Nimitz, King, Leahy, and General Vandergrift of the Marines—were uniformly opposed to the single command-line concept. Nor was the element of civilian control ignored. Mr. Hensel introduced two charts depicting the Army proposal's "subordinate civilian control" in budgetary matters compared with the Navy's existing system, which was labelled "predominant civilian control."

Navy opposition was based in part on the belief that the several elements of military power must be properly balanced and in part on the fear that the Navy's jurisdiction over its aviation and amphibious forces (the Marine Corps) was seriously threatened. One commentator has suggested that "Secretary Patterson and the Army Generals wanted consolidation because they feared that otherwise the ground Army would be neglected under the greater glamor and popularity of the Air Force and the Navy".[13] It was generally believed that the vigorous Air Force sponsorship of unification stemmed in part from a conviction that by no other means could they attain the co-equal legal status they had long sought and which the Royal Air Force had enjoyed in England for more than two decades. These attitudes provided the emotional background for what one writer has called an "internecine war of almost unprecedented bitterness".[14] There were some in all uniforms who thought their service was fighting for its life. Yet the voluminous hearings convey the impression that a great deal of the testimony represented views that rose above service and career.

Intertwined with the controversy was the basic question on roles and missions of the various services. The proper emphasis should logically have been on the role which each might play in a future conflict. Inevitably, however, the matter developed endless debates over who had won the last war and legalistic arguments based on the obsolete Joint Action of the Army and Navy or various pre-war acts of Congress. Such statements as that of Admiral Leahy that "The Army did not appear to be able to recognize that the Navy, with some Army

Air assistance had already defeated Japan" [15] were typical of the more outspoken opinions. The questions of functions and roles and missions has been one of continuing debate, both before the National Security Act of 1947, and after, as with the 1949 Unification and Strategy hearings. Although *organization* can have little meaning without reference to *function,* discussion is best deferred to Chapter VIII and the Key West Conference of 1948.

In the fall of 1945 the viewpoints which for purposes of convenience have been identified with the Army, Navy and Air Force could have been summarized as follows: The Army favored a strong centralized Department of the Armed Forces, with an integrated top command. The Air Force generally favored the Army concept as most likely to give them a fully equal status.[16] The Navy view was that if unification was necessary at all, it should be as loose as possible.[17] The single, integrated command structure was opposed by Navy spokesmen as (a) contrary to the principle of "balance between components" (implicit in which was the Navy desire for as much autonomy as possible);[18] (b) unsuccessful when tried elsewhere—for example, in Germany; (c) contrary to our own experience which had proved itself in World War II, and (d) tending to weaken the effectiveness of civilian control.

THE EBERSTADT REPORT

As the pressures for unification mounted, it became apparent that, as the Chairman of the Senate Naval Affairs Committee pointed out to Forrestal, the Navy must offer a "constructive alternative." The report submitted to Forrestal by Ferdinand Eberstadt in October 1945[19] contained an outline of such an alternative: a structure with a large number of coordinating devices but without any superior authority above the service secretaries except the President. The details of the Eberstadt plan are shown in the chart on page 80. As noted in Chapter I, the Eberstadt Report drew on the American experience in politico-military coordination (such as with SWNCC[20]) and the British Committee of Imperial Defense[21] as well as the Navy's organizational concepts. The merger of these three streams produced the basic bluprint from which the National Security Act of 1947 was constructed. The basic scheme was to retain the separate but equal status for the services but to improve coordination by establishing permanent organizations—such as the Research and Development Agency and the Munitions Board—in which representatives of each service would meet on a regular basis. The Joint Chiefs of Staff, aided by a Joint Staff, was to furnish the main source of military advice for the National Security Council. As a comparison with the chart showing the organization established by the 1947 Act will show, the Eberstadt Report opened the way for an eventual compromise between the Army and the Navy concepts.

PRESIDENTIAL EFFORTS TO SECURE UNIFICATION

On December 19, 1945, President Truman submitted in a message to Congress his recommendation for unification under a single department. "The President as Commander in Chief, should not personally have to coordinate the Army, Navy, and the Air Force. With all the other problems before him, the President cannot be expected to balance . . . the several branches of the national defense. He should be able to rely for that coordination . . . at the Cabinet level." [22]

Shortly afterward, a subcommittee of the Senate Military Affairs Committee under Senator Elbert D. Thomas drafted a bill (S. 2044) which followed quite closely the President's recommendations and included some but not all of the Eberstadt proposals. Since the Navy opposed it, the Naval Affairs Committee started separate hearings. In general each of the military and naval committees agreed with the view of the service with which it was concerned. For example, following the President's message, Secretary Forrestal told Senator Ernest W. McFarland that "the greatest help he could be to us would be to insure that the bill was referred to the Naval Affairs Committee for consideration as well as the Military Affairs Committee." [23] It is of more than passing significance, therefore, that the Congressional Reorganization Act of 1946 set up one committee on the armed services in each house. In a sense this "unification" in Congress facilitated ultimate unification within the Executive. At the same time, however, the reduction from two focal points to one increased rivalry between the services. The Reorganization Act had passed the full force of the controversy down to the armed forces.

The spring of 1946 was marked by charges of lobbying by the services and insubordination by military officers. President Truman attempted to limit public discussion by the military to appearances before Congress. But this rule, according to the Navy, was not applied to the other services, and charges of "gag rule" were made. [24] Signs of change in Navy's position first became visible during the hearings on S. 2044. Eberstadt for example, testified on how a single secretary should function, if such a position were created, and Admiral Nimitz proposed a Director of National Security.

In May 1946, President Truman requested that the Secretaries of War and Navy attempt to reach agreement on a single plan for organization. Since they had already agreed on unified command in the field, it was possible to work backward. The Secretaries replied on May 31 that eight points had been agreed upon but that some were still disputed—for example, the basic concept of a single department and the status of the Air Force, the Naval Air arm, and the Marines. These, of course, were the ones that had always been the most controversial. The President again stated his view on June 15 that there should be one department and one secretary, with civilian heads of the three co-equal military services. The Navy view on retention of its aviation and its control over the Marines was supported by the President in his Twelve Point plan. The Thomas bill was accordingly revised and passed to the Naval Affairs Committee, which, however, failed to report it out before the 79th Congress adjourned in August.[25]

The War and Navy Departments announced in December that unified command arrangements had been made for seven command areas, with the commanders responsible to the Joint Chiefs of Staff. On February 26, 1947, further initiative was taken by President Truman. He approved the draft legislation on which the services had agreed and sent it to Congress with his blessing as an "admirable compromise". The proposals were introduced in the House by Representative Clare Hoffman[26] as HR 2319 and in the Senate by Senator Chan Gurney[27] as S. 758. During the ten weeks of hearings that were held by the two Committees, the testimony was generally favorable to overall coordination features. However, the disputed points—such as naval aviation—continued to produce heated discussion.[28] The roles and missions aspect was dealt with in an executive order—based on the Joint Chiefs' approval of the service agreement—which was to take effect with the legislation.

Three principal areas received thorough examination by Congress; although these can only be mentioned here, a condensed account can be found in the U.S. Code, Congressional Service.[29] The role of the Secretary of Defense was the subject of more than one third of the testimony. But Congress changed the draft bill in only two respects: first, to insert the word *general* before the "authority, direction and control" which the Secretary was to have over his establishment, and second, to prohibit a professional military officer from occupying the position.[30]

Of perhaps greater concern to Congress—especially supporters of the Navy—was the matter of safeguarding the independent status of each service and preventing a supreme military high command. Consequently there was great emphasis, especially in the House version of the bill, on spelling out functions in detail. Congress also added the provision that the services must be "administered as individual Executive Departments" and that powers not conferred upon the Secretary of Defense were "reserved" to the Secretaries of the Military Departments. A right of appeal to the President and the Director of the Bureau of the Budget over the head of the Secretary of Defense was expressly included.

Finally, the staff organization which was to aid the Secretary of Defense in providing unified "direction and control" was discussed at some length. The basic scheme was that proposed by the Eberstadt Report with such bodies as the Research and Development Board, the Munitions Board, and the War Council having their membership drawn from service components of the National Military Establishment. This is significant since the emphasis from the beginning was thus placed on *negotiation* among service representatives rather than on *decision* by independent authority in the Office of the Secretary of Defense. The Joint Chiefs of Staff were given a statutory charter for the first time. They were constituted the "principal military advisers to the President, the National Security Council, and the Secretary of Defense." In addition to the preparation of strategic plans, the Chiefs were given the responsibility for "establishment of unified commands in strategic areas." The organization as finally approved by Congress is illustrated graphically on page 81.

The Senate debated S. 758 on July 7, 1947, and passed it with only one amendment.[81] In the House debates on July 19, many more amendments were adopted. The House version—with its statutory definition of functions—is more clearly reflected in the final bill than that of the Senate.[82] After the usual process of conference, amendment, and adoption, the bill finally became law by the signature of the President on July 26, 1947. "Unification" was thus enacted as the National Security Act of 1947.[83]

Perhaps the most appropriate comment on the Act is a quotation from George Washington on the creation of the War Office in 1776:[84] "The Benefits derived from it . . . will be considerable tho' the plan upon which it is first formed may not be perfect. This like other great works in its first Edition, may not be entirely free from Error. Time will discover its Defects and Experience suggest the Remedy, and such further Improvements as may be necessary; but it was right to give it a beginning."

COMPARATIVE CHARTS ON UNIFICATION

The charts that follow are simplified versions for illustrative purposes. They do not purport to represent the actual organization charts attached to the various plans.

THE McNARNEY PLAN

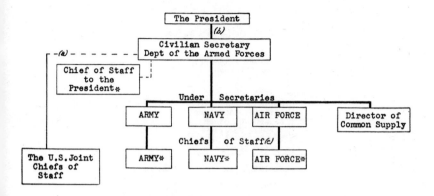

THE RICHARDSON COMMITTEE PLAN

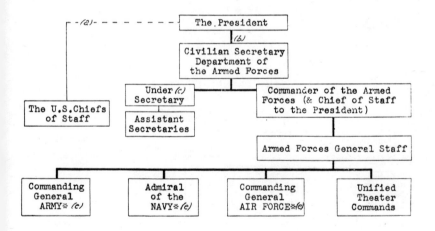

NOTES TO COMPARATIVE CHARTS

* Denotes membership in U.S. (or Joint) Chiefs of Staff.

(a)   To advise the President on military strategy and the budget.

(b)   To advise the President on politico-economic-industrial matters.

(c)   To coordinate business side of the department, including supply and logistics.

(d)   Can comment on but not change military recommendations while forwarding them to the President.

(e)   Has command authority over military service.

THE COLLINS PLAN

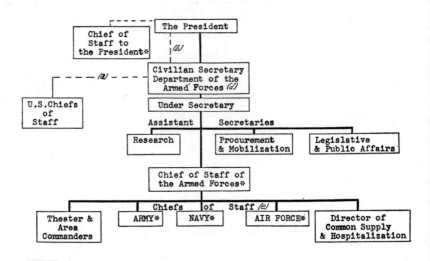

THE EBERSTADT PLAN

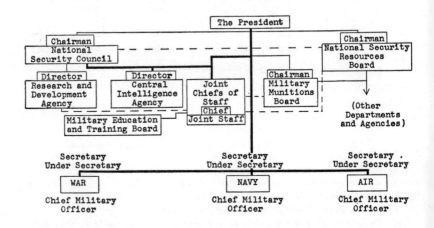

THE NATIONAL SECURITY ACT OF 1947

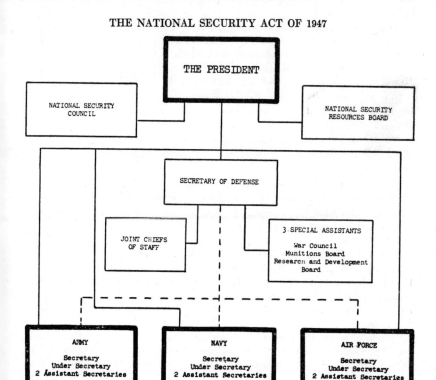

[1] One member of this Board was Admiral Joseph O. Richardson, who was later to dissent from a somewhat similar proposal. See page 73.

[2] General Dwight D. Eisenhower, *Crusade in Europe*, Doubleday & Co., New York, 1948, pp. 221-223, 263.

[3] See Admiral Frederick C. Sherman, *Combat Command*, Dutton & Co., New York, 1950, pp. 280-314.

[4] General H. H. Arnold, *Global Mission*, Hutchinson & Co. London, 1951, p. 153.

[5] Major Lawrence J. Legere, Jr., U.S.A., *Unification of the Armed Forces*, unpublished Ph.D. thesis, Harvard University, 1950.

[6] One good study, which however admittedly emphasized the air arm, is *Unification of the Armed Forces: Administrative and Legislative Developments, 1945-1949* by R. Earl McClendon, Documentary Research Division, Research Studies Institute, Air University, Maxwell Air Force Base, Alabama, 1952.

[7] See *Proposal to Establish a Single Department of Armed Forces*, Hearings before the House Select Committee on Post War Military Policy, 78th Congress, 2nd Session, 1944. Secretary of War Stimson was "at first reluctant to let his Department be involved in public discussion of an issue on which feelings would surely run high. Only the surprising discovery that Secretary of the Navy Knox favored a single unified

82 AMERICAN DEFENSE AND NATIONAL SECURITY

department overcame this objection." However Knox's views "were not shared by his successor, James V. Forrestal . . ." Stimson and Bundy, *op. cit.*, pp. 518-19.

[8] So called because it was chaired by Admiral James O Richardson, U.S.N. Retired. The other members were Major General William F. Thompkins, U.S.A., Lt. General Harold L. George, U.S.A.F., and Rear Admiral M. F. Shoeffel,, a Navy air officer.

[9] See *Department of Armed Forces, Department of Military Security, Hearings* before the Senate Military Affairs Committee, 79th Congress, 1st Session, 1945, pp. 386, 403, 389, 462.

[10] A list of witnesses interviewed, the terms of reference, and the report of the Richardson Committee will be found at pp. 411-439 of the *Hearings, op. cit. supra* note 9.

[11] This Act gave the President power to submit reorganization plans to Congress which would become effective within 60 days, if not disapproved.

[12] S. 84 and S. 1482, 79th Congress, 1st Session. See *Hearings, op. cit.* note 9 *supra*.

[13] Walter Millis in the background text to *The Forrestal Diaries*, p. 146.

[14] Hanson Baldwin, *N.Y. Times*, January 17, 1947.

[15] Admiral William D. Leahy, *I Was There*, McGraw-Hill, New York, 1950, p. 280.

[16] A full—if biased (from the Air Force viewpoint)— account of the pre-World War II struggles to establish the Air Force against both Army and Navy resistance can be found in General Arnold's *Global Mission*, especially pages 74-97, 91, 119-120. Also see William B. Huie, *The Fight for Air Power*, L. B. Fisher, New York, 1942, and *The Case Against the Admirals*, E. P. Dutton and Co., New York, 1946.

[17] Unless of course the unification merged the other services into the Navy. General Arnold in *Global Mission*, p. 246, reports the following statement by Admiral King: "Trouble with all this . . . reorganization is your Air Force, Hap. If you would take your Air Force and bring it over to the Navy, then the Navy would have an Army in the form of the Marines, and with your Air Force, real air power. With our battleships . . ., the Navy could be the largest and most powerful force in the world."

[18] Secretary Forrestal's own statement confirms this: "My own conduct has been governed by three main considerations (1) to keep the Navy intact as a Service as distinct from a merely subordinate branch of a vast Department: (2) to obtain the improvements in our national defense organization which the war indicated should be made, but without sacrificing the autonomy of the Navy; (3) to discharge my responsibilities to the President." *The Forrestal Diaries*, Walter Millis, editor, The Viking Press, New York, 1951, p. 167.

[19] See Chapter I, note 32.

[20] Pronounced "Swink" or "Swank". It is an abbreviation for the State-War-Navy Coordinating Committee which was formed in 1944 for the primary purpose of giving military advice to the State Department. *Department of State Bulletin*, Vol. XIII, 1945, No. 333, p. 745, and Chapter I, pp. 10-11 *supra*.

[21] Forrestal told Churchill that the "germinal basis" for Eberstadt's plan was the "minute by Lord Hankey on the operations of the Imperial General Staff in England." *Diaries*, p. 145. For comparative data on British Organization, see Appendix I *infra*.

[22] Forrestal considered this message a *"defeat"* for the Navy. *Diaries*, p. 119.

[23] *Diaries*, p. 121.

[24] *Cf. The Forrestal Diaries*, p. 121, *passim*. Chapter XI of the forthcoming book by R. G. Albion and R. H. Connery, "Forrestal and the Navy, 1940-1947", will contain an excellent account of this and other aspects of the unification controversy.

[25] One of the Navy's main objections to the Thomas bill was that "it rested on the

premise of 'merge now and organize later,' " rather than on an analysis of the practical problems of organization. *Forrestal Diaries*, p. 159.

[26] Chairman of the House Committee on Expenditures in the Executive Departments, which held hearings on the *National Security Act of 1947* (H.R. 2319), 80th Congress, 1st Session, 1947.

[27] Chairman of the Senate Armed Services Committee. This newly created Committee's *Hearings on the National Defense Establishment*, 80th Congress, 1st Session, 1947, contain a useful chronological statement of unification and a summary of major proposals, as well as the 1947 Executive Order on roles and missions drafted by Patterson and Forrestal. See pp. 2-12.

[28] Stimson, who by then had retired as Secretary of War, considered the bill a "triumph for all concerned" and he wrote to Senator Gurney that he saw nothing in the bill to justify "any fear that . . . naval aviation . . . will be lightly or carelessly discarded." Stimson and Bundy, *op. cit.*, pp. 519-523.

[29] Published by the West Publishing Company. See the volume on the 80th Congress, 1st Session, 1947, pp. 1487 and following, and Senate Report No. 239, June 5, 1947 on S. 758.

[30] Thus in September, 1950 when President Truman wanted to appoint General Marshall as Secretary of Defense, it was necessary to amend the National Security Act. See the debates on H.R. 9646 reported in the *Congressional Reeord*, September 15, 15091-15135 *passim*.

[31] That of Senator Taft, restricting the functions of the National Security Council to national security matters. Title I of the Act, "Coordination for National Security", is treated in Chapter I, *supra*. The discussion in this Chapter is limited to unification aspects.

[32] A good summarized account of the legislative history and debates will be found in the *Congressional Quarterly Almanac*, Vol. III, 1947, pp. 457-458.

[33] P.L. 253, 80th Congress, 1947, 61 *Stat*. 495, 50 U.S.C. 401, Appendix II, *infra*.

[34] This passage was selected by Major Legere for quotation on the flyleaf of his thesis on *Unification of the Armed Forces*, cited in note 5 *supra*.

CHAPTER VIII

ROLES AND MISSIONS

The National Security Act of 1947 was a major achievement, but it was also a compromise in which each side yielded upon matters of principle for the purpose of achieving an agreed solution. The end result would never have been proposed initially by anyone, nor when achieved, defended as a whole as a sound solution. It was simply the best attainable at the time—a recognition that politics is the science of the possible. This chapter traces the early turbulent history of unification.

The first two years of operation under the 1947 Act witnessed a series of developments that can be fairly described as extraordinary:

(1) The first appointee as Secretary of Defense was the man who had fought most effectively against the creation of the office, James V. Forrestal, Secretary of the Navy.

(2) During his administration Secretary Forrestal sought to proceed by conference, accommodation, and compromise to achieve interservice solutions. That is to say, even though he had the power of decision—or, as the act put it, "general authority, direction, and control"—he sought to establish a pattern of coordination rather than direction. A striking example was his attempt to get interservice agreement on roles and missions through conferences with the Joint Chiefs of Staff at Key West and Newport.

(3) As Secretary of Defense, Mr. Forrestal concluded that further integration of the armed forces and stronger authority of the Secretary were necessities—developments which as Secretary of the Navy he had done his utmost to prevent. His views on this subject were influential in the 1949 Amendments to the Act.

(4) Secretary Forrestal found the difficulties and frustrations of administering the 1947 Act overwhelming to the extent that he suffered a nervous breakdown ending in a tragic suicide shortly after his resignation in the spring of 1949.

(5) Forrestal's successor, Louis A. Johnson, a pre-war Assistant Secretary of War and former Chairman of the National Finance Committee of the Democratic National Committee, was determined to exercise his authority. His first venture as Secretary of Defense, the cancellation of the super-carrier the USS *United States,* led to the

resignation of the Secretary of the Navy, John L. Sullivan, the "revolt of the admirals" in the B-36 investigation of 1949, and the dismissal of Chief of Naval Operations Louis E. Denfeld. His attempts to impose "economy" upon the forces, especially upon the Air Force, later resulted in the resignation of Secretary of the Air Force W. Stuart Symington. When Secretary Johnson himself resigned after the outbreak of the Korean War, it can fairly be stated that the appointment of General George C. Marshall was a salvage operation to restore the prestige of the Office of the Secretary of Defense.

After the National Security Act of 1947, the armed forces had, if not unification, at least confederation, with a Secretary of Defense heading not a *department* but an *establishment*.[1] It was natural then that controversies should focus upon the first Secretary of Defense: upon the man, upon his office, and upon the way he exercised or failed to exercise his authority.[2] In the words of one official, the period 1947 to 1949 was marked by: ". . . the rapid growth of the indoor sport of debating the authority of the Secretary of Defense . . . The ramifications . . . of the term 'Establishment' versus 'Department' were explored with gusto. The phrase 'general direction, authority and control' contracted or expanded depending upon who was trying to prove what . . . Some practitioners of the art found that by concentrating one's gaze fixedly upon . . . the proviso that the Services should be administered as individual Executive Departments a good part . . . of the remaining schematic . . . structure gradually faded away."

The Forrestal Diaries convey a real flavor of the magnitude of the issues which inevitably found their way to the desk of the Secretary during the first year. The international situation deteriorated rapidly, with the threat to Greece and Turkey followed closely by the Palestine-Middle East problems. Throughout the spring of 1948, the Universal Military Training controversy coming as it did during the period of tension following the Czechoslovakian coup of February 24, 1948, occupied much of Forrestal's time.

THE ROLES AND MISSIONS PROBLEM

The division of labor in the national defense effort—in short, the problem of roles and missions—was still cloudy. President Truman had signed an executive order to take effect simultaneously with the National Security Act of 1947, embodying the service agreement that was the basis of the legislation.[3] But this order had proved inadequate.

The Navy still held firmly to its position that it must possess everything needed to carry out is mission. Naval aviation, by the terms of

the Act, was to "be integrated with the naval service as part thereof
. . ."; and it was specified that the United States Marine Corps, "within the Department of the Navy," should include "land combat and service forces and such aviation as may be organic thereto." These two controversial elements had thus been definitely fixed within the Department of the Navy. But the *role* of naval aviation was something else again. In anti-submarine warfare, in aerial mine laying, in conducting "air operations as necessary for the accomplishment of objectives in an area of naval operations", there was plenty of room for conflict with the Air Force. Authorization of "land operations" by the Marine Corps could equally conflict with the Army. The Navy has traditionally been oriented towards a task force type of organization designed to be self-sufficient. It has been reluctant to depend upon another service to accomplish primarily naval missions. The Marine Corps has a similar tradition; each Marine division has its own tactical air wing—a cause of considerable envy on the part of the Army.

The Army doctrine, based upon "unity of command," was designed to give the *ground* commander the means to accomplish his mission.[4] Although the Army was willing to borrow—transport and loading craft and naval gunfire from the Navy, and air transport and tactical air support from the Air Force—it has tended to think of itself as the major combat service which would furnish the unified commander. Although, unlike the Navy, it does not insist on possessing all elements necessary to land combat, it does stress the importance of a single *command*. However the Army has sought for a long time to expand its own air arm, particularly in reconnaissance and combat zone transport.[5]

The Air Force philosophy, simple in theory but difficult in practice, has favored the view that everything that flies should be under Air Force control. Conflict was, of course, inevitable. The development of atomic weapons and guided missiles made differences even more difficult to reconcile.

THE KEY WEST AGREEMENT

As international tensions increased during the spring of 1948, the urgency of settling these issues became apparent. Accordingly within a period of six months two conferences were held to seek agreement on roles and missions of the armed services.[6] Tentative steps were taken at Key West and then expanded into a more definite agreement at Newport. Since both conferences dealt with the same subject matter, the results may be summarized without distinguishing between them.[7]

Following a statement of the basic policy embodied in the National Security Act of 1947, the Key West Agreement discussed general principles, common functions of the armed forces, functions of the Joint Chiefs of Staff, and functions of each of the three military services.

The Principles emphasized "maximum practicable integration" of policies and procedures without actual merging of the armed forces—in short, "coordination" and "correlation". It noted that "collateral as well as primary functions will be assigned" and that "while collateral functions may establish further *justification* for stated force requirements . . . such assignment shall not be used as the *basis* for *establishing additional force requirements*". [italics added] This provision was to prove a significant one, for it was used when Secretary of Defense Johnson ordered the cancellation of the Navy's supercarrier *United States* and touched off the revolt of the admirals.

The section on "Common Functions of the Armed Forces" emphasized that all the services shared overall responsibility for the security of the United States, as well as such specific functions as bases, intelligence, reserve forces, weapons development, and procurement of equipment and supplies.

The section dealing with the duties of the Joint Chiefs of Staff was an entirely new addition to the 1947 Executive Order. For the most part the language of the National Security Act had been adopted as to preparing strategic and logistic plans and formulating policies. There were, however, two important additions: First, the Joint Chiefs were "to prepare and submit to the Secretary of Defense, for his information and consideration in furnishing guidance to the Departments for preparation of their annual budgetary estimates and in coordinating these budgets, a statement of military requirements which is based upon agreed strategic considerations, joint outline war plans, and current national security commitments." Second, the agreement further elaborated their responsibility (given by the National Security Act of 1947) for the "establishment of unified commands in strategic areas." The Key West Agreement gave them the duty of "general direction of all combat operations" and of designating "one of their members as their executive agent" for unified commands and certain other operations. The questions raised concerning the *command* authority of the Joint Chiefs were more than merely legalistic debates. There was strong feeling in some quarters that a corporate JCS, which possessed command authority, would, as in the case of a single chief of staff for the Armed Forces, render civilian control meaningless.[8] The executive agent system was subsequently to be modified, as discussed in Chapter IX.

The most important primary functions of the Army were stated in the Key West Agreement as follows:

"1. To organize, train and equip Army forces for the conduct of prompt and sustained operations on land."

"2. To organize, train, and equip Army antiaircraft artillery units." It was this provision which gave the Army entrée into the ground-to-air missile field. Among the other primary missions were providing Army forces for the defense of the United States against air attack, and for the occupation of territories abroad. The only collateral function given the Army was very general: "To interdict enemy sea and air power and communications through operations on or from land."

The Navy and Marine Corps was given primary functions among which were the following:

"1. To organize, train, and equip Navy and Marine Forces for the conduct of combat operations at sea, including operations of sea-based aircraft and their land-based naval air components. Specifically (a) To seek out and destroy enemy naval forces and to suppress enemy sea commerce. (b) To gain and maintain general sea supremacy . . .

"6. To be responsible for naval reconnaissance, anti-submarine warfare, the protection of shipping . . .

"11. To maintain the United States Marine Corps, which shall include land combat and service forces and such aviation as may be organic therein."

The provisions pertaining to the Marines did not, however, "contemplate the creation of a second land Army." The Navy's collateral functions included interdicting enemy land and air power and communications through operation at sea, conducting close air support for land operations and being "prepared to participate in the over-all air effort as directed by the Joint Chiefs of Staff."

The Air Force, with "primary interest in all operations in the air" except as otherwise assigned, had among others, the following primary functions:

"1. To organize train and equip Air Force forces for the conduct of prompt and sustained combat operations in the air. Specifically: (a) To be responsible for the defense of the United States against air attack . . . (b) To gain and maintain general air supremacy. (c) to defeat enemy air forces . . .

"2. To formulate joint doctrines and procedures, in coordination with the other services, for the defense of the United States against air attack, and to provide the Air Force units, facilities, and equipment required therefor."

"3. To be responsible for strategic air warfare.
"5. To furnish close combat and logistical air support to the Army.
"6. To provide air transport for the armed forces . . ."
The Air Force's main collateral functions were "To interdict enemy sea power through air operations. To conduct anti-submarine warfare and to protect shipping. To conduct aerial mine-laying operations."
It can readily be seen that some, but by no means all, of the areas of controversy were resolved.

Primary interest in the development of *amphibious* techniques was granted to the Marines, while primary concern with *airborne* operations was given to the Army. *Anti-submarine warfare* was made a primary function of the Navy and a collateral function of the Air Force. *Air transport* was assigned to the Air Force. But there were many areas of ambiguity. *Air Defense* was made a primary function of all three services. *Army aviation* was not discussed at all.[9] Nor was any mention made of *guided missiles.* Strategic bombing was made a primary function of the Air Force, but provision was made for Navy participation "in the over-all air effort as directed by the Joint Chiefs of Staff." The term *primary function* received further elaboration at Newport, and "an understanding was reached that the Navy will not be prohibited from attacking any targets, inland or otherwise, which appear necessary for the accomplishment of its mission."[10] The recognition that no clear line could be drawn between *strategic* and *tactical* use of air power temporarily laid to rest the Navy-Air Force controversy. But the word *temporarily* is used advisedly in view of the explosion over unification and strategy which was to occur only a year later.

The issue of control and direction of atomic weapons—which had hitherto remained in the civilian-run Special Weapons Project—was also discussed at Newport. A final decision was deferred until the relationship between the Atomic Energy Commission and the Department of Defense could be settled.[11]

Perhaps most important of all was the decision to establish a weapons evaluation group, which could objectively assess the comparative capabilities of particular weapons—and weapons systems—to which competing claims were advanced. There was, however, disagreement as to whether the group should be under the Joint Chiefs of Staff or under the Research and Development Board which was headed by a civilian.[12]

THE 1949 AMENDMENTS

Meanwhile the summer of 1948 saw increased international tension brought about by the Berlin blockade and the airlift which was undertaken as a counter measure. In addition to the daily problems of a substantive nature and to the continuing unification issues, there were broader problems of organization. The Commission on Organization of the Executive Branch (The Hoover Commission) had been created in 1947, and a task force under Ferdinand Eberstadt was set up in May, 1948, to examine the National Security Organization. Although Forrestal was himself a member of the Hoover Commission, he took no part in its report except to make recommendations to the Task Force which was studying his department.[13] Some of the basic recommendations were to increase the authority of the Secretary of Defense, give him a larger staff, and make him the sole representative on the National Security Council. The Report of the Commission itself emphasized freedom from the rigidity of statutory control of organization and clearer lines of control and responsibility running from the President. Another important recommendation of the Task Force was that an Under Secretary of Defense should be appointed to relieve the Secretary "of an impossible burden of work". The proposal was considered separately from the 1949 Amendments, and the Committee Report[14] stated that in 1947 "it could not be foreseen that the duties of the Secretary would be of such magnitude and diversity as to require an additional statutory official." The Committee recommended that the Under Secretary rank *above* the Service Secretaries so as to be able to act as an effective *alter ego* of the *Secretary*.

The first report of the Secretary of Defense, submitted to the President early in 1948, contained Forrestal's recommendations for legislative changes to meet some of the organizational defects revealed during the first year. It was similar in many respects to the reports of the Task Force and the Hoover Commission. Forrestal's draft, as approved by the President and the Bureau of the Budget, contained 14 points. The three principal areas of change, quite similar in some respects to the proposals of the Rockefeller Committee nearly four years later, are here summarized:

(1) *The nature of the organization:* Change the National Military Establishment to the Department of Defense and make it a regular executive department. Eliminate the statutory right of appeal to the President and Bureau of the Budget. Amend the "general direction authority and control" given to the Secretary by the 1947 Act by eliminating the word "general". Repeal the clause declaring that all powers not specifically given to the Secretary of Defense shall be reserved to the military departments. Eliminate the clause providing that the services shall be administered as individual executive departments. Make the Secretary of Defense the only defense representative on the National Security Council.

(2)   *The Office of the Secretary of Defense:* Transfer the functions of the Munitions and Research and Development Boards to the Secretary of Defense.[15] Give the Secretary three assistant secretaries and the power to appoint the Chairmen of the Munitions Board and the Research and Development Board and to fix the compensation (subject to civil service laws) for civilian personnel of the Department other than those of the three military departments.

(3)   *The Joint Chiefs of Staff:* Establish a Chairman of the JCS.[16] Transfer to the Secretary of Defense certain of their functions and have the Chiefs "assist the Secretary" in carrying them out.   Give the Secretary power to appoint the Director of the Joint Staff.

Secretary Forrestal sent a copy of the draft proposals to the Joint Chiefs of Staff for comment.   Their reaction, distinctly hostile to the proposed JCS changes, was based on the statement that their functions, as set forth in Section 211 of the National Security Act, were "purely military and as such, properly duties with which the JCS should be charged."   Since these views were not in accord with the President's program, they were not included in the official legislative program of the Secretary of Defense.   Nevertheless, the Joint Chiefs testimony before the Senate Armed Services Committee on April 7, 1949, was so strongly opposed to the draft bill provisions that the Committee followed their recommendations in eliminating them.   But the rest of the 14 points were adopted in the Senate, which passed the bill at the end of May.

The House Armed Services Committee held short and acrimonious hearings on the proposed legislative changes, but failed to take action. Instead they turned to the investigation of the B-36 bomber. Although the first phase of this investigation overlapped the enactment of the 1949 amendments, it seems best to take up the B-36 controversy and the hearings on unification and strategy separately.

With the original department bill (H.R. 4766) abandoned for the time being, the Armed Services Committee considered only a fiscal management bill, which passed the House on July 18, 1949[17]—the same day the President submitted his Reorganization Plan No. 8. This plan sought to put into effect the proposed changes of the Department's draft bill via reorganization plan in view of the B-36 diversion of the legislation.   However as finally enacted, Section 12 (j) of the Amendments specifically provided that the Reorganization Plan should not take effect.   The Senate combined the provisions of the House bill with its own version based on the original 14 points, and the 1949 Amendments were therefore actually written in Conference. The resulting amendments were passed by both Houses on August 2,

1949 and after approval by President Truman, they were enacted as the National Security Act Amendments of 1949.[18]

The authority of the Secretary of Defense was strengthened by making the National Military Establishment the Department of Defense and demoting the armed services to "Military Departments." The word *general* was removed from "direction, authority, and control", and the concept of powers "reserved" to the services was eliminated. But the armed services still had to be "separately administered." Furthermore, Congress, while strengthening the Secretary's authority also limited it. He was forbidden to transfer or consolidate any combatant function; that is to say, he could not eliminate the Marines or transfer the naval air arm to the Air Force. He was also required to report to Congress any reassignments of a non-combatant function, and was forbidden to merge the administration of the services. They could no longer appeal to the President or the Budget Bureau over the head of the Secretary of Defense, but any service secretary or member of the Joint Chiefs, after informing the Secretary of Defense, could make recommendations to Congress on his own initiative. This meant that Congress was not to be limited to one official channel for military advice.

The proposed changes in the Munitions Board and the Research and Development Board were not made at this time, but the Korean war gave such further proof of the inadequacy of the board form of organization that the changes were finally made in 1953.

A Chairman of the Joint Chiefs of Staff was created with a proviso that he "shall have no vote" and "shall not exercise military command . . ." Actually these limitations were meaningless since it was never proposed that the Chairman should have any command or authority to settle disputes. The Joint Chiefs of Staff have never acted by a majority vote[19]; if unanimous agreement is not reached, the issue is passed up to the Secretary of Defense for decision. Nevertheless these provisions were inserted to pacify those who did not want the office of Chairman in the first place, just as the word "general" had been inserted in the 1947 Act before the "direction, authority and control" which the Secretary was to exercise. Forrestal himself thought of the Chairman as the "person to whom the President and the Secretary of Defense look to see to it that matters with which the Joint Chiefs should deal are handled in a way that will provide the best military staff assistance to the President and the Secretary of Defense."[20]

Nevertheless, the institution of the Chairman has had a greater effect on the way in which the Joint Chiefs have worked than almost any other development. In practice, the Chairman has come to be the spokesman, and in numerous instances it is he, and only he, who has personal contact with the Secretary of Defense, the National Security Council, the President, and Congress. This saves the time of the other Chiefs, each of whom also has an armed service to administer, but it also dilutes their influence. The British, by the way, adopted the idea of a Chairman to their Chiefs of Staff Committee in 1955 and appointed an air officer.[21]

The three assistant secretaries who had been requested were authorized, and one of these was designated by Congress as the Comptroller. Actually, this addition merely changed the title of the three special assistants, who had already been set up by Secretary Forrestal. But, as some of the opponents of unification feared, this small expansion in the Office of the Secretary was but a preview of coming events.[22]

Finally, a new Title IV, "Promotion of Economy and Efficiency through Establishment of Uniform Budgetary and Fiscal Procedures and Organizations", was added to the National Security Act. This was of course the result of the House bill on fiscal management,[23] which in turn stemmed from the deficiencies noted by the first Hoover Commission. In fact, the need for better fiscal and budgetary management was a major factor in the establishment of the 1947 Hoover Commission. Title IV added comptrollers in the Department of Defense and in each military department and emphasized the "performance budget".[24] It thus greatly strengthened the budgetary control over programming and operations, and incidentally—but not accidentally—increased the power of the Defense Comptroller.

This particular aspect of unification—fiscal and budgetary matters —has progressed comparatively fast—in fact, too fast, for some. A "high Pentagon general" is quoted as saying, "McNeil has done a marvelous job" in controlling expenditures. "But when he takes upon himself the job of 'distributing shortages' as he did . . . [in the 1953 Air Force budget cuts] he's going beyond his proper function . . . He's deciding strategy, make no mistake about it."[25] The 1955 Hoover Commission *Report on Business Organization of the Department of Defense* states that the Defense Comptroller has been forced to use financial controls as a substitute for an adequate review of military requirements and urges that the other assistant secretaries take more responsibility for screening requirements.[26]

In the words of former Secretary of War Robert Patterson, the Amendments of 1949 "cleared away the clouds" obscuring the authority of the Secretary of Defense. But many problems remained, and some of these were almost immediately to receive a thorough airing.

REVOLT OF THE ADMIRALS

The strategic differences between the Navy and Air Force had begun to receive considerable publicity.[27] When Secretary of Defense Louis A. Johnson ordered work stopped on the aircraft carrier USS *United States* on April 23, 1949—less than a month after he had succeeded Forrestal—the so-called revolt of the admirals began.

Secretary of the Navy John L. Sullivan promptly resigned in protest. It was soon revealed that the Chief of Naval Operations differed strongly from the other Joint Chiefs in their recommendations concerning the super-carrier, and the Navy began to prepare for action. Meanwhile an anonymous letter circulating in Washington alleged political influence in procuring the B-36[28] and disparaged this aircraft as a weapon. Representative James E. Van Zandt, Captain USNR, produced the letter in the House, and on May 25, a resolution[29] was introduced calling for an investigation of the matter. The hearings, held in August, disproved the accusations, and discovered that the letter had been authored by a special assistant to the Under Secretary of the Navy. During the September recess, some spectacular fire works were set off by the release of correspondence between high ranking Navy officers and the Secretary of the Navy, deploring the "emasculating" of the Navy and the resulting low state of morale.[30]

On October 5, 1949 the House Armed Service Committee began, as the second phase of the B-36 investigation, hearings on Unification and Strategy."[31] Almost forty officers and officials testified and the subject matter ranged over practically all aspects of air operations. But the most significant result was the public revelation that unification was still an emotion-charged and controversial issue. The Committee noted the tortuous progress that had been made since 1947; it characterized the Army as "overardent," the Navy as "reluctant,"[32] and the Air Force as "exuberant." There were acrimonious exchanges on inter-service relations; and the perennial roles and missions problem—concerning the Army and Navy aviation branches and the Marines—was reexamined.

Possibly the major outcome of the hearings was the unanimous agreement that the Weapons Systems Evaluation Group was the necessary and proper forum before which claims to such competing weapons systems as the carrier or the long range bomber should be examined. Also important was the restatement of Congress' desire that military witnesses be permitted to testify frankly and without fear of reprisal. This last resulted from the criticism following President Truman's approval of the Secretary of the Navy's request to remove Admiral Louis E. Denfeld as Chief of Naval Operations.

The Committee report dealt at some length with what "unification" did and did not mean.[33] Unification was, in the view of the committee, a goal to which there might be more than one path. It did not involve operational control of the armed forces by the Joint Chiefs of Staff, nor the imposition of the views of any one—or two—of the armed services upon all three. It should not involve "triplification" of administrative costs, nor should it cause "savings" by reduction in fighting efficiency. The Committee particularly stressed that unification should not—and would not—cause a diminution of Congress' role in national defense policies, nor the denial of military advice to Congress by reprisals against officers who gave their personal views. Unification, said the Committee, should involve a comprehensive and well integrated program for national security based upon three separately administered military departments with effective strategic direction and unified control in the field. The Committee promised that the progress of unification of the land, sea, and air forces into an integrated and efficient team would receive its continued assistance.

An atomic explosion in the Soviet Union in August, 1949—during the B-36 controversy—served as a timely reminder that unification was more than a matter of service squabbling. A few months later, the U.S. announced its decision to proceed with development of the hydrogen bomb, and the world moved a step further into the era of nuclear warfare.

---

[1] An entity which was unique in the history of the executive branch. From 194 until the legislative changes of 1949 there was some doubt as to whether various statutes—some going back to 1789—giving certain legal powers to the "heads of Executive Departments" applied to the Secretary of Defense.

[2] James Forrestal became Secretary of Defense on September 17, 1947. He served until March, 1949. His tragic mental breakdown and suicide in May 1949, were an indication of the superhuman stresses and tensions to which the new office was subjected. His own 1944 statement that the responsibilities of a single Defense Secretary would be too great for any one man to handle was thus prophetic.

[3] Executive Order 9877 (12 F.R. 147) was based upon the Patterson-Forrestal agreement and had been tentatively approved by the JCS in March, 1947. Actually, however, the executive order was less specific on some points than the National Security Act itself. However, unlike the Act, the roles and missions provisions of the executive order could be amended at the will of the President. Executive Order 9877 was revoked by Executive Order 9950 on April 21, 1948, when the Key West Agreement became effective.

[4] It is of historical interest to note that twenty-five years ago the Army and Navy positions were exactly reversed. In a dispute over the control of troop transports, the Army claimed a need on the basis of the "task force" concept while the Navy argued

that *they* should have them because transports were sea-going. The task force approach to organization, if carried to an extreme, could lead to a claim by the infantry for their own guided missiles, tactical air, ground and air logistics, and naval transport.

[5] In 1956 the Army has about as many aircraft, either on hand or on order, as the entire Army Air Force had in 1939. See note 9 *infra*.

[6] The first meeting was held at the Key West Naval Base from March 11 to 14, 1948, between Secretary Forrestal and the Joint Chiefs (Leahy, Bradley, Denfield and Spaatz). A minor flurry was caused by the Air Force's objection to a press release which referred to an "agreement on all major areas". According to Forrestal, the Air Force felt there was still going to be two air forces instead of one. *Diaries*, pp. 389-399. The Key West Agreement was first promulgated as a Secretary of Defense Memorandum on April 21, 1948, entitled "Functions of the Armed Forces and the Joint Chiefs of Staff." The second meeting between Forrestal and the Chiefs was held at Newport, Rhode Island, August 20-22, 1948. See pp. 475-479 of the *Forrestal Diaries*.

[7] The Agreement has been further refined, as discussed in Chapter IX. The full text of the present version is reproduced in Appendix III.

[8] There were several staff studies made of this problem, and a legal opinion by the Office of the Secretary of Defense concluded that any command authority posssesed by the JCS was a delegation from the Secretary of Defense under the Key West Agreement and was revocable at the pleasure of the Secretary. According to this opinion, the command authority was not vested by the National Security Act, and it did not gain any increased status by having been sub-delegated to an executive agent. The JCS, however, did not concur in this conclusion, even though no "appeal" was attempted.

[9] A later agreement, which, to further confuse matters, was also known as the "Key West Agreement" did take up the matter. In 1952 the Secretary of the Air Force and the Secretary of the Army signed a memorandum of agreement which restricted the Army to certain types of fixed-wing and helicopter aircraft within prescribed weight limits.

[10] See *First Report of the Secretary of Defense*, U. S. GPO, Washington, 1948, p. 80.

[11] This relationship ultimately took the form of the Military Liaison Committee, headed by an Assistant to the Secretary of Defense (Atomic Energy). The problem was created by the firm separation of the Atomic Energy Commission and the Defense establishment which Congress had imposed.

[12] Eventually the Weapons Systems Evaluation Group (WSEG) was established under the Research and Development Board, but it worked under the direction of the JCS. It remained responsible to Board's successor—the Office of the Assistant Secretary of Defense (Research and Development)—and in 1955 it was shifted to a contract basis at Massachusetts Institute of Technology and subsequently to a contracting agency formed by a group of universities. See *Forrestal Diaries*, p. 477.

[13] See *The Forrestal Diaries* pp. 433, 465, and 497 (for comments on Forrestal's relation to the Hoover Commission and the Task Force) and Appendix G, Report of the Commission on Organization of the Executive Branch of Government, Washington-1949. An excellent abridgement of the Report may be found in McGraw-Hill's *The Hoover Commission Report*, New York, 1949. See also Chapter III *supra*.

[14] See House Committee on Armed Services *Report to Accompany H.R. 2216:* "Amending the National Security Act of 1947 to Provide for an Under Secretary of Defense", House Report No. 143, 81st Congress, 1st Session, February 17, 1949. The bill was subsequently enacted in April as P.L. 36, 81st Cong. (61 *Stat.* 495; 5 U.S.C.

171a)   The title was changed to *Deputy* Secretary of Defense by 1949 Amendments.
[15]The Eberstadt task force sought to correct this deficiency by conferring upon the Chairmen "broad powers of decision", subject to the authority of the Secretary of Defense, rather than transferring the functions to the Secretary himself.
[16] The position which Admiral William D. Leahy had held was not that of Chairman of the Joint Chiefs, but rather that of Chief of Staff to the President. Nevertheless that post was named in the 1947 Act as a member of the JCS. Forrestal recommended the deletion of this provision.
[17] H.R. 5632. 81st Congress, 1st Session, 1949.
[18] P.L. 216, 81st Congress. 61 *Stat.* 499, 5 U.S.C. Supp. 171.
[19] Contrary to some opinions, the decision to cancel the U.S.S. *United States* was made by the Secretary of Defense on the basis of split papers coming up from the JCS. It was *not* the JCS who made the decision by a 2-1 vote.
[20] *First Report of the Secretary of Defense*, 1948, p. 4. Forrestal was willing to accept either a fourth officer as Chairman or the designation of one of the Chiefs of Staff as Chairman. The Hoover Commission Task Force recommended only the latter.
[21] See Appendix I, p. 151.
[22] For a discussion of the subsequent history of attempts to strengthen the Chairman and increase the number of assistant secretaries, see Chapter IX.
[23] See House Committee on Armed Services, *Full Committee Hearings on H.R. 5632*, 81st Congress, 1st Session. The Hearing lasted only two hours and is contained in 34 pages. The primary testimony was that of Wilfred J. McNeil, the Defense Comptroller, who had had a major hand in drafting the bill.
[24] Another important provision was the grant of authority to establish working capital and management funds similar to those employed in private industry. Title IV also required annual reports to be made to the President and to Congress. These reports contain much useful material for the student of government fiscal policy. See *Implementation of Title IV, National Security Act of 1947, as amended, Interim Report of the Preparedness Subcommittee No. 3* of the Senate Committee on Armed Services, 83rd Congress, 1st Session, 1954, and the hearings before the same sub-committee held during both sessions of the 83d Congress.
[25] "Mystery Man of the Pentagon" by Charlotte Knight, *Colliers*, January 22, 1954, pp. 30-36.
[26] See Part IV of the Report, "Fixing Responsibility for Managing Defense Dollars."
[27] The Air Force view had been emphasized by the reports of two study groups a year before. The President's Air Policy Commission, headed by Thomas K. Finletter, had recommended a 70 group Air Force in its report of January 13, 1948. The Congressional Aviation Policy Board under Senator Brewster and Representative Hinshaw submitted a report on March 1, 1948, entitled *National Aviation Policy*. It agreed with the 70 group Air Force, but also urged an increased Naval Air Arm. The Board noted that the separate Air Force and Navy statements of requirements "in nowise represent a unified plan as might have been anticipated from the Unification Act" because of the "inability of the Joint Chiefs of Staff to prepare a unified plan."
[28] Those allegedly involved were Secretary of Defense Johnson, Secretary of the Air Force Stuart Symington, and aircraft manufacturer Floyd Odlum. Johnson as Chairman of the Finance Committee of the Democratic National Committee was said to have induced Symington to get Odlum to make a $6 million "contribution'" in order to get the B-36 contract. Johnson had been a director of a company making B-36's, but according to *The Forrestal Diaries*, he had asked Forrestal to make any decisions regarding them before leaving office. See *Diaries*, p. 551.

[29] H. Res. 227. The investigation was authorized by H. Res. 234, 81st Congress, 1st Session.

[30] The release was primarily the work of Navy Captain John G. Crommelin, but he was supported by his Navy superiors. What might otherwise have been treated as insubordinate conduct was thus allowed to pass.

[31] Hearings before the Committe on Armed Services House of Representatives, on the *National Defense Program—Unification and Strategy*, 81st Congress, 1st Session, 1949. The Report is entitled *Unification and Strategy, a Report of Investigation by the Committee on Armed Services,* House of Representatives, House Doc. No. 600, 81st Congress, 2nd Session, 1950.

[32] The Navy witnesses particularly stressed that Navy views on major matters of national strategy were either not solicited, or, if they were, did not receive full consideration. The Navy, according to some, felt itself to be a junior partner in the defense establishment—that is, a subject to being overruled on vital matters by the other services.

[33] See *Unification and Strategy,* op. cit., pp. 44-45.

CHAPTER IX

THE KOREAN WAR

On June 25, 1950, war broke out when the North Korean People's Republic launched a full scale invasion of the Republic of Korea by crossing the thirty-eighth parallel. The new Department of Defense was thus to receive its first trial by fire. Some have said that the Department was caught unprepared because of the policies of its second Secretary, Louis A. Johnson. He had used his increased authority to impose economy measures, which, despite assurances to Congress and the public, seriously affected our military posture. But the reductions in force of the Johnson regime cannot be blamed on him alone, nor on the defense organization; for an economy-minded President and Congress took a narrow view of how much the national economy could afford for defense. The Secretary of State had publicly defined the U.S. defense perimeter in a way which indicated that Korea was not within it. In any event, on behalf of the United Nations, we were quickly committed to what was initially referred to as a "police action", but which soon assumed the characteristics of a major military conflict.

Initial reverses nearly pushed the United Nations forces off the Korean peninsula. But a build up of U.S. forces and the deep amphibious envelopment through a landing at Inchon resulted in substantial victory. Pursuit of the disorganized North Korean Forces and the probability of United Nations occupation of the whole peninsula up to the Yalu river brought Chinese Communist forces into the war on a massive scale in November and December, 1950. U.N. forces were compelled to withdraw and stabilize a defense line at approximately the thirty-eighth parallel.

In the face of the unsatisfactory course of military events in Korea, Secretary of Defense Johnson was unable to survive in office. In September, General George C. Marshall was brought back from retirement to succeed him as the third Secretary of Defense. Appropriations for the military establishment, which had been reduced to $14 billion for fiscal 1950 under the Johnson regime rose in the following year to $48 billion.

99

THE GREAT DEBATE

The spring of 1951 saw two major airings in Congress of defense issues reminiscent—in terms of controversy, if not in subject matter—of the unification and strategy hearings two years earlier.

Shortly after the Chinese Communist and North Korean forces had launched their offensive, on January 8, 1951, Senator Wherry introduced a resolution challenging the authority of the President to send ground troops to bolster the defenses of Western Europe. Actually, the President had announced his intention the previous fall, but he had repeated it in his State of the Union Message. Senator Taft immediately charged that President Truman had "usurped authority . . . in violation of the laws and the Constitution."[1] Senator Wherry's resolution formally raised the Constitutional issue. The opponents of the substantive policy of "troops to Europe," preferring to fight on Constitutional grounds, planned their attack accordingly. Thus was launched the Great Debate of 1951, involving joint hearings before the Senate Armed Services and Foreign Relations Committees which lasted for 28 days with over 800 pages of testimony by legislative and executive leaders.[2]

The Hearings focused attention on over-all U.S. strategy, especially the "balanced forces" concept and the role of ground troops. Although the Senate approved the deployment to Europe of four divisions in a resolution on April 4,[3] the Administration promised to consult with Congress before making further additions of ground forces.

THE MacARTHUR HEARINGS

This debate had scarcely ended before President Truman's recall of General Douglas MacArthur on April 11, 1951, launched another and even more searching examination of strategic problems. The hearings which resulted[4] ranged over events in the Far East from the Wedemeyer Report, to the alleged "China Lobby," and to the decisions of Yalta relating to Soviet participation in the war against Japan. The problems of "civilian supremacy," of politico-military relationships—especially in regard to the non-military factors which permitted the Yalu "sanctuary"—and to the relations of the Joint Chiefs of Staff with the field commander all received attention.[5] Although no formal report was ever issued by the Committees, a statement of June 27, 1951, claimed that there had been no serious disagreement among the military on strategy—a somewhat debatable point—and generally supported the President's removal of MacArthur.[6]

The spring of 1951 was also marked by sharp clashes between military leaders and congressional supporters of the Marine Corps. Senator Paul Douglas, a World War II Marine veteran, introduced a bill to fix a statutory minimum strength for the Corps (at 3 divisions and 3 air wings) and to permit the Commandant to sit with the Joint Chiefs as a co-equal on matters affecting the Marines. (This latter had been recommended by the House Armed Services Committe report on Unification and Strategy.) Although the bill passed the Senate, it was held up in the House until June, 1952, when it was finally passed under the leadership of Carl Vinson of the Armed Services Committee.[7]

By autumn the Joint Chiefs of Staff, after serious initial disputes, unanimously recommended expanding the armed forces: an army of 20 divisions, a Navy of 409 major combat ships with 3 Marine Divisions and 3 Marine Air Wings, and an Air Force of 143 wings. After submitting this program to an *ad hoc* committee, chaired by James R. Killian of the Massachusetts Institute of Technology, Secretary of Defense Robert A. Lovett (who had succeeded General George C. Marshall) approved the Joint Chiefs' forces and successfully presented them to the National Security Council and the President for approval. Congress, however, imposed cuts on all three services in the appropriations bill for fiscal 1953.

CONGRESSIONAL CRITICISM OF DEFENSE

The Korean "police action" induced the Senate Armed Services Committee to establish Preparedness Investigating Subcommittees, modelled after the Truman Committee of World War II. Some seven reports, issued in 1952, stressed waste in use of manpower and extravagance in overseas air base construction. This latter criticism was in large part responsible for creating an Assistant Secretary of Defense for Properties and Installations a year later. In the House, considerable publicity was given to a "chamber of horrors" exhibit stressing service differences in purchasing. Procurement methods of the services and the lack of unification which various investigations had disclosed brought about demands for standardization.[8] The net result was the passage in June, 1952, of the Defense Cataloging and Standardization Act, which is still in effect.

During 1951 and 1952 the Munitions Board and the Research and Development Board were criticized as inefficient and unwieldy. Various Congressional investigating committees again urged reforms in procurement and supply, particularly the need for "standardization". A Johnson Preparedness Subcommittee report in July 1952, called for drastic reorganization of the services.[9] At the same time, Secretary Lovett was urged to create an advisory committee on manpower utilization. He finally chartered a "Citizens Advisory Committee on Manpower Utilization in the Armed Services" on August 15, 1952, but the Committee, chaired by reserve General David Sarnoff of RCA, did not meet until after the elections. On February 17, 1953, the Committee—which held only five sessions—submitted its report, which urged "an overall reduction of at least ten percent in men, money, and material."[10]

The Joint Chiefs of Staff were subjected to a constant line of fire, especially from Senator Taft. It started with the setback to United Nations forces in North Korea, continued through the MacArthur hearings and the great debate, and culminated in Taft's promise to remove the incumbent Joint Chiefs of Staff if he were elected. President Eisenhower, in a major campaign speech at Baltimore on September 25, 1952, offered "security with solvency" and a three point program: a Republican administration, a commission to study Department of Defense operations, and revitalization of the National Security Council. He stressed particularly the need for increased unification and efficiency.[11]

On November 18, 1952, Secretary of Defense Robert A. Lovett, in a long letter to President Truman, listed "subjects or general areas where work already begun might be profitably continued by the new administration". These major areas were the authority of the Secretary of Defense, the Joint Chiefs of Staff, the Munitions Board, and the organization of the Armed Services. Secretary Lovett emphasized the need for a strong hand at the top to force needed changes over the resistance of the services.[12]

After the election, President Eisenhower appointed a three-man committee, composed of Nelson Rockefeller, Arthur S. Flemming (who was to become Director of the Office of Defense Mobilization) and Milton S. Eisenhower, to investigate the need for reorganization in federal departments.[13] Two weeks after the President's State of the Union address on February 2, 1953, a new Rockefeller Committee was appointed, consisting of the original three members plus David Sarnoff, Robert A. Lovett, General Omar Bradley, and Dr. Vannevar Bush. Dr. Bush was apparently included partly because of his wide experience in military research and development (especially on atomic weapons) and partly because he had been making speeches highly critical of defense organization—particularly the unresponsiveness of the Joint Chiefs to civilian control.[14] The appointment was only two days before the Army's admission of ammunition shortages in Korea, and during the next two months—the period during which the Rockefeller Committee was in session—Senate hearings on these shortages kept Army, Department of Defense and JCS organizational problems in the headlines daily.[15]

The Rockefeller Committee held hearings with leading military officers, civilian administrators, and consultants. Apparently, however, they did not confer with individual Congressmen or with Congressional committees. Some criticism of the Committee—made even before its report—was based on the charge that the members favored a stronger chairman for the Joint Chiefs. This raised the "man-on-horseback" spectre and foreshadowed objections later to be made to Reorganization Plan No. 6.[16] Other critics noted that out of 22 persons heard by the Committee, 9 had Navy backgrounds, 5 had Army experience and only 3 had been associated with the Air Force. Moreover, the Air Force was displeased that its plea for changes in the Joint Chiefs of Staff to end the "inevitable compromises" resulting from the "practical requirement of unanimity" and to provide for JCS scrutiny of service budgets was not answered in the recommendations.

REPORT OF THE ROCKEFELLER COMMITTEE

The report of the Rockefeller Committee on Defense Organization was completed on April 11, 1953.[17] This study, followed as it was by Reorganization Plan No. 6 carrying out its recommendations, was the third of three major steps in the development of the defense organization. The first two, it will be recalled, were the National Security Act of 1947, following lengthy hearings and studies, and the National Security Act Amendments of 1949, pursuant to recommendations by the Hoover Commission and Secretary of Defense Forrestal. Since the committee, according to the letter transmitting its report, "concentrated its attention on the basic organization and procedures of the Department of Defense . . ." and since the set-up recommended is essentially what now exists, it is worthwhile to examine its findings in some detail. These dealt with five major areas.

First, the Secretary of Defense was said to require complete and effective control over the entire Department of Defense. The Report noted that there is "a long record of challenges [to the Secretary's authority] based on a legalistic argument that the phrase . . . which requires that the three military departments be 'separately administered' is a limitation on the authority of the Secretary of Defense . . ." The Committee's counsel, with the General Counsel and Assistant General Counsel of the Department of Defense, wrote an opinion which indicated that such challenges had no basis in statute or in legislative history. The committee adopted this interpretation and printed the opinion as an appendix to its report.

Second, the committee urged that the secretaries of the military departments should be in all respects the operating heads of their respective departments—both military and civilian elements. Rejecting proposals for two parallel lines of command, one for military affairs and one for such civilian matters as political, economic, and industrial affairs, the committee stated that the proper way to enforce responsibility is "to have a single channel of command or line of administrative responsibility within the Department of Defense and each of the military departments."

Third, the committee considered it "unfortunate" that the intention of the National Security Act, which stressed the planning and advisory role of the Joint Chiefs of Staff, had been obscured in practice. It was therefore recommended that the Key West Agreement be revised to remove the command function from the Joint Chiefs of Staff and that the Secretary of Defense—not the JCS—should assign executive responsibility for unified commands. The report noted the "difficulties inherent in the dual role of the service members of the Joint Chiefs of Staff"—as members of the JCS and the military chiefs of their services. Although it recognized these difficulties, the committee did not feel that proposals to create a single Chief of Staff or single General Staff—or to give the chairman of the Joint Chiefs authority to settle disagreements—should be adopted. However, it was recommended that the JCS chairman should be given the responsibility for organizing the structure of the Joint Chiefs and Joint Staff and emphasizing their joint planning role. Moreover, the members of the Joint Chiefs should be encouraged to delegate administrative duties to their service deputies and to delegate within the Staff to subordinate committees. The report stated that "the importance of a close relationship between the Secretary of Defense and the Joint Chiefs of Staff cannot be overemphasized." While thus stressing the importance of coordination with the Office of the Secretary of Defense, the committee cautioned that this direct relationship does not relieve individual chiefs of the obligation to keep their own secretaries fully informed.

Fourth, finding that the Munitions Board and the Research and Development Board were unwieldy, the Rockefeller Committee recommended that they be abolished and that their functions be transferred to assistant secretaries of defense. To absorb those duties and to strengthen further the administrative staff of the Secretary of Defense, six additional assistant secretaries were proposed (making a total of nine in all) plus a General Counsel, who has the rank but not the name of an assistant secretary.

Finally, to free military officers on duty in the Office of the Secretary of Defense from service influence the Committee urged that efficiency reports on such officers be made by civilians rather than by officers from the individual's own service. It further recommended emphasis on the procurement of highly qualified officers for assignment to that office, in view of the importance of personnel relationships to the whole progress of unification.

PRESIDENTIAL ACTION

On April 30, 1953, President Eisenhower sent Reorganization Plan No. 6 with an accompanying message to Congress.[18] As indicated by Reorganization Plan No. 6, reproduced in Appendix III, most of the recommendations of the Rockefeller Committee were adopted by the President. The Plan provided for the abolition of the Boards, the transfer of their functions to the Secretary, and the appointment of the additional assistant secretaries and General Counsel. It give the Chairman of the Joint Chiefs of Staff power to manage the Joint Staff and its Director and made appointments to the Joint Staff subject to the approval of the Chairman.

CONGRESSIONAL ACTION

In Congress the plan was referred to the House Committee on Government Operations, Representative Clare E. Hoffman, Chairman, and by special agreement, to the Armed Services Committee of the Senate, Senator Leverett Saltonstall, Chairman.[19] Some of the Rockefeller Committee proposals, particularly provisions concerning the Joint Chiefs of Staff, had aroused public criticism—for example, by David Lawrence, Hanson Baldwin, and Arthur Krock.[20] Chairman Hoffman introduced a resolution in the House to eliminate these provisions and then held hearings on the resolution.

On May 7, 1953—one week after the Plan had been submitted— General Nathan F. Twining replaced General Hoyt S. Vandenberg as the Air Force representative on the Joint Chiefs of Staff. A few days later the appointments of Admiral Arthur W. Radford as Chairman, General Matthew B. Ridgeway (Army), and Admiral Robert B. Carney (Navy) were announced.[21] This complete change in personnel did not, however, help to quiet the criticism. Representative Leslie C. Arends, Republican leader in the House, wrote President Eisenhower requesting assurance that the JCS provisions would not result in the emergence of a general staff. The President's reassuring reply was

placed before the House on May 28, and the hearings on Joint Resolution 264 continued during June.[22] Several Congressmen—notably
Hoffman—were annoyed at what they considered an "end-run," that
is, using a reorganization plan rather than legislation. Some members
implied that the administration had brought pressure to bear to allow
the plan to go through without hearings or debate.[23] In any case,
because of the restricted nature of Hoffman's resolution—and because
dissension within the committee prevented attempts to broaden it—
the hearings rarely if ever touched on the main points of the reorganization plan, except for the opening statment of Deputy Secretary of
Defense Roger M. Kyes.

One complaint was that the Plan was an unconstitutional delegation of power from the President to the Secretary of Defense. Another,
especially from Navy critics, was that it violated the intention of the
National Security Act, which had emphasized the autonomy of the
services. Present also was the fear that in granting new powers to
the Chairman over the Joint Staff, the Plan was taking an additional
step toward the creation of a German-type general staff. The rea-
soning here was that the Chairman, by controlling the selection of
the Joint Staff, could eventually create a staff with views so like his
own that they would become a "personal" general staff. That the
Director of the Joint Staff was to be selected with the approval of the
Secretary of Defense and that the Chairman did not appoint, but
merely *approved,* selections for the Joint Staff was conveniently ignored by these critics. Moreover, the *management* of the Joint Staff
was construed by the opponents to mean *control,* whereas the supporters of the Plan interpreted it as mere administration.

The committee failed in its attempt to obtain detailed information on the proposed revision of the Key West Agreement.[24] A request
for transcripts of the testimony before the Rockefeller Committee was
also refused on the ground that the witnesses had been promised
complete secrecy.[25] Congress' general acceptance of the Plan and the
lack of support behind its critics were indicated by the final vote of
235 to 108 against the resolution disapproving the Plan. Reorganization Plan No. 6 went into effect on June 30, 1953.

THE 1953 REVISION OF THE KEY WEST AGREEMENT

On October 1, 1953, a Directive of Secretary of Defense Charles E.
Wilson revised the Key West functions paper to conform to the recommendations of the Rockefeller Committee. Although no changes
were made in the roles and missions of the three services, the sections
on the Joint Chiefs were amended in several respects.[26] Primarily

affected was the "executive agent" system. Before, the Joint Chiefs of Staff appointed one of *their members* as their executive agent for a unified command or some other responsibility, such as mutual assistance. That member then acted for the Joint Chiefs through his own service, which had the effect of short circuiting the civilian secretary. Now the *Secretary of Defense*, with the advice of the Joint Chiefs, appoints a *military department* as *his* executive agent, and that department, *through its civilian secretary*, has the responsibility for the unified command.[27] To insure that there would be no temptation for the Secretary to make military decisions, he was directed to "forthwith authorize the military chief of such department . . . to act for [it]". However, the military chief was instructed to keep his secretary, the Secretary of Defense, and the Joint Chiefs fully informed on all decisions and actions taken.

There can be no doubt that Reorganization Plan No. 6 provides a tighter form of unification by giving increased authority to the Secretary of Defense and the Chairman of the Joint Chiefs of Staff. With nine assistant secretaries of Defense—dubbed "Vice-presidents"— reporting to him the Secretary of Defense is bound to assume a degree of detailed direction of the affairs of the military establishment which was impossible with the small staff of the pre-1953 period. The line between policy and administration—the former being the sphere of the Office of the Secretary of Defense and the latter the sphere of the Military Departments—is always a matter of interpretation. Inevitably nine assistant secretaries delve more deeply into details than could three. Just how deep is indicated by an Instruction from the Assistant Secretary of Defense (Properties and Installations) covering "Refuse Collection and Disposal", a document lampooned in a Navy League publication under the title, "The Boundless Blessings of Unification."[28] Also inevitable was that more policy decisions would be made at the level of the assistant secretaries without consultation with the Secretary of Defense.

Along with these developments has come increased influence by the Chairman of the Joint Chiefs of Staff. The new powers conferred by Reorganization Plan No. 6 were in and of themselves, not of great importance, but it is significant that a trend towards centralization of authority in the Chairman was established. He has increasingly become the major point of contact between the Joint Chiefs of Staff and the President, the Secretary of Defense, and the National Security Council.

There has been a certain amount of rather metaphysical discussion about single and double lines of authority and channels of civilian control. The effect of Reorganization Plan No. 6 has been debated between Mr. Eugene S. Duffield, co-editor of the *Forrestal Diaries*, and Mr. H. Struve Hensel, originally a leading opponent of unification but subsequently counsel for the Rockefeller Committee and the Department of Defense. This discussion[29] is a survey of the difficult issues of organizational philosophy and practical political judgment inherent in any organizational changes in the military establishment. A clear cut issue, however, does exist as to whether the Joint Chiefs of Staff as a corporate body are to be both planners and commanders. There are two possible command channels from the President and the Secretary of Defense to the operating military echelons: one via the civilian secretary and the military chief of staff, who acts on the advice of the Joint Chiefs *as strategic planners;* the other via the Joint Chiefs as a "corporate command body" and the military chief of staff as a member of that body.

Despite protests that the Joint Chiefs were intended to have, and should have, command authority, the present trend is contrary. The Rockefeller Committee and the present Administration have stressed that the single chain of command from the Secretary of Defense to the Military Departments is not only the proper interpretation of the National Security Act but is also preferable as a matter of policy. It remains to be seen whether a period of crisis with the need for speedy coordination of military advice and military decision will not cause a short circuit and result in a complete delegation of command to the military chief of staff. This would leave the Secretary with the administrative and support duties that the Navy feels is the proper area for civilians. Actually, delegation and readjustment by administrative action may represent a suitable compromise between partisans of the Navy's "horizontally spread and bi-lineal" organization and advocates of the Army's "vertical, single channel" pattern.[30] Defense organization may require flexibility among the functions of administration, planning, and operations as the international situation changes from cold war, to local war, to "relaxed tension," and back again.[31] During combat operations, strategic and tactical planning and command may well require "short circuiting" the civilian hierarchy. But during periods of "non-military" warfare, the adjustment of military policies with the economic, political, and diplomatic ingredients of national security may equally require the fullest use of civilian secretariats.

[1] *N.Y. Times, January 6,* 1951.
[2] *Hearings, Assignment of Ground Forces of the United States to Duty in the Euro-*

pean Area, on S. Con. Res. 8, Senate Committee on Foreign Relations and Senate Committee on Armed Services, 82nd Congress, 1st Session, 1951.

[2] S. Res. 99 and S. Con. Res. 18 (which thus brought in the House of Representatives), 82nd Congress, 1st Session, 1951.

[4] Hearings on *The Military Situation in the Far East,* Senate Committee on Foreign Relations and Senate Committee on Armed Services, 82nd Congress, 1st Session, 1951.

[5] For further discussion of the Korean war and the problem of politico-military coordination, see Chapter I *supra.*

[6] For an account from a somewhat partisan point of view, see Arthur M. Schlesinger, Jr. and Richard H. Rovere, *The General and the President,* Farrar-Straus, New York, 1951.

[7] P.L. 416, 82d Congress, 2d Session, 1952. Actually the original bill had proposed full JCS membership for the Commandant. The co-equal status was a compromise reached in the conference committee. See *The Joint Chiefs of Staff, 1941-1954* by Arthur O. Sulzberger, the U. S. Marine Corps Institute, Washington, D. C., 1954, (S-A235.3) Chapter XV

[8] For a general account of these and other Congressional activities in the defense field, see the *Congressional Quarterly Almanac,* Volume III, under "Military and Veterans".

[9] See *N.Y. Times,* July 7, 1952. Hanson Baldwin criticized the Johnson Report in the *N.Y. Times* on August 3.

[10] DOD Directive 5120.7. The Committee Report is available as a Committee Print, Senate Committee on Armed Services, 83d Congress, 1st Session and was. criticized in *Army, Navy, Air Force Journal,* Vol. 90, February 21, 1953, p. 725.

[11] See *N.Y. Times,* September 26, 1952.

[12] The letter was issued as a press release on November 18, 1952, and is printed in full in *Army, Navy, Air Force Journal,* Vol. 90, 1953, p. 542.

[13] Articles dealing with the Committee appeared in the *N.Y. Times* on December 1, 10, and 22, 1952; January 4, 14, 21; and February 15 and 20, 1953.

[14] See, for example, *N.Y. Times,* September 27, 1953, p. 7, and Dr. Bush's article "What's Wrong at the Pentagon?" in *Colliers,* December 27, 1952.

[15] See *Ammunition Shortages in the Far East, Hearings* before the Senate Committee on Armed Services and Preparedness Subcommittee, No. 2, 83d Congress, 1st Session, 1953.

[16] See *Congressional Record,* 83d Congress, 1st Session, Vol. 99, pp. 1871, A 1561, A 1481, 2447, A1665, A 2040 (1953).

[17] *Report of the Rockefeller Committee on Department of Defense Organization,* April 11, 1953, Committee Print, Senate Committee on Armed Services, 83d Congress, 1st Session, 1953. A list of the witnesses heard and the statements, or documents considered by the Committee will be found at pp. 22-25 of the *Report.*

[18] "Reorganization Plan No. 6 of 1953, Message from the President of the United States", House Doc. No. 136, 83d Congress, 1st Session, 1953.

[19] 99 *Congressional Record* 4209 (1953)

[20] The articles are reprinted in the hearings. See House Committee on Government Operations, *Reorganization Plan No. 6 of 1953, Hearings on H.J. Res. 264,* 83d Congress, 1st Session, 1953, pp. 255-9.

[21] See *N.Y. Times,* May 8, 13, 1953, and *Joint Chiefs of Staff Nominations, Hearings* before the Senate Armed Services Committee, 83d Congress, 1st Session, May 28, 1953.

[22] Meanwhile, the new Secretary of Defense, Charles E. Wilson, had been defending

budget cuts by referring to economies to be obtained through the Plan. See *Depart-partment of Defense Appropriations for 1954, Hearings,* House Appropriations Committee, 83d Congress, 1st Session, 1953, pp. 376, 386.

[23] See especially the questions asked of John Adams (the Department's Deputy General Counsel for Legislative Services) at pp. 170-1, 240-244 of the Hearings on H.J. Res. 264, *op. it.*

[24] Hearings on H.J. Res. 264, *op. cit.,* pp. 240-244.

[25] *Ibid.,* pp. 72-73.

[26] See DOD Directive 5100.1, March 16, 1954, "Functions of the Armed Forces and the Joint Chiefs of Staff". The 1953 changes are indicated in Appendix III which gives the revised version of the Key West Agreement as set forth in this Directive.

[27] As of March, 1954, the Department of the Army had responsibility for three unified commands (Far East, Europe, and Caribbean), the Department of the Navy, two unified and one specified commands (Atlantic, Pacific, and U.S. Naval Forces, Eastern Atlantic and Mediterranean), and the Department of the Air Force two unified and two specified commands (Alaska and U.S. Northeast, and USAF-Europe and Strategic Air Command.)   See DOD Directive 5100.2, March 16, 1954, "Executive Agent Responsibility for Unified and Specified Commands".

[28] *Now Hear This,* November-December, 1955.

[29] Eugene S. Duffield, "Organizing for Defense", *Harvard Business Review,* September-October, 1953 and H. Struve Hensel, "Changes Inside the Pentagon, *Harvard Business Review,* January-February, 1954.

[30] Mr. Hensel's article, takes an opposing viewpoint to that of Mr. Duffield. Although the issues are not always clearly drawn, Mr. Duffield in general sees a tendency toward centralization into a "monolithic" and fully vertical organization. He also feels that the Navy's bi-lineal system is the appropriate form for civilian control, since there is no "whisper of a challenge" to that control. Mr. Hensel on the other hand urges that civilian control must be "active" and demonstrative to prevent military domination of policy. He, however, believes that *decentralization* "is today's reality" in view of the delegation of operational authority to the service secretaries under a single channel of responsibility.

[31] The letter of transmittal accompanying the Rockefeller Report seems to recognize this by stating: "We believe that it [the proposed defense organization] will be suitable not only for the present period of localized war, but also in time of transition to either full war or relatively secure peace."

CHAPTER X

THE OFFICE OF THE SECRETARY OF DEFENSE

Although there have been a number of minor reorganizations since 1953, the basic structure of the Department of Defense has continued to follow the plan proposed by the Rockefeller Committee and Reorganization Plan No. 6. The main components are the three military services—Department of the Army, Department of the Navy, and Department of the Air Force—and the Office of the Secretary of Defense (OSD). As noted earlier, the other two armed services, the Marines and the Coast Guard, are under the Navy except in peacetime when the Coast Guard operates under the Treasury Department. The details of the defense organization are shown in Appendix V.

The most significant yardstick against which to measure the progress of unification and evolution of the defense structure is the Office of the Secretary of Defense. That office has grown from a small personal staff under Secretary Forrestal to an organization employing over 1500 civilians and nearly 700 military personnel. Compare, for example, Admiral Nimitz' 1947 views on the size of the Office of the Secretary of Defense with the present situation. The Chairman of the Senate Armed Services Committee had confused the staff of the Secretary of Defense with the Joint Staff and had mentioned the figure of 100 during the hearings. Admiral Nimitz replied: "That is for the Joint Staff, the staff to the Joint Chiefs. As for the Secretary of Defense, I do not visualize him having a staff that large".[1] From three special assistants in 1949, the office has developed a structure which includes ten officials with the rank of Assistant Secretary of Defense (ASD). (Within the Department as a whole, some thirty individuals rate the designation "Mr. Secretary." (The *number* of civilians in the office of the Secretary of Defense has not increased since 1949 as much as these statements might imply. On December 31, 1949 the figure was 1616, and on January 20, 1953 it was 2082. But by December 31, 1955, the number had been reduced to 1760.) It is necessary to have some idea of the functions of these "vice presidents" and of their relationships with the military departments to understand how the Department operates.[2]

111

THE SECRETARY AND DEPUTY SECRETARY OF DEFENSE

The Secretary of Defense is the principal assistant to the President in all matters relating to the Department of Defense. The Deputy Secretary acts for and exercises the powers of the Secretary during his absence or disability and also represents the Department on the Operations Coordinating Board. Special Assistants to the Secretary of Defense are appointed from time to time as required; two, for example, were appointed to assist the Secretary in evaluating recommendations of the 1955 Hoover Commission. At any given time there may be from three to five or more persons acting with this title.

The Assistant Secretaries of Defense (sometimes referred to as *functional* vice presidents to distinguish them from the Service Secretaries as *operating* vice presidents) have been designated[3] as follows: Comptroller, General Counsel, Legislative and Public Affairs, Manpower, Personnel and Reserve, Supply and Logistics, Research and Development, Applications Engineering, Properties and Installations, Health and Medical, and International Security Affairs.

THE COMPTROLLER

The Comptroller advises the Secretary on financial matters and supervises the preparation of budget estimates. He is, in official Pentagonese, "responsible for the establishment of uniform policies and procedures in the preparation and execution of budgets, accounting, statistical reporting and auditing and the expenditure and collection of funds." Despite the administrative nature of these duties, the Comptroller is in reality on of the most powerful influences in defense. In part this is due to the personality and ability of the present incumbent[4] and the fact that the budget is the *one* place where requirements, resources, manpower and funds are brought together. Inevitably the Comptroller gets into substantive policy—if only to point out that, for example, an Air Force request for airplane bodies for a certain period is in conflict with the number of engines requested. The Comptroller's office will also point out to the Army that a request for high performance aircraft—even if within the 5000 pound weight limitation agreed upon with the Air Force—is not in accordance with their mission and require the Army to justify it. Although in theory the Comptroller's staff function is separated from the command function of programming, in fact the screening of requirements is ultimately done by the Comptroller. As pointed out in Chapter VIII, the 1955 Hoover Commission urged that this situation be remedied.

THE GENERAL COUNSEL

The chief legal officer, the General Counsel, is responsible for all legal services within the Department or involving it. In addition to advising on legal aspects of defense activities, he gives interpretations on such matters as the power of the Secretary of Defense and the command authority of the Joint Chiefs of Staff. Actually his overall responsibility is largely theoretical since legal staffs in the military departments operate with a large degree of independence and there are, in addition, many lawyers in uniform working for the Judge Advocate General of each service. There are a number of assistant general counsels who service the various functional areas on a client basis, just as the partners of a large law firm handle their own accounts while still working within a partnership.

LEGISLATIVE AND PUBLIC AFFAIRS

As indicated by his title, this Assistant Secretary has two areas of responsibility: (1) developing and presenting legislative programs to Congress and providing liaison, and (2) determining policies for the Department's public information and public affairs activities. He works closely with other assistant secretaries, particularly the Comptroller and the General Counsel, and is responsible for coordination of legislative and public information programs within the Department. He must maintain a close check on all Congressional activities concerned with defense, although each service maintains its own legislative liaison office.

MANPOWER, PERSONNEL AND RESERVE

This Assistant Secretary advises and assists the Secretary of Defense in the fields[5] of manpower and personnel (including security programs) armed forces information and education, and administration and maintenance of reserve forces. He also must coordinate civil and military defense planning and industrial relations. Within this office there is a Reserve Forces Policy Board, which is "the principal policy adviser to the Secretary of Defense on matters pertaining to the reserve components"; it consists of a civilian chairman, Under or Assistant Secretaries of each military department, and 16 regular and reserve officers representing all branches of the services.[6] This official also performs management and housekeeping services for the entire office of the Secretary through a Director of Administrative Services.

SUPPLY AND LOGISTICS

Included here are procurement, production, distribution, transportation, communications, storage, cataloging, requirements, and mobilization planning. Although basically a coordinator among the military services, the Assistant Secretary is responsible for "appraising the feasibility of strategic plans with respect to the availability of materials, end items, components and support."[7] He also determines priorities of various segments of the military procurement programs. Prescribing a single supply catalog system in order to standardize the nomenclature in the entire defense inventory is currently receiving considerable emphasis. However, during the summer of 1956 the standardization function was transferred to the Air Force as the operating agency. Because of the size and diversity of military procurement, Supply and Logistics is the largest segment of the Office of the Secretary of Defense.

RESEARCH AND DEVELOPMENT

The Research and Development vice president establishes "policies and procedures necessary to achieve a sound and integrated research and development program," and assures "interaction of research and development with strategy." His office provides the Joint Chiefs of Staff with highest level operations analysis services through the Weapons Systems Evaluation Group now operating under contract to a group of universities. As with intelligence, there is a nation-wide "research and development community" which includes industry, universities, laboratories, the military services and such government agencies as the Atomic Energy Commission and the National Science Foundation. The Office of the Assistant Secretary of Defense (Research and Development) mobilizes the resources of science and industry for defense purposes through some thirteen coordinating committees and eleven technical advisory panels. It also operates the Research and Development Policy Council jointly with the Office of the Assistant Secretary of Defense for Applications Engineering.

APPLICATIONS ENGINEERING

Applications engineering, a novel term in Pentagonese, covers the engineering phases of the cycle that begins with research and stops with the production of an end item—that is, those areas that are partly development and partly production which lie between the scientist and the production official. Its relationship with its sister office, Research and Development is a very close one—for example, the Weapons Systems Evaluation Group was originally intended to come under Applications Engineering. A separation between these two divisions was deliberately made, however, because it was felt that putting both in the same hands would mean the neglect of one or the other. Research and Development people have been heard to comment that Applications Engineering is currently emphasized because that field was Mr. Wilson's specialty at General Motors.

PROPERTIES AND INSTALLATIONS

The programs with which this official is concerned include: real estate acquisition,[8] utilization and disposal, construction, real property maintenance and management, and family housing. He administers the duties of the Secretary of Defense with respect to the reserve of commercial and industrial plants—such as those for machine tools—included in the National Industrial Reserve. However, the office is *not* concerned with civil projects of the Army Engineers. It works closely with other areas, especially Supply and Logistics and Research and Development. Although the Assistant Secretary is, like the others, in theory merely a staff adviser to the Secretary, in fact he gets closer to the administration and operations of the services than any of the others. His office works through the assistant secretary of each military department responsible for properties and installations and also with the various chiefs of staff for logistics, and through them with military commands and installations.[9]

HEALTH AND MEDICAL

The area covered here is medical services and hospitals, where the principal problems are eliminating duplicated services, standardizing medical manpower requirements, and planning the medical aspects of mobilization and disaster situations. On such touchy problems as the doctor draft, he deals with the American Medical Association and with manpower officials in the Office of Defense Mobilization. In 1955 he established a Health and Medical Planning Council to bring together his personnel with the medical profession and other officials of the Department.

INTERNATIONAL SECURITY AFFAIRS

This vice president is the defense representative on the National Security Council Planning Board, and in token of his close relationship to strategic problems, he has an office adjacent to the Chairman of the Joint Chiefs of Staff. He handles military aid, North Atlantic Treaty Organization affairs, United Nations matters, intergovernmental conferences, and the like, insofar as these lie within the authority of the Secretary of Defense. His office furnishes the support for defense participation in both the National Security Council and the Operations Coordinating Board. He advises the Secretary of Defense on the politico-military and economic aspects of foreign military affairs, as well as on policies for base negotiations with foreign governments. As noted in Chapter V, International Security Affairs must obtain the position of the Department of Defense on a proposed policy and represent the Department in dealings with other agencies, such as the State Department or the International Cooperation Administration. Since this area of activity involves not only the three military departments but also the rest of the executive branch—especially the State Department—foreign governments, and international organizations, the office has special administrative duties as well as functional responsibilities. For example, it has its own comptroller and it has an assistant general counsel for which it is the only "client." Some of its legislative liaison must be performed outside normal channels because it collaborates with State in preparing requests for Mutual Assistance funds and other military aid programs.

ATOMIC ENERGY

An Assistant to the Secretary of Defense advises on atomic energy aspects of defense policies and programs. He furnishes liaison with various other government agencies in these matters. Just as there was an "intelligence community" and a "research and development community," there is a community of interest throughout the government and nation on atomic energy matters. The key agency of course, is the Atomic Energy Commission, and there is a Military Liaison Committee to the AEC. The chairman of this committee (a full time statutory position) has always doubled as Assistant to the Secretary on atomic energy matters. He has *direct* liaison with the Joint Committee on Atomic Energy in Congress—that is, he does not go through the normal legislative and public affairs channels. The activities of the three services, especially in connection with the Armed Forces Special Weapons Project, have a close relationship with the field operations of the Atomic Energy Commission. They are coordinated at the headquarters level primarily through the Military Liaison Committee and the Office of the Assistant to the Secretary of Defense for Atomic Energy.

OFFICE OF SPECIAL OPERATIONS

The Office of Special Operations, headed by a Director, handles the intelligence duties of the Secretary of Defense. It operates through the established channels, such as the Joint Intelligence Group of the Joint Chiefs and maintains defense contacts with the Central Intelligence Agency, the National Security Agency (which is actually a part of the Defense Department)—and with other intelligence and special operations organizations. It also has some responsibilities in the field of psychological warfare.

THE JOINT CHIEFS OF STAFF

The Joint Chiefs of Staff, it should be noted, are located within— and are a unit of—the Office of the Secretary of Defense. However, by statute they have broader responsibilities than the other agencies of the Office of the Secretary. The service members of the Joint Chiefs of Staff (the military heads of the three services) serve in a dual capacity. They are appointed by the President with the advice and consent of the Senate.

There are a number of Joint Chiefs of Staff committees, some of which, like the Joint Intelligence Committee and the Joint Strategic Survey Committee, were formed as early as 1942.[10] These are staffed by officers from the three services who serve in both capacities. Since 1949 there has been a Chairman of the Joint Chiefs of Staff who, while holding office, takes precedence over all other officers of the armed forces. Although he manages the Joint Staff and presides over JCS meetings, he has no authority to settle issues upon which there is disagreement, except by suggesting a basis for compromise or making recommendations to the Secretary of Defense to guide him in making a decision.[11] He is expressly forbidden to exercise military command over the Joint Chiefs or the military services.

The Joint Staff includes officers from all the services assigned on a full time basis to provide assistance to the Joint Chiefs of Staff. It is limited by statute to 210 members. It is important to understand that the Joint Staff is the staff of the Joint Chiefs, and *not* of the Secretary of Defense, who is prohibited by the National Security Act from establishing a military staff other than the Joint Chiefs themselves. It is headed by a Director—who is junior to all members of the JCS and who is appointed subject to the approval of the Secretary of Defense. The role of the Joint Chiefs of Staff in determining national security policy was discussed in Chapter V, and the problem of JCS relations with the Office of the Secretary of Defense will be mentioned in Chapter XI.

THE JOINT SECRETARIES

This body, composed of the Secretary of Defense, the Deputy Secretary, the Secretaries and Under Secretaries of the three services and the Assistant Secretary of Defense for International Security Affairs meets regularly to act as another source of inter-service civilian advice for the Secretary of Defense.[12] It provides a convenient forum in which differences of opinion on matters of broad administrative policy can be discussed and reconciled. Such a matter as the extension of the *single manager system* for supply and procurement would be discussed by this body.

THE ARMED FORCES POLICY COUNCIL

The Armed Forces Policy Council, established by the National Security Act of 1947 as the War Council and renamed by the 1949 Amendments, combines the membership of the Joint Secretaries (minus the Assistant Secretary of Defense for International Security Affairs) with that of the Joint Chiefs of Staff. Other officials participate from time to time when appropriate. Since the Joint Secretaries are solely civilians and the Joint Chiefs of Staff, military officers, the Armed Forces Policy Council is the one place where military and civilian views may be threshed out before the Secretary of Defense. Although it was originally designed to serve as the major point for coordinating politico-military matters, it proved inadequate in this capacity. It now has wide flexibility in the matters of broad policy relating to the armed forces which it considers and on which it reports to the Secretary of Defense.

THE ROLE OF THE OFFICE OF THE SECRETARY OF DEFENSE

The major components having been reviewed, it is desirable to take a closer look at the whole organization. In a sense the Office of the Secretary is the *management* echelon of the Defense Department. If one defines management as the effective utilization of money, men, and materials, then the Office of the Secretary—as represented by the Comptroller, the Assistant Secretary (Manpower, Personnel and Reserve) and the Assistant Secretary (Supply and Logistics)—certainly fulfills the definition. As noted earlier, the defense budget is the universal solvent of management and policy, or, stated another way, of means and ends. The Budget cycle for fiscal 1957 (which commences on July 1, 1956) started in July, 1954 with plans by the Joint Chiefs of Staff and the development of departmental programs. During the spring of 1955, budget guidances were furnished and the service estimates reviewed in the military departments. During the fall, these were reviewed by the Office of the Secretary of Defense and the Bureau of the Budget, culminating in the President's budget submitted to Congress in January, 1956. Congressional review and appropriations hearings took place during the spring of 1956. Simultaneously, the Department is going through a *funding* process—apportioning and allocating the appropriations. The point here is that much of the time the budget and fiscal offices are working on three different years: doing a post-audit on the past year, supervising the allocation and allotment of current appropriations, preparing estimates for the next fiscal year—and perhaps developing advanced planning for the year after that.[18]

Thus it seems safe to say that a good many of the officials in the Office of the Secretary consider their major job to be reviewing past, present or future programs—and the policies and procedures on which programs are based—whether or not they are actually working on the budget itself. Since most of those programs involve more than one functional area, the relationships among the various offices are important. Supply and Logistics has common interests in medical supplies with Health and Medical; Applications Engineering and Research and Development are closely related; both are concerned to some extent with Manpower and Personnel problems. Coordination therefore becomes important both to insure that all relevant views are considered in making a decision and to keep all areas informed of what is going on. This may take the form of liaison by a simple phone call, by a "conference"—which is where every official in the Pentagon is when not at his desk—or by more formal committees and working groups. In matters of major importance, a forum such as the Joint Secretaries or the Armed Forces Policy Council may be used to bring the Assistant Secretaries of Defense together with the service secretaries in the presence of the Secretary.

The Hoover Commission commented that the "assignment of responsibilities among members of the Secretariat in the Office of the Secretary of Defense impedes effective coordination. This is due to the numerous interrelationships among the function for which these executives are responsible."[14] To remedy this alleged defect, it proposed a new civilian position to aid in coordination[15] and urged a regrouping of the assistant secretaries into four major management areas: Logistics, Research and Development, Personnel, and Financial Management.[16] But coordination is not the answer to everything; it is quite possible to coordinate something to death.

Certain of the assistant secretaries play an important part in the smooth workings of the Office. The General Counsel and his staff work across the board. Legislative and Public Affairs must iron out inconsistencies between functional areas in preparing the Department's legislative program. International Security Affairs particularly must pull together all aspects of defense as they apply to foreign relations—bases, alliances, military aid, and so on. The Office of Administrative Services[17] produces a certain amount of cohesion by providing centralized personnel, supply, and housekeeping services. But the Comptroller, perhaps more than any of the other assistant secretaries, serves as a focus for coordination. This sometimes creates problems in his relationship to the assistant secretary responsible for a program area. During the questioning of the Assistant Secretary of Defense (Properties and Installations) in an appropriations hearing before Congress, the following exchange took place:

The Chairman "Now the next question is this: We have now established that you are the boss, so far as construction is concerned. But I would like to know what your relationship is as far as Mr. McNeil, the Department Comptroller, is concerned. Can he refuse to give you the money or refuse to give the Department money and thus prove that he is the boss and not you?

Secretary Floete: "That is on the nose." (Laughter) [18]

Actually, the Comptroller looks to the functional assistant secretary for advice and guidance and usually accepts his views, although as the quotation indicates, the man who controls the money may ultimately have the last word.

AN ILLUSTRATIVE CHARTER

Each Assistant Secretary has a "charter" in the form of a directive from the Secretary of Defense which establishes his assigned field and delegates authority to require information from the appropriate officials in the military departments. Thus, for example, Department of Defense (DOD) Directive No. 5126.1, 13 August 1953, sets out the detailed responsibilities of the Assistant Secretary of Defense (Supply and Logistics). A few excerpts are quoted below by way of illustration.

"Pursuant to the authority vested in me by the National Security Act of 1947, as amended, and by Reorganization Plan No. 6 of 1953, the Assistant Secretary of Defense (Supply and Logistics) . . . shall, in addition to such responsibilities as may hereafter be assigned have the following responsibilities: . . .

"(1) Developing policies and procedures for the Department of Defense in the broad fields of procurement, production, distribution, transportation, storage, cataloging, requirements, and mobilization planning.

*   *   *   *

"(23) Insuring effective implementation of established Department of Defense policies, plans, and programs in the above listed areas and taking all necessary or appropriate action to insure that the procedures, methods, and practices of the military departments are in compliance therewith.

"The Assistant Secretary of Defense (Supply and Logistics) is herewith delegated the authority to obtain such reports and information from the military departments as are necessary to carry out his responsibilities and is authorized to request the military departments to issue the necessary directives to obtain such reports and information . . .

"[He] . . . will to the extent practicable utilize the advice, assistance, and appropriate facilities of the military departments. Such utilization shall not, however, be so construed or so utilized as to circumvent the established command channels through the Secretaries of the military departments . . .

"Directives recommended by the Assistant Secretary (Supply and Logistics) which intend to change established policies or procedures will be signed by the Secretary or Deputy Secretary of Defense and their implementation will be accomplished by the Secretaries of the military departments . . .

"[He] is specifically prohibited from negotiating contracts with suppliers.

*   *   *   *

The carefully drafted terms of the directive indicate the delicate balance between overall responsibility for a functional area and the need to maintain the status of the assistant secretaries as *staff* aides of the Secretary.

It should be noted that this directive refers to "Directives recommended by the Assistant Secretary" having to be signed by the Secretary of Defense or the Deputy Secretary. Emphasized here is an important distinction between a DOD Directive and a DOD Instruction. The former is ". . . used to . . . promulgate fundamental policies and . . . orders." It is the "medium through which the Secretary of Defense publishes policy guidance, instructions and orders for the direction and control of all Department of Defense activities."[19] An instruction, on the other hand, is signed by "the Assistant Secretary of Defense having cognizance over the particular functional area involved." It is used "primarily to implement or supplement policies, plans, and programs" established by directives.[20] A directive therefore has the full authority of the Secretary of Defense, carries his signature, and goes to the service secretaries for compliance. The instruction goes direct from the Assistant Secretary and is more in the nature of administrative guidance.

A HYPOTHETICAL EXAMPLE OF AN
ADMINISTRATIVE POLICY DECISION

By tracing a policy decision throughout the defense organization, we can examine the operations of an Assistant Secretary. The hypothetical policy is to deal with the utilization of manpower by the military services—specifically, to fix a ratio of various types of overhead personnel to total personnel. This imaginary example merely illustrates the general procedures which might be followed in any one of the various offices.

Attention to the problem might have been called in any number of ways: by one of the services, by a Congressman, or by someone in the Manpower and Personnel office. In any case, once brought to the attention of the latter, the problem will eventually reach the Office of Manpower Utilization and the Quantitative Manning Standards Division. From information already on file in reports submitted by the services, a study is in progress on clerical manning standards— *i.e.*, the number of clerical personnel per 1000 assigned to operations. The Manning Standards Division concludes that the ratio is too high, and a field inspection team visits seven major headquarters from each service. Its report shows that the average Navy ratio is x clerks per thousand, while the Army and Air Force average y and z. All are deemed too high, and the Manpower Utilization staff writes a draft memorandum indicating this fact and suggesting appropriate criteria for fixing a better ratio to be incorporated in a proposed directive.

This draft is forwarded from the Manpower and Personnel office to the Assistant Secretary of the Army (Manpower and Reserve Forces), the Assistant Secretary of the Air Force (Manpower and Personnel) and the Assistant Secretary of the Navy (Personnel and Reserve Forces). Each of these would route the memorandum to his manpower utilization staff officer, either within his own office—or more probably, in the Air Force to the Deputy Chief of Staff, Personnel; in the Army, to the Deputy Chief of Staff, Personnel; or in the Navy to the Bureau of Personnel. Assuming that the matter is important enough to warrant such treatment, staff members from each service meet together with the staff of the OSD Manpower Utilization Office. There the process of "negotiation and persuasion" takes place.

The final draft, which is thus a joint staff product, repeats the cycle described above, going down to the assistant secretaries of each service for concurrence. Each in turn calls on his staff for advice as to whether he should concur or not. If the Army has refused to go along in this final draft, the various staff officers for manpower utilization— or the nearest equivalent—from each service meet with the head of the OSD Manpower Utilization Office to attempt to adjust the difficulty. If they still can not agree and feel strongly enough about it, the Assistant Secretary of Defense (Manpower, Personnel and Reserve) meets with the Assistant Secretaries of the three services. In all but the most vital matters, the decision will be arrived at here. But if not, it will be passed up the line for ultimate judgment by the Secretary of Defense, in consultation with the service secretaries if necessary.

Assuming then that the Army disagreement is overcome in the conference of assistant secretaries, the final draft of the directive passes through the Comptroller's office for budgetary concurrence and eventually is forwarded to the Directives Section (under the OSD Administrative Secretary) which reviews it for possible conflicts with other directives and obtains the signature of the Secretary of Defense.

The Directive is then sent down to the services where each takes the necessary action, in terms of its own regulations, tables of organization, etc. to comply. This is important. The DOD directive operates on the *Secretariat* level of each military department, and *not* on the operating echelons. Further action is necessary to put it into effect, and the Assistant Secretary of Defense (Manpower, Personnel and Reserve) may by an instruction require that copies of the amended service regulations be sent to him for approval, or that reports be made to his office on the implementation. In this hypothetical case, the directive furnishes policy guidance and lists the criteria to be used in fixing the administrative personnel ratio. It does *not* attempt to fix this ratio for the various service units. The military departments therefore often seek to keep the guidance as broad as possible to allow themselves a great deal of latitude. The Office of the Secretary, on the other hand, often tries to make the guidance quite specific, and conflict is likely.

The final Directive represents the culmination of several weeks (often months) of hard staff work within the OSD and each military department. It is the official decision for the record on matters which have been argued, negotiated, and discussed at a number of different levels. In this negotiation process the *ad hoc* committee composed of representatives of each service and one from the Office of the Secretary of Defense is therefore perhaps the most common working device. This "committee" may be extremely informal and be arranged as a "conference" by a telephone call. Or, it may be a task force with a charter of its own and with formal appointments made to it. Similar coordinating devices—the most common being the interdepartmental committee—are used in matters of concern to other departments and agencies as well as defense. It is not uncommon for the head of a section or division to be the defense representative on anywhere from ·one to a dozen such committees.

The foregoing account has greatly oversimplified the decision-making process. It scarcely requires emphasis that the personal relationships—who sees whom, when, how, and where—are as important as titles on an organization chart.

¹ *National Defense Establishment, Hearings on S. 758,* Senate Armed Services Committee, 80th Congress, 1st Session, 1947, Part I, p. 134.

² The summaries which follow are taken primarily from the May, 1956 "Brief of the Organization and Functions, Office of the Secretary of Defense," prepared by the Office of the Director of Administrative Service, OSD. It was drawn from the Directives and "Charters" outlining the functions of each ASD, and is duplicated in large measure in the current *U. S. Government Organization Manual.*

³ With the exception of the Comptroller, a position established by the National Security Act Amendments of 1949, all the other functions have been designated by the Secretary of Defense—generally in accordance with the recommendations of the Rockefeller Committee. Both the National Security Act of 1947 as amended (Section 202 (f) and Reorganization Plan No. 6 of 1953 (Section 5) authorize the Secretary of Defense to delegate or assign any of the functions with which he is charged.

⁴ Mr. Wilfred J. McNeil was in charge of the Navy budget under Forrestal, and became Special Assistant to Forrestal when the latter became Secretary of Defense. He has thus been in OSD longer than any other official of equivalent rank, and has remained through the administration of five Secretaries of Defense—a good testimony to his ability and vital role. Many of the key officials on McNeil's staff also came over with Forrestal in 1947.

⁵ It is impossible to outline these fields, since each is a subject in itself. A considerable number of diverse and unrelated activities are grouped under this ASD simply as a matter of convenience, in order to avoid having them attached to the immediate office of the Secretary. With the exception of Supply and Logistics, Manpower, Personnel and Reserve has by far the largest number of personnel in OSD.

⁶ When the Armed Forces Reserve Act of 1955 was being prepared in the Defense Department the major responsibility fell to *ad hoc* task forces working directly under the ASD (MP & R). The Reserve Forces Policy Board was opposed to certain aspects of the reserve plan as drafted by the task forces and its role was less significant than its title might indicated. T. W. Stanley and R. G. Stevens, "The Formulation of the National Reserve Plan Within the Department of Defense," unpublished staff study, Office of the Secretary of Defense, 1955.

⁷ Had there been a fourth service or a "common supply agency" as proposed by the 1955 Hoover Commission, this office probably would have furnished the organizational nucleus. It is of some interest therefore to note that probably a majority of the officials in this area do not think such a separate agency would be feasible. The *single manager* concept on the other hand has received considerably greater support. See the article by General Thomas R. Phillips in the *St. Louis Post-Dispatch,* November 17, 1955.

⁸ The ASD (P & I) has recently completed the first full inventory of real property owned by the Defense Department. It was disclosed that the Department owned

some 29.4 million acres with a total real property inventory valuation of $21.5 billion.

[9] The "operations" of this Assistant Secretary have perhaps raised more claims by the Military Departments—particularly the Air Force—of interference with service independence than any of the others.

[10] See "The Joint Chiefs of Staff," *op. cit.* note 7, Chapter IX.

[11] The Chairman is charged by Section 211 (e) (3) of the National Security Act of 1947, as amended, with the duty of informing the Secretary of Defense of "those issues upon which agreement among the Joint Chiefs of Staff has not been reached."

[12] Although it has no statutory basis, it currently plays an important role. The Joint Secretaries do not, however, have a staff of their own.

[13] For a comprehensive and up-to-date treatment of the budget, see Arthur Smithies, *The Budgetary Process in the United States*, McGraw-Hill, New York, 1955.

[14] *Report on Business Organization of the Department of Defense.* p. 16.

[15] Recommendation No. 1. *Ibid.*, p. 19.

[16] Recommendation No. 2. *Ibid.*, p. 21.

[17] Although this office is within the Office of the Assistant Secretary of Defense (Manpower, Personnel, and Reserve) there do not seem to have been many serious complaints of favoritism—*i.e.*, that Manpower and Personnel gets more than its share of the OSD budget or other items administered by this office.

[18] See House Armed Services Committee, *Military Public Works Hearings*, 84th Congress, 1st Session, 1955, pp. 2930-2940 *passim.*

[19] DOD Directive No. 5025.1, February 2, 1954, "Department of Defense Directives System."

[20] *Ibid.*

CHAPTER XI

PROBLEMS: PRESENT AND FUTURE TENSE

It would be possible to select a half dozen problem areas in defense and write a book about each of them. The three critical relationships to be discussed in this chapter were selected because they are perennial and current and because they concern structure. These are (1) those between the civilian Assistant Secretaries of Defense and the military departments; (2) those of the Joint Chiefs of Staff to the Office of the Secretary of Defense; and (3) those among the services as expressed in disputes over roles and missions and strategic concepts.

THE ASSISTANT SECRETARIES AND THE MILITARY DEPARTMENTS

The largest expansion in the Office of the Secretary of Defense followed the creation of six additional assistant secretaries by Reorganization Plan No. 6 in 1953. The President's message transmitting this plan to Congress states that "Without imposing themselves in the direct line of responsibility and authority between the Secretary of Defense and the Secretaries of the three Military Departments . . ." the Assistant Secretaries of Defense will "provide the Secretary with a continuing review of the programs . . . and help him institute major improvements in their execution. They will be charged with establishing systems, within their assigned field, for obtaining complete and accurate information to support recommendations to the Secretary."

However sound this may be in theory, in practice the assistant secretaries inevitably create supplementary lines of authority between themselves and the functional offices in the services whose duties fall within their assigned fields. But this, it should be noted, is not peculiar to the Office of the Secretary of Defense. The S-1 (Personnel) or S-3 (Plans and Operations) staff officer of a military unit is certainly not within the "direct line of responsibility" between the commander and the subordinate unit commanders. Yet if the regimental personnel officer tells the company clerks how to fill out the morning reports, they follow his advice without requiring him to "advise the commander to order the company commander to tell the clerks" to do it. There is always a certain amount of friction between the *staff* and *line* personnel of any organization. And the staff usually develops a cer-

126

tain amount of *de facto* authority, even though it is not in the chain of command authority. In the Department of Defense, this situation is complicated by the fact that the relationship between the Office of the Secretary and the services is a new one. Before 1947—and really until 1949—the services were "sovereign" departments. In addition to a natural chafing at new authority there is the perennial problem of rivalry among the services which now causes them to compete for fiscal, manpower, and material resources administered from above. Although there is no challenge whatever to civilian authority at the level of the President and Congress there is a feeling on the part of some of the military that, since national defense is by nature a military enterprise, the OSD civilians—particularly the politically appointed secretariat, not a few of whom have been lawyers—are really just making work for themselves; that if they would just quietly pack up and let the military go about its business of running the defense of the nation, things would operate much more efficiently.[1]

Inherent in the OSD-service relationship is this problem of civilian control.[2] But in the view of most Americans, this doctrine is so firmly rooted in our national philosophy that there is not the remotest possibility that the kind of military clique which runs many South American countries could exist here.[3] So the problem becomes one of civilian *participation* to insure that military policies respond to the needs of the country.

There are three areas where such participation—if not absolutely essential—is at least desirable. First, as the 1955 Hoover Commission points out, "The management of the Defense establishment is no longer principally one of managing tactical operations. Of equal importance today is the development and production of implements, supplies and services of war . . . and this aspect of Defense management has come to require as much specialized knowledge and expert direction as is traditional in the command of tactical operations."[4] Second, there are defense problems in which non-military factors are of great importance and which require the views of other departments and agencies, as for example foreign military assistance, which is covered in Chapter V. Finally, some situations demand a compromise between military needs and domestic politics. One such issue was involved in the National Reserve Plan, which formed the basis for the Armed Forces Reserve Act of 1955. The President and Congress insisted that all must have an equal obligation to serve in order to avoid repetition of the recall injustices of Korea. But there were more men in the manpower pool than the military could train and use with their existing establishments. The solution of Universal Military

Training was unacceptable in Congress, and to draft everyone for a short period of service did not meet the military's need for a two or three year term in which to train technicians.

In short, a compromise had to be found, and the way in which it was sought illustrates all three of these civilian participation areas. The great mass of statistics that had to be analyzed and projected called for skilled analysts both from the services and from the Office of the Secretary. There had to be constant negotiation with the Office of Defense Mobilization and the Department of Labor. Detailed plans for screening out occupational skills essential to the civilian economy had to be drawn up for the recall procedure. This liaison was in fact done by civilians in the office of the Assistant Secretary of Defense (Manpower, Personnel, and Reserve.) Finally, a politically responsive civilian—the Assistant Secretary—had to bear the brunt of the lobbies and the pressures. On one hand he had to explain the military viewpoint to Congress and the public and on the other shield the military from a flood of criticisms and demands. Moreover he had to have the authority to make the compromise stick —both outside the Department where it was strongly attacked and in the services themselves.[5]

So it can be seen that civilians would be needed even if there were only one service—and in fact civilians do perform important duties within each military department; there, the constant rotation of military officers increases the value of civilians. But there are three services, not one. Coordinating, adjusting, and compromising their plans, policies, and procedures is really the major function of the staffs in the Office of the Secretary. Why coordinate them? Because in the long pull of the cold war, the U. S. cannot afford the cost of overlapping and duplicated functions nor the inefficiency of the right hand not knowing what the left is doing—as was the case at Pearl Harbor. Most observers agree that such coordination is desirable. But there is disagreement on whether efficiency is best obtained through centralization or decentralization [6]—and indeed as to which of these two alternatives is being followed at the present time.[7]

ADJUSTMENT OF SERVICE ORGANIZATION TO DOD ORGANIZATION

The 1955 Hoover Commission Report on Business Organization of the Department of Defense stated that "the responsibilities of the Assistant Secretaries in the Military Departments differ significantly in nature and scope—a condition which complicates coordination and understanding between each department and the office of the Secretary of Defense."[8] Accordingly, it recommends that the "Secretary of

Defense should revise the assignments of Departmental Assistant Secretaries to secure uniform grouping of management responsibilities similar to that proposed . . ." for the OSD.[9]

On June 14, 1954, a plan for Army reorganization[10] was formally submitted by the Secretary of the Army. The cover sheet contains the following note: "This plan was approved by the Secretary of Defense on 17 June 1954." It seems likely that one factor in this prompt approval was the inclusion of a paragraph on "responsiveness to the Department of Defense" and a chart illustrating liaison between the two groups of assistant secretaries.

It is not possible to discuss the organizational structure of the three military departments, for each is governed not only by the National Security Act as amended, but by various organization acts of Congress pertaining to that service. Each has its own peculiar history and problems, and each has been studied by a number of management consultants and other groups. The emphasis in Part Two of this book has been to indicate the organizational pattern which has influenced defense as a whole—that is, the relationships among the services and between them and the Office of the Secretary of Defense.

However, in transmitting Reorganization Plan No. 6 of 1953 to Congress, the President stated that "other improvements are badly needed in the Department of the Army, the Navy and the Air Force. Accordingly, the Secretary of Defense is initiating studies by the three Secretaries . . . to apply to the organization of the Military Departments some of the same principles of clearer lines of accountability which we are applying to the Department of Defense as a whole." The Army plan for organization resulted from these studies, as did certain changes in the Navy[11] and the Air Force.[12] It remains to be seen whether further reorganizations will result from the 1955 Hoover Commission recommendations.

The terms *horizontal* and *vertical* forms of organization are used by several writers. A glance at the organization charts for the military departments in Appendix V will show that this terminology has some basis. Whereas the Army and Air Force structure is a single pyramid, the Navy has what amounts to two pyramids, one reporting to the Under Secretary and one to the Chief of Naval Operations, tied together at the top in the Office of the Secretary. This explains in part why some of the Navy's attitudes toward defense organization as a whole differ from those of the other services.

MILITARY OFFICERS ON DUTY IN THE OFFICE OF THE SECRETARY

Another aspect of the civilian-military relationship concerns the career officers detailed to duty on the various staffs which make up the Office of the Secretary of Defense. They comprise more than one third of the total number of personnel in OSD. For example, in the Office of the Assistant Secretary of Defense (International Security Affairs) as of August 1955, military officers occupied over 60 out of a total of 140 non-clerical positions. And a majority of the sixty were Chiefs or Deputy Chiefs of branches. The relationship of military and civilian personnel is on the whole very good. A civil servant will have an adjoining desk with a Colonel or a Navy Captain and by working with him on the same problem, will develop a high degree of mutual esteem. This overlapping has brought criticism from Congressional committees and the Hoover Commission.[18] But delineating the proper spheres for civilians and for military personnel and other problems inherent in a dual personnel system are not at issue here.[14]

The fact that the Office of the Secretary of Defense has found it useful in its dealings with the services to have part of its staff composed of military men does, however, raise important questions of conflict of loyalty. The officers assigned have generally been able and effective representatives of the Secretary of Defense in dealing with their services. But since these officers are generally selected by their services, the criteria of their selection is important. Sometimes they are chosen for their ability to respond to the needs of the Secretary of Defense; sometimes for their reliability in supporting the interests of their service. Almost every day some military officer makes a decision on behalf of a joint organization which a superior in his own service may consider "against the best interests" of that service. It is not difficult to see how these men may feel that their career will suffer as a result. It will be recalled from Chapter IX that this point was raised by the Rockefeller Committee in 1953. Changes in preparing efficiency reports on military officers assigned to OSD have brought some improvement. But the fact remains that the officer must eventually return to his service for duty. That this question of joint versus service values and receptiveness to the views of civilians as criteria for service promotion is not purely academic is illustrated by a study which has recently been made.[15] It was found through questionnaires that joint values—as opposed to service values—have been most highly developed at the OSD level, next at the Joint Staff level, and least in service staff assignments.

Some observers urge that the real key to unification is to have one service, one uniform, and one academy for all military personnel.[16] Regardless of merit, the chances of this step being taken seem somewhat remote. It is therefore encouraging to note that at least in the

Office of the Secretary—and to some extent within the Joint Staff—it has proved possible to establish a group of capable officers whose loyalty can be directed to national defense as a whole rather than entirely to their own service.

THE JOINT CHIEFS AND THE OFFICE OF THE SECRETARY

As noted earlier, the Joint Chiefs of Staff have a statutory responsibility to the President, the National Security Council, and the Secretary of Defense. At the same time, their box on the organization chart is indistinguishable from that of any assistant secretary, and they are legally a unit of the Office of the Secretary of Defense.

But every major group who has studied defense—from the first Hoover Task Force to the Rockefeller Committee and the 1955 Hoover Commission—has noted that the Joint Chiefs tend to be isolated from the rest of the secretariat. Gordon Dean has referred to their "unfortunate isolation".[17] Vannevar Bush has criticized their unresponsiveness to outside factors,[18] and the Rockefeller Committee Report emphasized "the importance of a close relationship". Physical arrangements in the Pentagon contribute to their isolation.[19] A 1954 directive stated that the entire JCS structure "shall effectively, fully, and completely collaborate with all parts of the Office of the Secretary of Defense to insure broadened participation in strategic and logistic planning at the early stages of staff work . . ."[20] But almost a year later the Hoover Commission claimed that one of the "obstacles to fully effective administration in the Department of Defense" is the fact that "decisions and information do not flow freely between the Joint Chiefs of Staff to the Assistant Secretaries of Defense."[21]

This difficulty is perhaps unavoidable. Since the JCS is supposed to be the fountainhead of military advice, its prestige is not something to be taken lightly. But where military advice begins and ends, is a difficult problem, some aspects of which—particularly regarding international security affairs—were discussed in Chapter V.[22] But the fact remains that organizationally the Joint Chiefs of Staff tend to be a closed corporation. Some critics have even concluded that a thorough overhaul is necessary to end service rivalry and a tendency toward compromise—a "trading post" outlook. Even war plans, say such critics, are not really *joint;* instead, they are merely the separate services' plans clipped together.[23] Although there may be considerable merit in the often-made proposal to subject the JCS to a complete study, most observers with experience in the Joint Chiefs of Staff would probably agree that considerable progress has already been made. As a planning team (on matters in which there is no serious inter-service disagreement) the Joint Chiefs and the Joint Staff seem to function effectively. The difficulty lies not so much with the JCS as an institution as in the fact that its members are also career officers from the three armed forces. In the case of the Joint Chiefs themselves, they are the operating heads of their services and feel themselves bound to represent those interests. It is perhaps expecting too much of any individual to assume that, by putting on a different hat —in this case as one of the Joint Chiefs of Staff—he can change the basic outlook he holds while sitting in the office of the Chief of Staff. It is to the credit both of the seniors and their subordinates on the Joint Staff that they have been able to see problems from a non-parochial standpoint as much as they have. Proposals have been made to meet this problem by establishing a Joint Chiefs of Staff group composed of men who would have no dual role as heads of their services. The real objection to this is not that it would lead to a German-type general staff (although this produces the most emotional opposition) but that it violates the principle that *advice* and *responsibility* are inseparable. In any case, the question of service disagreements leads to the last problem area to be discussed.

INTER-SERVICE RELATIONS: THE 1956 DISPUTES

Although this book is concerned with structure rather than strategy, the different service views on the nature of future wars, and the size of the forces, and weapons systems, needed to fight them may have a profound effect on structure. Conversely the way the military is organized influences strategy. Specifically, 1956 has seen a flare up of rivalry over roles and missions and suggestions that tighter unification is needed.

To trace even a bare outline of these developments requires reviewing the Eisenhower Administration's so-called New Look at defense policies. Following the President's State of the Union Message on February 2, 1953, discussions of defense focused on "attaining maximum security at minimum cost". According to Drew Pearson, Deputy Secretary of Defense Roger Kyes issued a highly restricted order on March 9, 1953, stating that the Bureau of the Budget had proposed, and had secured National Security Council agreement to, certain "assumed total (defense) expenditure limits" of $41.2 billion for fiscal 1954 and $34.6 billion for fiscal 1955.[24] In May, 1953, announcement was made of the appointment of an entirely new group of officers to constitute the Joint Chiefs of Staff. During June, in the hearings on 1954 defense appropriations, the new Secretary of Defense,

Charles E. Wilson, stated that during the summer and fall of 1953 "a new look at the entire defense picture" was planned.[25]

In December, this New Look finally emerged with an increase in the Air Force (from 110 to 127 wings, still considerably short of the 143 wing goal set in 1951 but postponed by President Truman's "stretch-out" action) and "increasing reliance upon atomic weapons of all types—including as a principal deterrent and retaliatory force, massive atomic and hydrogen attack upon cities."[26] Shortly thereafter, in a speech at the New York Council on Foreign Relations, Secretary of State John Foster Dulles, stated that "local defenses must be reinforced by the further deterrent of massive retaliatory power."[27] Thus was born the controversy that was to rage over the "massive retaliation" strategy.

Air power advocates maintained that strategic air-atomic capability was the great deterrent to war with Russia.[28] But some military leaders and civilian commentators were beginning to speak of an atomic stalemate. This power of mutual destruction, it was said, would depreciate the effectiveness of American retaliatory air power particularly for local wars in peripheral areas such as Southeast Asia. During 1955 various writers urged that a graduated deterrent, not relying on atomic weapons, was needed to meet Soviet threats in those areas.[29] This view not surprisingly was in accord with that of the Army.[30] The Navy likewise stressed mobility, dispersion, and a balanced force able to deter aggression short of total war.[31]

Each side conceded a need for both kinds of forces. The issue was —and is—one of degree. Since resources available for national defense cannot satisfy all claims upon it, each service feels that it must fight for a share of the budget adequate to provide the kind of forces believed necessary for its mission. The revolt of the admirals, discussed in Chapter VIII, was the Navy's reaction to what seemed to be the first step in a serious depreciation of its role in national defense. Similarly, General Matthew B. Ridgeway's 1955 dissent from cuts in Army strength represented a similar—although less successful—challenge to the strategy of primary reliance upon strategic airpower.[32]

In the spring of 1956, the Symington Subcommittee of the Senate Armed Services Committee began an investigation into the "conditions and progress of the Department of the Air Force to ascertain if present policies, legislative authority, and appropriations are adequate to maintain a force capable of carrying out its assigned missions."[33] The inquiry was broadened at the suggestion of Republican members to include Navy and Marine air components. In a press conference on May 4, when President Eisenhower was asked to comment on testimony by Strategic Air Command General Curtis E. LeMay that the Soviet Union under present programs would surpass the United States in long-range modern bombers, he stated that the whole air power picture had not yet been brought out by the Symington investigation and that "we have got . . . a mobile air power in the sea forces." Four days later Defense Secretary Wilson, testifying before the Senate Appropriations Committee, also mentioned the "strategic capability that our carrier-based aircraft add to our retaliatory striking power." Subsequent press conferences failed to clarify the question of whether or not carrier-based air power was being counted upon to meet any weakness that might exist in the Air Force's Strategic Air Command.[34] Air Force Chief of Staff Nathan F. Twining and General LeMay replied to Senator Symington's questions that the Navy's strategic mission was strictly corollary and its contribution "small"; they stressed that the strategic retaliatory mission was still the sole *responsibility* of the Strategic Air Command. Chief of Naval Operations Admiral Arleigh A. Burke did not attempt to challenge this estimate of the Navy's role in strategic bombing. He simply asserted that the Navy's primary mission was control of the sea. However Secretary of the Navy Charles S. Thomas took a stronger position than his service's operating chief and referred to the "powerful atomic punch" of the Forrestal-class carriers.[35] It should be noted in this connection that about six months before, the Air Force and the Navy had been at odds on a related question: the right to develop and use atomic powered sea-planes such as the Navy's Seamaster.[36]

Coincident with these developments, Army and Air Force feuding which had long been smouldering, broke out into the open during the last ten days in May. According to *Time* magazine, the Army, fearing that the publicity of the Symington investigation would result in still greater Air Force appropriations—and possibly further reductions in its own forces—"saw its future closing in. It attacked."[37] At any rate, unidentified Army officers leaked to members of the press certain staff studies charging that the "airpower concept can only lead the U.S. to disaster." Over the weekend of May 19-20, as the Air Force quickly followed suit, a virtual battle of press releases and leaked documents occurred, each critical of the strategic concepts and weapons of the other service.[38] The problem of roles and missions in the era of atomic warfare was thus reopened for public debate.

The present assignment of roles and missions is still based upon the 1948 Key West Agreement, discussed in Chapter VIII. As indicated in Appendix III, no changes in the roles of the services were made in the 1953 revision. In 1948 it was thought that the Soviet Union would not have an atomic capability for several years, and our own weapons systems, except for the Strategic Air Command, had not as yet been geared to atomic warfare. Guided missiles, for example, were not mentioned in the 1948 functions paper, with the result that each service has been developing its own arsenal. Faced with the necessity for some kind of jurisdictional lines, the Secretary of Defense and the Joint Chiefs of Staff agreed that the Army would be responsible for missiles designed for less than a specified range and the Air Force for the others. Each service has some basis for its claims, since a guided missile can be viewed as an air weapon by the Air Force, as artillery by the Army, and as "sea-based" by the Navy.

Defense of the United States was made a primary mission of all three of the services under the terms of the Key West Agreement. Air defense was a chief responsibility of the Air Force, but also, through its anti-aircraft artillery mission, of the Army. The Air Force, in much the same way as the Navy had sought to disparage the B-36 in the 1949 revolt of the admirals, has attempted to cast doubt on the Army's Nike as an effective air defense weapon, and is urging the superiority of its own ground-to-air missiles. Since guided missiles now represent a sizeable portion of the military budget, this dispute is by no means merely a struggle for prestige.

Another area of controversy has been the role of Army aviation. With the increased emphasis upon mobility and dispersion which atomic warfare demands, the Army has become less and less content with the restrictions imposed upon its aviation.[39] These limits are stated both in terms of weight (5000 pounds for fixed wing aircraft) and use (within a combat zone up to 100 miles deep). While denying that the Army wants its own air force again, officers such as Lieutenant General James M. Gavin, Chief of Army Research and Development, have sought "a change in policy on air mobility" and expressed dissatisfaction with air logistics and troop carrier transportation furnished by the Air Force.[40] As noted in the earlier discussion of roles and missions (Chapter VIII), the Army stresses *control* by the ground commander of aircraft engaged in the ground struggle. Although the distinction is not always made clear, the difference between control and *operation* may provide a basis for adjustment of Army and Air Force differences. But as newer developments, such as vertical-take-off aircraft and the "flying platform," come into common use, adjustments in the role of Army aviation seem likely.

Although the Secretary of Defense met with the Joint Chiefs of Staff in Puerto Rico during March, 1956, apparently no decision was made to revise the Key West functions paper. When questioned about roles and missions at a press conference, Admiral Arthur W. Radford, Chairman of the Joint Chiefs, would not commit himself to the need for change and conceded only that "some (service officers) think they should be changed . . ." Secretary Wilson added that much of the controversy concerned developments which were still at the drawing board stage—the implication being that an immediate revision of roles and missions was premature.⁴¹

The 1956 inter-service disputes over carriers, guided missiles, and Army aviation brought to the fore the question how far it was proper for the services to go in seeking public and Congressional support for their respective positions. The American separation of powers between Congress and the executive coupled with the existence of politically influential reserve organizations backing—and backed by—each service have given publicity a key role. Even when the services themselves are comparatively silent, various military journals carry on the battle. The February, 1956, issue of *Army* (published by the Association of the U.S. Army) carries an article on the Strategic Air Command entitled "$13 Billion Scarecrow," which headlines the question: "How many superbombers are enough? If an apple a day keeps the doctor away, a bushel a day won't make you any healthier." The same month the Air Force Association's *Air Force* features a story urging a "truly Air Age cabinet member." The April issue is completely devoted to the Strategic Air Command and its vital role. And last, but not least, the Navy. The piece on "The Boundless Blessings of Unification," published by the Navy League has already been mentioned. But at least the Navy has not lost its sense of humor, for the article comments (with reference to the mail-carrying tricycles which "infest" the corridors of the Pentagon): "Realizing that there are those who can think only of a single monolithic service, we are surprised that they do not seek to replace these tricycles with unicycles. That would be a telling blow for unification . . ."

The problem of restraining service rivalry has been heightened by the fact that Congress and the public have increasingly tended to expect a unified position at the top. This expectation is reflected in the unusual press conference held by Secretary Wilson and the chief civilian and military officials of the three services on May 21.⁴² All of these leaders stressed that the release of documents had been unauthorized and that they were not prepared to support the more extreme partisans lower down in the hierarchy. At least for public record, each of the service chiefs supported the Secretary of Defense. Perhaps the greatest significance of this press conference is that it probably could not have been held successfully as recently as 1949. The related problem of leaks to the press (which led one official to facetiously remark that future announcements should have a notation "not to be leaked" before the specified date) was referred in August to a special committee headed by Charles A. Coolidge, a Boston lawyer and former Special Assistant to Secretary Wilson.

But every new outburst of inter-service rivalry brings new demands for greater unification, even to the extent of a single service. Thus *Time* in its June 4, 1956, issue published a box explaining "how a single service works." As the "most workable plan" *Time* suggests (without identifying the source) a proposal almost identical to the Richardson Committee's plan and the Army's Collins Plan of 1945 which were discussed in Chapter VII. The reader may be tempted to say, "But that is where I came in!" And the writer is tempted to reply, "Precisely so!" But this ignores the evolutionary progress of the past decade which has been outlined in this book.

It is worth noting that the Defense Department has no monopoly on bureaucratic rivalries. In other "holding company" departments there are equally strong differences of opinion, as between the Soil Conservation Service and the Federal Extension Service of the Department of Agriculture, or the Bureau of Land Management and the National Park Service of the Department of the Interior. The point is that putting two or more agencies with a particular approach to a national problem into one executive department does not necessarily reduce the conflict between them. Even if the military services were some day to be completely merged, those officers whose specialty is air warfare would very likely have a different view of force requirements, weapons systems, and the nature of future wars than those concerned with land warfare. Both, very likely, would differ in their views with the naval specialists. Perhaps the solution is to be found in the direction of reorganizing completely on the basis of missions, rather than assigning missions to land, naval, and air forces. That is, have one component for the strategic air mission, another for continental defense, another for peripheral wars and so on. But in any case, it is not necessary nor even desirable that unanimity of opinion should result—certainly not if it is imposed. For reliance on and pre-preoccupation with one weapons system may prove as disastrous as did the French dependence on the Maginot Line. The problem is to keep dissension within tolerable limits, to avoid unnecessary duplication, while permitting more than one viewpoint.

The surprising thing then is not that there are still snags in the operation of the unified Department of Defense. Rather it is that those who argued that such a system could never work have been proved as wrong as they have been. For the system *does* work. As in any organization, there is room for improvement. Unification was and is an evolutionary process. The vast majority of the men, civilian and military, who operate the defense structure are genuinely concerned with providing the best national security that the money they are given can buy. To be sure there are differences of opinion as to where the best "security" can be bought. But if the day comes when only one voice is heard on the subject, the goal may be further away than ever. Surely more has been accomplished toward achieving truly effective team work for national defense in the past ten years than in the previous one hundred and fifty.

[1] Those who would condemn the military too quickly for this should consider that the problem is not unlike the situation which would exist in the Department of Justice if the Attorney General and his top aides were West Point graduates who had never had any legal training.

[2] The history, theory, and practice of this doctrine cannot be discussed in detail. However a selected list of works dealing with civilian control will be found in Appendix IV, *infra*.

[3] In fact, those who do see dangerous trends in our present government are much more concerned with the forces responsible for *internal* security—*e.g.*, loyalty boards and the FBI—than they are with the military forces whose concern is security from *external* threats.

[4] Commission on Organization of the Executive Branch, *Report on Business Organization of the Department of Defense*, 1955, p. 10.

[5] Stanley and Stevens, *op. cit., supra*.

[6] Some critics have noted that whereas Mr. Charles E. Wilson's former Detroit establishment follows a firm policy of decentralization with the various divisions of General Motors competing against each other, his Potomac establishment seems to operate on the assumption that the greater the centralized control, the greater the efficiency. Perhaps the answer is that national defense is dissimilar from even big business—which is small by comparison—and that unlike defense, there are few political considerations in General Motors policies.

[7] Compare, for example, Eugene S. Duffield's conclusion that "The Department of Defense will have to decentralize . . ." ("Organizing for Defense," *op. cit.*) with Mr. H. Struve Hensel's statement that "The tendency toward centralization in the Department of Defense has been ended. Decentralization is today's reality" ("Changes Inside the Pentagon," *op. cit.*)

[8] *Report on Business Organization of the Department of Defense*, p. 16.

[9] *Ibid.*, p. 25.

[10] *Secretary of the Army's Plan for Army Organization*, a mimeographed document of the department of the Army. The internal organization of the Army is based upon the Army Organization Act of 1950 (64 *Stat.* 263, 10 U.S.C. 1 b); it provides the statutory framework within which changes must be made just as the National Security Act of 1947 provides the framework for Defense as a whole.

[11] The so-called Gates Report (named for Under Secretary Gates), submitted in

1953, resulted in the addition of two assistant secretaries and clarified the relationship of the Bureau Chiefs to the Under Secretary on the one hand and the Chief of Naval Operations on the other.

[12] See, for example, Secretary of the Air Force Order No. 100.1, August 4, 1955, which outlines the functions of the Secretaries and Assistant Secretaries. These were originally revised in 1953 as a result of studies undertaken following Reorganization Plan No. 6.

[13] Which urged that Congress enact Title V to the National Security Act to establish criteria for distinguishing the "proper roles for civilian and miltary support managers . . ." Report on Business Organization of the Department of Defense, pp. 59-67.

[14] Congressional criticism of "dual staffing" has been primarily directed at the military departments where a particular office may have both a civilian and a military officer doing the same job; for instance, a military chief who is rotated every 3 years and a civilian deputy who is permanently assigned.

[15] See "Armed Forces Unification and the Pentagon Officer" by Henry, Masland, and Radway in Public Administration Review, Summer, 1955, p. 173.

[16] Field Marshal Montgomery has made this point a number of times, as in his 1954 address to the Royal United Services Institution (reprinted in Air Force magazine, November, 1955). He refers to "additional bureaucracies for coordination and arbitration above those already existing" being the necessary result of failure to combine service cadet and staff colleges preparatory to organizing "one fighting service." One important step in the United States has been the establishment of such joint schools as the National War College, the Industrial College of the Armed Forces, and the Armed Forces Staff College. However, each service maintains its own war college and academy.

[17] Report on the Atom, Knopf, New York, 1953, p. 140.

[18] See Chapter IX, p. 102.

[19] The JCS area of the Pentagon is a maximum security area. This requires special passes—even for OSD officials to be admitted, which cuts down informal contacts. Since 1953, however, a greater number of outside consultants have worked with the JCS and Joint Staff.

[20] DOD Directive 5158.1, July 26, 1954, "Method of Operation of the Joint Chiefs of Staff and Their Relationships With Other Staff Agencies of the Office of the Secretary of Defense."

[21] Report on Business Organization of the Department of Defense, p. 16.

[22] For one analysis of the problem see Sapin and Snyder The Role of the Military in American Foreign Policy, Doubleday, New York, 1954, pp. 27-31. This study is one of the most thoughtful which has yet appeared, although many military men tend to be critical of its approach and conclusions.

[23] See for example the staff paper prepared for the Task Force on Procurement of the 1955 Hoover Commission: "Defense Procurement: The Vital Roles of the National Security Council and the Joint Chiefs of Staff,' pp. A-31 to A-79. This paper is not generally available, but an article summarizing some of the conclusions was printed in the N.Y. Herald-Tribune, May 25, 1956.

[24] See Drew Pearson, "Kyes Orders Drastic Budget Cuts", Washington Post, March 21, 1953.

[25] Hearings on Department of Defense Appropriations for 1954 Senate Committee on Appropriations, 83d Congress, 1st Session, 1953, p. 6.

[26] Hanson W. Baldwin, N.Y. Times December 13, 1953. This article gives a concise breakdown and analysis of the "New Look".

[27] The full text is reported in the *N.Y. Times* for January 13, 1954, and is also available in the *Department of State Bulletin*, Vol. 37, pp. 107-110, January 25, 1954.

[28] Sir John Slessor's *Strategy for the West* (Morrow, New York, 1954) and Thomas K. Finletter's *Power and Policy* (Harcourt Brace, New York, 1954) are reasonably representative of the air power viewpoint. An excellent summary of materials giving all the opposing arguments has been prepared in mimeographed form by the Harvard Defense Studies Program: "Planning for Peripheral War," Serial No. 59, by Robert W. Berry, February, 1956.

[29] See for example Henry A. Kissinger, "Military Power and the Defense of the 'Grey Areas'" *Foreign Affairs*, April 1955; "Force and Diplomacy in the Nuclear Age", *Foreign Affairs*, April 1956; William W. Kaufmann, *The Requirements of Deterrence*, Center of International Studies, Princeton, 1954.

[30] Thus the May 1956 issue of *Army* devotes a feature article to the book edited by Kaufmann on *Military Policy and National Security*, (Princeton University Press, 1956). This article quotes Lieutenant General James M. Gavin as saying: "This [book] is the Army's story."

[31] See Commander Ralph E. Williams, Jr., U.S.N., "The Great Debate; 1954," *United States Naval Institute Proceedings*, March 1954.

[32] General Ridgway expressed his views in a letter to Secretary of Defense Charles E. Wilson on the occasion of his retirement. It was printed in full in *U.S. News and World Report*, July 29, 1955. See also General Ridgway's memoirs, *Soldier* (Harper, New York, 1956) Chapters 31 and 34. Materials on the ensuing "Debate over Military Forces" have been prepared as mimeographed readings by the Harvard Defense Studies Program: Serial No. 41, by Harry H. Ransom, November 10, 1955.

[33] For an analysis of the comparative airpower issue being investigated, see *U.S. News and World Report*, "Is U.S. Really Losing in the Air?", May 18, 1956, p. 25.

[34] See "Bombers, Carriers, Secretaries and Senators, a Review of the Record", by Robert W. Berry, *Air Force*, July 1956.

[35] *N.Y. Times*, May 20, 1956.

[36] *Ibid.*, October 9, 1955.

[37] *Time*, June 4, 1956, p. 21.

[38] The *N.Y. Times* for May 19-22 carried full coverage of the developments.

[39] These restrictions are contained in the Army-Air Force "Memorandum of Understanding Relating to Army Organic Aviation," November 4, 1952, which superseded an earlier 1951 agreement.

[40] Testimony on this question by Army and Air Force leaders will be found respectively in *Hearings, Department of the Army Appropriations for 1956*, House Appropriations Subcommittee, 84th Congress, 1st Session, 1955, pp. 576-7, 648, 719-20, and *Hearings, Department of the Air Force Appropriations* for 1956, House Appropriations Subcommittee, 84th Congress, 1st Session, 1955, pp. 11-16, 38, 127-8, 259.

[41] See the *N.Y. Times*, May 22, 1956, p. 14.

[42] The transcript of this press conference is printed in the *N.Y. Times*, May 22, 1956.

PART THREE

APPENDICES

COMPARATIVE NOTES ON BRITISH DEFENSE ORGANIZATION

(PREPARED BY LAURENCE W. LEVINE)

*A. Some Differences Between British and
American Defense Policy Formulation*

Defense policy in Great Britain is formulated within the framework of the general organization for defense. Before giving an account of this organization, some of the constitutional principles which distinguish the British form of government from ours should be noted:

(1)   The Cabinet, which controls the executive government of the country, is composed of ministers who are at the same time members of Parliament. These ministers are responsible both individually and collectively to the legislature for their departments. The policy once formed is that of the government, and a majority vote against this policy would lead to its fall; thus the program is usually passed as presented. In the United States, Congress has no hesitation in making changes in the substance of defense programs submitted to them, since criticism cannot result in having to assume executive responsibility.

(2)   Cabinet ministers normally occupy a leading position in the party or parties which attain a majority of Parliament. Party discipline is relatively stricter in England than in the United States. When dissension does arise, as it did in March 1955 when Mr. Bevan took a stand against his party's position in the field of defense, it is met by all possible measures to preserve party unity—and as a last resort by expulsion.

(3)   Members of the public service and armed forces are responsible to their minister and he is responsible to Parliament. Thus, the Chiefs of Staff are not examined by Parliament as they are by our Congress. Instead, the Minister must answer for the entire administration of his department and he is expected to resign if he cannot do so.

(4)   In Britain, the right of the House of Commons to be the main forum of discussion is jealously guarded. In the United States on the other hand detailed examination of the Administration's program takes place more in the various committees of Congress than on the

floor. In the British Parliament the Prime Minister or the Minister of Defense (who is a senior Cabinet minister) reads a statement of the government's policy at the opening of the annual debate on the defense budget. He may, and usually does, answer questions: the matter is then thrown open to debate. The discussion closes in the Commons with speeches by the leader of the opposition and by the Prime Minister.

The most striking difference between discussion in Congress on defense matters and those in Parliament is that the average member of the House of Commons is much better informed than his American counterpart. This is due in part to the fact that the Member of Parliament has available to him a concise statement of the government policy set out in four small pamphlets devoted to (a) defense policy in general, (b) Navy estimates, (c) Army estimates, (d) Air Force estimates. These so-called White Papers contain brief explanations of the government's policy on the particular Department to which they refer, and they contain all the relevant details in 10 pages or less. They are authoritative, have been carefully framed, and since they represent the government's position, they will be supported by all members of the party in power. They show the important financial implications and are capable of being read in two hours. They are distributed at least a week and generally a month before the debates, usually in February.

There is no such concise annual review available to members of Congress. The closest approach in the United States occurs at the time the budget is considered by the Congress.[1] The Congressman and Senator is the confronted by a thick green book some three thousand pages long filled with graphs, tables and numbers. He must rely for interpretation upon Presidential messages, departmental memoranda and the testimony of witnesses before the Congressional committee. It is particularly difficult for the layman to assess what the major issues are.[2] Questions from Committee members are apt to draw a mass of detailed analysis and facts, which are overwhelming in their complexity. However, there are annual and semi-annual reports of the Secretary of Defense which include reports by each of the Secretaries. These are of considerable value to the student of American defense policy, but of little value to Congress because they are a summary of past work rather than future plans.

The British have the additional advantage that in their debates, both in Lords and Commons, there are present a comparatively large number of men who have occupied positions of responsibility in the sphere of defense. Although the House of Lords now has comparatively little constitutional authority, it is nevertheless important because it has as members many widely experienced leaders whose views are unrelated to personal interests. The debates in the House of Lords have an elevated tone and are widely read by those in positions of power, as well as reported carefully in the London papers.

B. *British Defense Organization*

THROUGH WORLD WAR II

The Central Organization for Defense was set up in its present form in 1946, but its real beginning was in 1904. The Esher Committee (War Office Reconstitution Committee) was appointed as a result of the weakness revealed in the Boer War. It pointed out that no machinery existed for coordinating defense problems, for dealing with them as a whole, nor for defining the \proper functions of various elements. The committee also noted that in time of emergency no long range war policy could be formulated in advance. It therefore recommended the setting up of the Committee of Imperial Defense, hereafter abbreviated C.I.D. This proposal met with approval by the government and the C.I.D. was established as an advisory rather than executive body. The Prime Minister was chairman and he had discretion as to the ministers who would attend each meeting. The Committee was served by a small but highly competent secretariat headed by Lord Hankey.[3] It undertook comprehensive strategic duties formulating both defense plans and policies as well as the measures needed for the smooth transition from peace to war. Because of this, Britain entered the 1914-1918 war better prepared than she had been in the past. But the First World War proved that the functions of the C.I.D. did not go far enough. First, it was not designed for executive control, a defect which was not remedied until the end of 1916 with the creation of the War Cabinet. Second, it had not developed any central machinery for inter-service planning. Each service at the time was entirely responsible for the planning and conduct of its own operations without any central coordination. After the first World War, the emergence of the Air Force as a separate service emphasized the need for a joint service planning organization. Thus in 1924, the Chiefs of Staff Committee was established and the foundations of the Joint Staff system laid.

In 1939 a War Cabinet was immediately established which worked with the assistance of the Chiefs of Staff Committee and other committees taken over from the old Committee of Imperial Defense. There was, however, still a defect in the organization. This was the absence of a guiding hand for the formulation of a unified defense policy for the three services. The strategic roles and missions of each service were at this time still considered separately rather than as parts of a larger whole. During World War II this weakness was largely overcome by the appointment of the Prime Minister as Minister for Defense. A Defense Committee (Operations) under the chairmanship of the Prime Minister and a Defense Committee (Supply) were set up in an attempt to coordinate matters. It was left for Mr. Churchill to develop a method of working through the Defense Committee and the Chiefs of Staff Committee which enabled him to provide direction for wartime operations.

POST WORLD WAR II

There were several possible alternatives for the achievement in the post World War period of the necessary centralization of defense policy.[4] One was to amalgamate the three services completely under a single minister and department of defense. This had many supporters and the Government did not entirely dismiss it as a possibility, although it was abandoned as an immediate objective. A second alternative was the creation of a combined General Staff—that is, a General Staff on the German conception, drawn from the three services. This body would formulate defense policy, issue directives, freed, it was claimed, from the service bias and tendency toward compromise which was present in the existing Joint Staff system. Having regard particularly to weaknesses revealed by a study of the German wartime General Staff, the government decided that it was unsafe in practice and unsound in principle to divorce responsibility for planning from responsibility for the execution of those plans. This had proved one of the cardinal defects of the German system.

The British decided therefore to continue with their Chiefs of Staff Committee served by Joint Staffs. Thus the men who formulate the plans are those who have the responsibility for carrying them out in the Service Departments. This principle had been adopted in the international sphere during World War II with the creation of the combined Chiefs of Staff organization, and the American Joint Chiefs of Staff have operated on the same basis. To remedy such defects in pre-war organization as the lack of a central ministry, a Minister of Defense and a Defense Ministry were created. This gave the necessary top level authority and direction in the organization for formulating and applying unified defense policy.

NEW POST-WAR ORGANIZATION FOR DEFENSE

The form of the new organization may be described as follows: The

Prime Minister retained the ultimate responsibility for defense. A Defense Committee, under the Chairmanship of the Prime Minister, took over the functions of the old Committee of Imperial Defense. It is responsible to the Cabinet for the review of current strategy and for coordinating departmental action in preparation for war. A new post of Minister of Defense with a Ministry was created. The Minister of Defense is responsible to Parliament for certain subjects affecting the three services and their supply. In addition, he is Deputy Chairman of the Defense Committee. He also presides over meetings with the Chiefs of Staff whenever he or they so desire. The Ministry of Defense is a secretariat for the British defense organization. In 1955-1956 it had a budget of 18,300,000 pounds ($41,240,000) and had a total of 1204 personnel which included 288 from the services and 44 locally recruited in foreign countries. The Minister of Defense is as his title implies, the politically responsible head of the Defense Ministry. However, there is a permanent Secretary of Defense and two Under Secretaries, who are the top civil servants in Britain's defense organization. They have a small staff to assist them in carrying out the administrative and coordinating responsibilities of the Ministry of Defense.

The service ministers, whose official titles are: the Secretary of State for Air, the Secretary of State for War, and the First Lord of the Admiralty, are each members of Parliament. Each is the head of his Service Ministry, that is, the Air Ministry, War Office, and the Admiralty, and is responsible to Parliament for the administration of his service in accordance with the general policy approved by the Cabinet and within the resources assigned to his service.

The Chiefs of Staff Committee—composed of the three service Chiefs of Staff plus a chairman—remain responsible for preparing strategic appreciations and military plans and for submitting them to the Defense Committee. The position of chairman was created in 1955, an air officer being the first appointee to the post. The Joint Staff system was retained and developed under the direction of the Chiefs of Staff Committee.

Great Britain, unlike the United States, has a single Ministry of Supply which except for the construction of heavy Navy equipment, does most of the purchasing for the three services. It is responsible both for procurement of supplies—including aircraft—guns and ammunition, and guided missiles. The Admiralty is responsible for the procurement of ships and maritime equipment. The Ministry of Supply is also responsible for research and development, acting in this field on behalf of the War Office and the Air Ministry and, for certain aspects such as naval aviation, for the Admiralty. However research and development on ships and naval weapons is carried out by the Admiralty.

The single Ministry of Supply was adopted on July 13, 1939— seven weeks before Britain went to war—after a ten year battle. A summary of the British experience with a single service for supply is included here because, of the many proposals considered in the United States for a similar system, few if any have made reference to the British counterpart. It was first proposed by the Haldane Committee on the machinery of government—Britain's equivalent of the Hoover Commissions—in 1918-1920. But the idea was pigeonholed for sixteen years due to opposition from the Navy and Air Force. As late as 1937 the Committee of Imperial Defense was against it because, first, it might disrupt the plans which were already being drawn up for the defense of the island, and second because critics might see it as a sign of crisis and preparation for war. But the Committee studied the matter and recommended that, when and if a central supply organization was needed, the Admiralty should be included. The Royal Navy, however, was firmly against central procurement and supply of any navy equipment.

In 1938, Winston Churchill defended the proposal for a single supply service and stated, "In war why should you divorce strategy from supply? Supply will dictate the strategy of most of the wars that are apt to be fought in the future." [5]   The Government however, in defense of separate systems, maintained that the Air Minister was the "only person who can satisfactorily decide on the number of aircraft and their efficiency" and denied that a Minister of Supply "can be the authority for the standardization of destroyers, tanks, and aircraft." [6]

Because of the opposition of the Air Ministry and the Admiralty, the Ministry of Supply Act, as passed, required that consent of the other government departments concerned must be obtained before any transfer of powers could be made to the Ministry of Supply. If such consent were obtained, the powers could be transferred by the King's Order in Council—the British equivalent of an executive order. Initially, only the munitions responsibilities of the Secretary of State for War were transferred, but, as the war progressed, ammunition for all three services, medical supplies, transport, helmets, textiles, clothing, and ball bearings were taken over by the Ministry of Supply. As of 1942, research and development was similarly assigned. The planning was done by a Supply Council which coordinated and reviewed the progress of mobilization with reference to raw materials, tools, construction, and labor. Because of the urgent priorities, a special

Ministry of Aircraft production was set up in 1940 and functioned throughout the war in charge of design, development, inspection and repair of all aircraft. Atomic Energy was likewise initially handled by an independent organization. In 1945 it was transferred from the Department of Scientific and Industrial Research to the Ministry of Supply. However, in 1954 it was retransferred to the Atomic Energy Authority leaving the Ministry of Supply responsible only for testing and for supply of completed nuclear weapons.

As of 1956, the Ministry of Supply is responsible for all procurement of the Army and Air Force and certain weapons, such as guided misiles, used by the Navy. The Royal Navy orders, buys, and builds its own ships on a contract basis. The Royal Ordnance Factories and Dockyards—some 24 in number—are operated jointly by the Admiralty and the Ministry of Supply.

C. *British Defense Policy Formulation.*

The foregoing is necessarily a brief summary. In considering the decision-making process for defense policy the following additional details should be taken into account.

1. *The Defense Committee*

The Prime Minister is chairman of the Defense Committee. Its organization is flexible. The Prime Minister, the Minister for Defense, the Lord President of the Privy Council, the Foreign Secretary, the Chancellor of the Exchequer, the Service Ministers, the Minister of Labor, and the Minister of Supply are all regular members of the committee. The Chiefs of Staff are in attendance. Such other ministers, officers and officials as may be required are invited to attend the meetings of the committee according to the subjects under discussion. It will be observed that almost all the members of the Defense Committee are also members of Parliament and, as leaders of the majority party, are members of the Cabinet. The Defense Committee is therefore in effect a Cabinet committee concerned with national security. Generally speaking, it is comparable to a kind of combination of the National Security Council and the Armed Forces Policy Council in the present United States system.

2. *Functions of the Minister of Defense*

Among other functions, the Minister of Defense is responsible for the apportionment of available resources between the three services in accordance with the strategic policy laid down by the Defense Committee on the advice of the Chiefs of Staff. This included policies on research and development and production. The Minister's proposals on such matters are brought before the Defense Committee and the Cabinet. The Cabinet's decisions are then presented to Parliament for approval. The Minister of Defense has the power to decide questions arising between the three services on matters of practical application of approved policies. But he is not responsible for the execution of the approved program by each of the services, this being the task of the Service Ministers and the Minister of Supply.

3. *Procedure for Apportionment of Resources*

The Chiefs of Staff advise the Defense Committee on strategic requirements from year to year. It is then for the Service Departments to translate these requirements into terms of men, money and supplies, and for the Minister of Defense to coordinate the results with the help of the Chiefs of Staff and a committee of Service Ministers. He then presents to the Defense Committee a coherent scheme of expenditure which will give the country forces and equipment in properly balanced proportions. On production questions there is a standing Ministerial Production Committee consisting of the Service Ministers, the Minister of Supply and the Minister of Labor, over which the Minister of Defense presides. Working for this committee there is a Joint War Production Staff, composed of service officials and representatives of the service and civil departments concerned, under a permanent chairman appointed to the staff of the Minister of Defense.

With the help of this organization, the Minister of Defense is able to frame comprehensive defense proposals in the form of a consolidated estimate for presentation to the Defense Committee and the Cabinet.

4. *Relations of the Minister of Defense with the Chiefs of Staff*

The Chiefs of Staff organization was highly developed during the war and its value was fully proved. No change was therefore made in the organization of the Chiefs of Staff Committee. It was continued, as were the Joint Staffs for Strategic Planning, Intelligence, and Administrative Planning. The Chiefs of Staff Committee retained its responsibility for preparing strategic military plans and submitting them to the Defense Committee on which they sit in an advisory capacity. On all technical questions of strategy and plans it was deemed essential that the Cabinet and Defense Committee should be able to have presented to them directly and personally the advice of the Chiefs of Staff. It can thus be seen that their advice to the Defense Committee or to the Cabinet is not presented only through the Minister for Defense. At the same time the staff organization on which the Chiefs of Staff rely in their collective capacity is within the Ministry of Defense, and they meet under the chairmanship of the Minister of Defense.

In October 1955 the Ministry of Defense had two substantial changes. One strengthened the power of the Minister of Defense so that he now has the authority not only to divide money and weapons among the three service but also to see that the "composition and balance within the three services is proper and in accordance with the decisions of the Defense Committee." [7] While the Minister has more power in theory, it will be observed from the debates in Commons and the Prime Minister's answers to opposition questions that the Chiefs of Staff still retain their veto power over any suggestion made by the Minister. [8] Thus if a Service Chief does not like a decision of the Committee or the Defense Ministry he can theoretically prevent it from being put into effect. Anthony Eden maintained that this would not happen because of the calibre of the men chosen for the job. And yet the Chiefs of Staff are still to work under a system of collective responsibility and the independence of each service is unimpaired. It would therefore be extremely difficult for the Ministry of Defense to impose any radical reorganization upon the services.

The other major change was the appointment in 1955 of a Chairman of the Chiefs of Staff. This was advocated in the 1946 White Paper on the Central Organization for Defense, and has been widely advocated by Field Marshal Montgomery and other high ranking officers. This post initially went to the Marshal of the Royal Air Force, Sir William Dixon and its official title is Chairman of the Chiefs of Staff Committee. One reason given for this new job was the growing burden of international work which the Chiefs of Staff must do. The move probably also strengthens the hand of the Minister of Defense and the civilian members of the Defense establishment by providing one individual to whom they can look for coordination of the senior military officers of each of the three services.

5. Responsibility of the Cabinet

The 1946 White Paper states "there are problems which engage the collective responsibility of the government as a whole." These are described as (a) the organization of national defense in its broader aspects, including both current questions of high policy in the sphere of defense and also in the preparation of plans in the whole field of government activity in both its civil and military aspects; and (b) mobilizing the entire resources of the nation in a major war. It is clearly laid down that such problems must be handled under the authority of the Cabinet itself. It can thus be seen that the Cabinet holds somewhat of a veto power over all defense policy matters in England.

CONCLUSION

Until very recently, Britain's Defense Ministry was most closely paralleled in America by the Office of the Secretary of Defense in the years 1947 to 1949. With the changes of 1955, Britain has taken steps toward increased central authority just as the United States did with the National Security Act Amendments of 1949. "Unification" in Britain, even more than in the United States, remains primarily a matter of coordination, even though the conflicts are mitigated by the cabinet system. In two aspects however, Britain has outdistanced the United States. The coordination of foreign and military policy achieved by the War Cabinet was the envy of Secretary of War Stimson, and it was working smoothly to harmonize the means and ends of national security long before the American National Security Council was conceived. Indeed, that body was modelled to a considerable degree on the Committee of Imperial Defense, and its successor, the Defense Committee. Secondly, faced with serious shortages of war materials, Britain has achieved a higher degree of standardization and unified supply than has the United States.

On the whole, it is a safe generalization that, stemming from the World War II Combined Chiefs of Staff and even before, the two systems of defense organization have influenced each other to a not inconsiderable degree. To give but two examples: the British established a separate air force shortly after World War I, and this was constantly held up as a shining example by the air power advocates in the United States although it was not adopted here until 1947. The American Chairman of the Joint Chiefs of Staff—and his predecessor, the Chief of Staff to the President, undoubtedly influenced the British when they established a comparable office in 1955.

---

[1] For an examination of this problem in the United States see, Arthur Smithies, *The Budgetary Process in the United States,* a Committee for Economic Development Research Study, McGraw-Hill, New York, 1955, especially Chapters VI and XI.

[2] The English public may inform itself by buying these White Papers which are available at a cost of 2 shillings (28 cents) and by reading papers such as the *London Times* which carries a full account of the debates. It is easier for the press to follow the debates and reports with accuracy since they have available to them the same data as the members of Parliament.

[3] One of the best and most concise studies of British Defense Organization is Lord Hankey, *Government Control in War,* Cambridge University Press, Cambridge, 1945. Lord Hankey was the Secretary of the Committee of Imperial Defense from 1912 to 1938 and held many important defense posts during World War II. Another valuable source is E. J. Kingston-McCloughry's *The Direction of War,* Jonathan Cape, London, 1955.

[4] For a discussion of the problem see *Central Organization for Defense,* Command

paper 6923 presented by the Prime Minister to Parliament, October 1946.

[5] House of Commons *Debates*, Vol. 341, Col. 1087, November 17, 1938.

[6] *Ibid.*, Col. 1202.

[7] Statement by Prime Minister Eden to the House of Commons, October 25, 1955, Hansard, *Parliamentary Debates*, Vol. 545, Col. 33.

[8] The *London Times*, October 25, 1955.

THE NATIONAL SECURITY ACT OF 1947

Public Law, 253, 80th Congress, July 27, 1947 (61 *Stat.* 495), as amended to June 1953. From Committee Print No. 3, Committee on Armed Services, 83rd Congress, 1st Session, December 1, 1953. (Title III, "Miscellaneous," and Title IV, Fiscal Management, are omitted).

DECLARATION OF POLICY

SEC. 2. In enacting this legislation, it is the intent of Congress to provide a comprehensive program for the future security of the United States; to provide for the establishment of integrated policies and procedures for the departments, agencies, and functions of the Government relating to the national security; to provide three military departments, separately administered, for the operation and administration of the Army, the Navy (including naval aviation and the United States Marine Corps), and the Air Force, with their assigned combat and service components; to provide for their authoritative coordination and unified direction under civilian control of the Secretary of Defense but not to merge them; to provide for the effective strategic direction of the armed forces and for their operation under unified control and for their integration into an efficient team of land, naval, and air forces but not to establish a single Chief of Staff over the armed forces nor an armed forces general staff (but this is not to be interpreted as applying to the Joint Chiefs of Staff or Joint Staff).[1] Intent of Congress.

TITLE I—COORDINATION FOR NATIONAL SECURITY

NATIONAL SECURITY COUNCIL

SEC. 101. (a) There is hereby established a council to be known as the National Security Council (hereinafter in this section referred to as the "Council"). National Security Council. Establishment.

The President of the United States shall preside over meeting of the Council: *Provided*, That in his absence he may designate a member of the Council to preside in his place. President to preside.

The function of the Council shall be to advise the President with respect to the integration of domestic, foreign, and military policies relating to the national security so as to enable the military services and the other departments and agencies of the Government to cooperate more effectively in matters involving the national security. Function.

The Council shall be composed of—
(1) the President;
(2) the Vice President;
(3) the Secretary of State;
(4) the Secretary of Defense;

---

[1] Amended by section 2, Public Law 216, 81st Congress, August 10, 1949 (63 Stat. 578).

(5) the Director for Mutual Security; [2]
(6) the Chairman of the National Resources Board; [3]
(7) the Secretaries and Under Secretaries of other executive departments and of the military departments, the Chairman of the Munitions Board, and the Chairman of the Research and Development Board, when appointed by the President by and with the advice and consent of the Senate, to serve at his pleasure.[4]

Duties. (b) In addition to performing such other functions as the President may direct, for the purpose of more effectively coordinating the policies and functions of the departments and agencies of the Government relating to the national security, it shall, subject to the direction of the President, be the duty of the Council—

(1) to assess and appraise the objectives, commitments, and risks of the United States in relation to our actual and potential military power, in the interest of national security, for the purpose of making recommendations to the President in connection therewith; and

(2) to consider policies on matters of common interest to the departments and agencies of the Government concerned with the national security, and to make recommendations to the President in connection therewith.

Staff and Executive Secretary. (c) The Council shall have a staff to be headed by a civilian executive secretary who shall be appointed by the President, and who shall receive compensation at the rate of $10,000 [5] a year. The executive secretary, subject to the direction of the Council, is hereby authorized, subject to the civil-service laws and the Classification Act of 1923, as amended, to appoint and fix the compensation of such personnel as may be necessary to perform such duties as may be prescribed by the Council in connection with the performance of its functions.

Recommendations and Reports. (d) The Council shall, from time to time, make such recommendations, and such other reports to the President as it deems appropriate or as the President may require.

---

[2] Reorganization Plan 7 of 1953, effective August 6, 1953, abolished the Mutual Security Administration and established the Foreign Operations Administration.
"SEC. 2. TRANSFER OF FUNCTIONS TO THE DIRECTOR.—There are hereby transferred to the Director:
"(a) All functions vested by the Mutual Security Act of 1951, as amended, or by any other statute in the Director for Mutual Security provided for in section 501 of that Act, or in the Mutual Security Agency created by that Act, or in any official or office of that Agency, including the functions of the Director for Mutual Security as a member of the National Security Council."
[3] Reorganization Plan 6 (section 2) (see appendix II) abolished the National Security Resources Board. Executive Order 10438, March 13, 1953 (see appendix III), named the Director of the Office of Defense Mobilization to replace the Chairman of the National Security Resources Board.
[4] Reorganization Plan 6, 1953 (section 2 (b)) abolished the offices of the Chairman of the Munitions Board and Chairman of the Research and Development Board (see appendix II) and transferred their functions to the Secretary of Defense.
[5] Subsection (a) amended by section 3, Public Law 216, August 10, 1949 (63 Stat. 578), as amended by section 501 (e), Public Law 165, 82d Congress, October 10, 1951; subsection (c) supplemented by section 2 (a) Public Law 359, 81st Congress, October 15, 1949 (63 Stat. 880), under which authority the President fixed the salary of the Executive Secretary at $15,000 per annum; subsections (b) and (d) from section 101, Public Law 253, July 26, 1947 (61 Stat. 495).

CENTRAL INTELLIGENCE AGENCY [6]

SEC. 102. (a) There is hereby established under the National Security Council a Central Intelligence Agency with a Director of Central Intelligence who shall be the head thereof, and with a Deputy Director of Central Intelligence who shall act for, and exercise the powers of, the Director during his absence or disability. The Director and the Deputy Director shall be appointed by the President, by and with the advice and consent of the Senate, from among the commissioned officers of the armed services, whether in an active or retired status, or from among individuals in civilian life: *Provided, however,* That at no time shall the two positions of the Director and Deputy Director be occupied simultaneously by commissioned officers of the armed services, whether in an active or retired status.

(b) (1) If a commissioned officer of the armed services is appointed as Director, or Deputy Director, then—
    (A) in the performance of his duties as Director, or Deputy Director, he shall be subject to no supervision, control, restriction, or prohibition (military or otherwise) other than would be operative with respect to him if he were a civilian in no way connected with the Department of the Army, the Department of the Navy, the Department of the Air Force, or the armed services or any component thereof; and
    (B) he shall not possess or exercise any supervision, control, powers, or functions (other than such as he possesses, or is authorized or directed to exercise, as Director, or Deputy Director) with respect to the armed services or any component thereof, the Department of the Army, the Department of the Navy, or the Department of the Air Force, or any branch, bureau, unit, or division thereof, or with respect to any of the personnel (military or civilian) of any of the foregoing.

(2) Except as provided in paragraph (1), the appointment to the office of Director, or Deputy Director, of a commissioned officer of the armed services, and his acceptance of and service in such office, shall in no way affect any status, office, rank, or grade he may occupy or hold in the armed services, or any emolument, perquisite, right, privilege, or benefit incident to or arising out of any such status, office, rank, or grade. Any such commissioned officer shall, while serving in the office of Director, or Deputy Director, continue to hold rank and grade not lower than that in which serving at the time of his appointment and to receive the military pay and allowances (active or retired, as the case may be, including personal money allowance) payable to a commis-

[6] Section 102 (a) and (b) amended by Public Law 15, 83d Congress (67 Stat. 19, 20).

sioned officer of his grade and length of service for which the appropriate department shall be reimbursed from any funds available to defray the expenses of the Central Intelligence Agency. He also shall be paid by the Central Intelligence Agency from such funds an annual compensation at a rate equal to the amount by which the compensation established for such position exceeds the amount of his annual military pay and allowances.

(3) The rank or grade of any such commissioned officer shall, during the period in which such commissioned officer occupies the office of Director of Central Intelligence, or Deputy Director of Central Intelligence, be in addition to the numbers and percentages otherwise authorized and appropriated for the armed service of which he is a member.[7]

Termination of employment. (c) Notwithstanding the provisions of section 6 of the Act of August 24, 1912 (37 Stat. 555), or the provisions of any other law, the Director of Central Intelligence may, in his discretion, terminate the employment of any officer or employee of the Agency whenever he shall deem such termination necessary or advisable in the interests of the United States, but such termination shall not affect the right of such officer or employee to seek or accept employment in any other department or agency of the Government if declared eligible for such employment by the United States Civil Service Commission.

Duties. (d) For the purpose of coordinating the intelligence activities of the several Government departments and agencies in the interest of national security, it shall be the duty of the Agency, under the direction of the National Security Council—

(1) to advise the National Security Council in matters concerning such intelligence activities of the Government departments and agencies as relate to national security;

(2) to make recommendations to the National Security Council for the coordination of such intelligence activities of the departments and agencies of the Government as relate to the national security;

(3) to correlate and evaluate intelligence relating to the national security, and provide for the appropriate dissemination of such intelligence within the Government using where appropriate, existing agencies and facilities: *Provided*, That the Agency shall have no police, subpena, law-enforcement powers, or internal-security functions: *Provided further*, That the departments and other agencies of the Government shall continue to collect, evaluate, correlate, and disseminate departmental intelligence: *And provided further*, That the Director of Central Intelligence shall be responsible for protecting intelligence sources and methods from unauthorized disclosure;

---

[7] As amended by Public Law 15, 83d Congress (67 Stat. 20).

(4) to perform, for the benefit of the existing intelligence agencies, such additional services of common concern as the National Security Council determines can be more efficiently accomplished centrally;

(5) to perform such other functions and duties related to intelligence affecting the national security as the National Security Council may from time to time direct.

(e) To the extent recommended by the National Security Council and approved by the President, such intelligence of the departments and agencies of the Government, except as hereinafter provided, relating to the national security shall be open to the inspection of the Director of Central Intelligence, and such intelligence as relates to the national security and is possessed by such departments and other agencies of the Government, except as hereinafter provided, shall be made available to the Director of Central Intelligence for correlation, evaluation, and dissemination: *Provided, however,* That upon the written request of the Director of Central Intelligence, the Director of the Federal Bureau of Investigation shall make available to the Director of Central Intelligence such information for correlation, evaluation, and dissemination as may be essential to the national security.

(marginal note:) Intelligence of other Departments and Agencies of Government.

(f) Effective when the Director first appointed under subsection (a) has taken office—

(1) the National Intelligence Authority (11 Fed. Reg. 1337, 1339, February 5, 1946) shall cease to exist; and

(marginal note:) National Intelligence Authority, Termination of.

(2) The personnel, property, and records of the Central Intelligence Group are transferred to the Central Intelligence Agency, and such Group shall cease to exist. Any unexpended balances of appropriations, allocations, or other funds available or authorized to be made available for such Group shall be available and shall be authorized to be made available in like manner for expenditure by the Agency.[8]

(marginal note:) Central Intelligence Group, Transfer of.

NATIONAL SECURITY RESOURCES BOARD [9]

SEC. 103. (a) There is hereby established a National Security Resources Board (hereinafter in this section referred to as the "Board") to be composed of the Chairman of the Board and such heads or representatives of

(marginal note:) National Security Resources Board. Establishment. Composition.

---

[8] Subsections (a) and (b) supplemented by section 4, Public Law 359, 81st Congress, October 15, 1949 (63 Stat. 880), which increased basic compensation to $16,000 per annum; subsections (c), (d), (e), and (f) from section 102, Public Law 253, 80th Congress, July 26, 1947 (61 Stat. 495).

[9] Reorganization Plan 3 of 1953, effective June 12, 1953, abolished the National Security Resources Board and also created the Office of Defense Mobilization and transferred all functions of the Chairman of the National Security Resources Board to the Director of the Office of Defense Mobilization. See appendix I for text of Reorganization Plan 3 of 1953.

158

the various executive departments and independent agencies as may from time to time be designated by the President to be members of the Board. The Chairman of the Board shall be appointed from civilian life by the President, by and with the advice and consent of the Senate, and shall receive compensation at the rate of $14,000 a year.

(b) The Chairman of the Board, subject to the direction of the President, is authorized, subject to the civil-service laws and the Classification Act of 1923, as amended, to appoint and fix the compensation of such personnel as may be necessary to assist the Board in carrying out its functions.

(c) It shall be the function of the Board to advise the President concerning the coordination of military, industrial, and civilian mobilization, including—

(1) policies concerning industrial and civilian moblization in order to assure the most effective mobilization and maximum utilization of the Nation's manpower in the event of war;

(2) programs for the effective use in time of war of the Nation's natural and industrial resources for military and civilian needs, for the maintenance and stabilization of the civilian economy in time of war, and for the adjustment of such economy to war needs and conditions;

(3) policies for unifying, in time of war, the activities of Federal agencies and departments engaged in or concerned with production, procurement, distribution, or transportation of military or civilian supplies, materials, and products;

(4) the relationship between potential supplies of, and potential requirements for, manpower, resources, and productive facilities in time of war;

(5) policies for establishing adequate reserves of strategic and critical material, and for the conservation of these reserves;

(6) the strategic relocation of industries, services, government, and economic activities, the continuous operation of which is essential to the Nation's security.

(d) In performing its functions, the Board shall utilize to the maximum extent the facilities and resources of the departments and agencies of the Government.

TITLE II—THE DEPARTMENT OF DEFENSE

SEC. 201. (a) There is hereby established, as an Executive Department of the Government, the Department of Defense, and the Secretary of Defense shall be the head thereof.

(b) There shall be within the Department of Defense (1) the Department of the Army, the Department of the Navy, and the Department of the Air Force, and each such department shall on and after the date of enactment of the National Security Act Amendments of 1949 be military departments in lieu of their prior status as Executive Departments, and (2) all other agencies created under title II of this Act. *Army, Navy, Air Force—military departments.* *Other Agencies.*

(c) Section 158 of the Revised Statutes, as amended, is amended to read as follows: *Department of Defense—Executive-Department.*

SEC. 158. The provisions of this title shall apply to the following Executive Departments:

First. The Department of State.
Second. The Department of Defense.
Third. The Department of the Treasury.
Fourth. The Department of Justice.
Fifth. The Post Office Department.
Sixth. The Department of the Interior.
Seventh. The Department of Agriculture.
Eighth. The Department of Commerce.
Ninth. The Department of Labor.

(d) Except to the extent inconsistent with the provisions of this Act, the provisions of title IV of the Revised Statutes as now or hereafter amended shall be applicable to the Department of Defense.[10] *Applicability of title IV.*

THE SECRETARY OF DEFENSE

SEC. 202. (a) There shall be a Secretary of Defense, who shall be appointed from civilian life by the President, by and with the advice and consent of the Senate: *Provided*, That a person who has within ten years been on active duty as a commissioned officer in a Regular component of the armed services shall not be eligible for appointment as Secretary of Defense. *Secretary of Defense. Appointment. Eligibility.*

(b) The Secretary of Defense shall be the principal assistant to the President in all matters relating to the Department of Defense. Under the direction of the President, and subject to the provisions of this Act, he shall have direction, authority, and control over the Department of Defense.[11] *Principal Assistant to President on Defense.*

(c) (1) Notwithstanding any other provision of this Act, the combatant functions assigned to the military services by sections 205 (e), 206 (b), 206 (c), and 208 (f) hereof shall not be transferred, reassigned, abolished, or consolidated. *Combatant functions of military services not to be changed.*

(2) Military personnel shall not be so detailed or assigned as to impair such combatant functions. *Detail of military personnel.*

---

[10] Subsections (a) and (b) amended by section 4, Public Law 216, 81st Congress, August 10, 1949 (63 Stat. 578) ; subsections (c) and (d) added by section 4 above.
[11] Reorganization Plan 3 of 1953, effective June 12, 1953 (see appendix I), abolished the National Security Resources Board and also :
SEC. 5. "(b) So much of the functions of the Secretary of Defense under section 202 (b) of the National Security Act of 1947, as amended, as consists of direction, authority, and control over functions transferred by this reorganization plan is hereby abolished."

(3) The Secretary of Defense shall not direct the use and expenditure of funds of the Department of Defense in such manner as to effect the results prohibited by paragraphs (1) and (2) of this subsection.

(4) The Departments of the Army, Navy, and Air Force shall be separately administered by their respective Secretaries under the direction, authority, and control of the Secretary of Defense.

(5) Subject to the provisions of paragraph (1) of this subsection no function which has been or is hereafter authorized by law to be performed by the Department of Defense shall be substantially transferred, reassigned, abolished, or consolidated until after a report in regard to all pertinent details shall have been made by the Secretary of Defense to the Committees on Armed Services of the Congress.

Recommenda-
tions to the
Congress by
Secretaries
of military
departments
and members
of Joint Chiefs
of Staff.
(6) No provision of this Act shall be so construed as to prevent a Secretary of a military department or a member of the Joint Chiefs of Staff from presenting to the Congress, on his own initiative, after first so informing the Secretary of Defense, any recommendation relating to the Department of Defense that he may deem proper.

(d) The Secretary of Defense shall not less often than semiannually submit written reports to the President and the Congress covering expenditures, work, and accomplishments of the Department of Defense, accompanied by (1) such recommendations as he shall deem appropriate, (2) separate reports from the military departments covering their expenditures, work, and accomplishments, and (3) itemized statements showing the savings of public funds and the eliminations of unnecessary duplications and overlappings that have been accomplished pursuant to the provisions of this Act.

(e) The Secretary of Defense shall cause a seal of office to be made for the Department of Defense, of such design as the President shall approve, and judicial notice shall be taken thereof.

(f) The Secretary of Defense may, without being relieved of his responsibility therefor, and unless prohibited by some specific provision of this Act or other specific provision of law, perform any function vested in him through or with the aid of such officials or organizational entities of the Department of Defense as he may designate.

(g) Under such regulations as he shall prescribe, the Secretary of Defense with the approval of the President is authorized to transfer between the armed services, within the authorized commissioned strength of the respective services, officers holding commissions in the medical services or corps including the Reserve components thereof. No officer shall be so transferred without (1) his consent, (2) the consent of the service from

161

which the transfer is to be made, and (3) the consent of the service to which the transfer is to be made.

(h) Officers transferred hereunder shall be appointed by the President alone to such commissioned grade, permanent and temporary, in the armed service to which transferred and be given such place on the applicable promotion list of such service as he shall determine. Federal service previously rendered by any such officer shall be credited for promotion, seniority, and retirement purposes as if served in the armed service to which transferred according to the provisions of law governing promotion, seniority, and retirement therein. No officer upon a transfer to any service from which previously transferred shall be given a higher grade, or place on the applicable promotion list, than that which he could have attained had he remained continuously in the service to which retransferred.

> **Appointment to grade by President.**

> **Place on promotion list.**

(i) Any officer transferred hereunder shall be credited with the unused leave to which he was entitled at the time of transfer.[12]

> **Credit for unused leave.**

DEPUTY SECRETARY OF DEFENSE; ASSISTANT SECRETARIES OF DEFENSE; MILITARY ASSISTANTS

SEC. 203. (a) There shall be a Deputy Secretary of Defense, who shall be appointed from civilian life by the President, by and with the advice and consent of the Senate: *Provided*, That a person who has within ten years been on active duty as a commissioned officer in a Regular component of the armed services shall not be eligible for appointment as Deputy Secretary of Defense. The Deputy Secretary shall perform such duties and exercise such powers as the Secretary of Defense may prescribe and shall take precedence in the Department of Defense next after the Secretary of Defense. The Deputy Secretary shall act for, and exercise the powers of, the Secretary of Defense during his absence or disability.

> **Deputy Secretary of Defense. Appointment. Qualifications, powers, duties, and precedence.**

(b) There shall be three Assistant Secretaries of Defense, who shall be appointed from civilian life by the President, by and with the advice and consent of the Senate. The Assistant Secretaries shall perform such duties and exercise such powers as the Secretary of Defense may prescribe and shall take precedence in the Department of Defense after the Secretary of Defense, the Deputy Secretary of Defense, the Secretary of the Army, the Secretary of the Navy, and the Secretary of the Air Force.[13]

> **Assistant Secretaries of Defense.**

---

[12] Subsections (a), (b), and (c) amended by section 5, Public Law 216, 81st Congress, August 10, 1949 (63 Stat. 578); subsections (d), (e), and (f) added by section 5 above; subsections (g), (h), and (i) added by section 3, Public Law 779, 81st Congress, September 9, 1950.

[13] Reorganization Plan 6 of 1953 (effective June 30, 1953), sections 3 and 4, provided for six additional Assistant Secretaries of Defense and a General Counsel with the rank of Assistant Secretary. (See appendix.)

(c) Officers of the armed services may be detailed to duty as assistants and personal aides to the Secretary of Defense, but he shall not establish a military staff other than that provided for by section 211 (a) of this Act.[14]

CIVILIAN PERSONNEL [15]

Civilian personnel.

SEC. 204. The Secretary of Defense is authorized, subject to the civil-service laws and the Classification Act of 1923, as amended, to appoint and fix the compensation of such civilian personnel as may be necessary for the performance of the functions of the Department of Defense other than those of the Departments of the Army, Navy, and Air Force.[16]

DEPARTMENT OF THE ARMY

Department of the Army. Department of War, redesignation of.

SEC. 205. (a) The Department of War shall hereafter be designated the Department of the Army, and the title of the Secretary of War shall be changed to Secretary of the Army. Changes shall be made in the titles of other officers and activities of the Department of the Army as the Secretary of the Army may determine.

Applicability of laws, orders, regulations and other actions of Department of War.

(b) All laws, orders, regulations, and other actions relating to the Department of War or to any officer or activity whose title is changed under this section shall, insofar as they are not inconsistent with the provisions of this Act, be deemed to relate to the Department of the Army within the Department of Defense or to such officer or activity designated by his or its new title.

Definition.

(c) The term "Department of the Army" as used in this Act shall be construed to mean the Department of the Army at the seat of government and all field head-

---

[14] Subsection (a) is former section 202 (d), Public Law 253, 80th Congress, July 26, 1947 (61 Stat. 495), as added by section 1, Public Law 36, 81st Congress, April 2, 1949 (63 Stat. 30), amended by section 6 (a), Public Law 216, 81st Congress, August 10, 1949 (63 Stat. 578) ; subsection (b) is former section 204 (a), Public Law 253, 80th Congress, July 26, 1947 (61 Stat. 495), as amended by section 6 (a), Public Law 216, 81st Congress, August 10, 1949 (63 Stat. 578) ; subsection (c) is former section 203, Public Law 253, 80th Congress, July 26, 1947 (61 Stat. 495), as amended by section 6 (a), Public Law 216, 81st Congress, August 10, 1949 (63 Stat. 578).

[15] Reorganization Plan 6 of 1953 (see appendix II) abolishes the office of Director of Installations which had been created pursuant to the directive to the Secretary of Defense to establish such an office as set forth in Public Law 534, 82d Congress (66 Stat. 625).

"SEC. 408. The Secretary of Defense shall maintain direct surveillance over the planning and construction by the military departments of all public works projects. Such surveillance shall be maintained through a civilian official of the Department of Defense to be known as the Director of Installations, who shall be appointed by and directly responsible to the Secretary of Defense and who shall receive compensation at the rate of $14,800 a year. The Director of Installations shall, from time to time, make such reports directly to the Secretary of Defense with respect to public works projects under construction by the military departments as he may deem necessary to keep the Secretary of Defense currently and fully informed with respect to the status, progress, and cost of, and all other pertinent matters concerning. such public works project. No person shall be appointed as Director of Installations unless the Secretary of Defense is satisfied that he has had a substantial amount of experience in the construction of public works of the types constructed by the military departments. The Secretary of Defense shall provide for furnishing the Director of Installations with such engineering, clerical, stenographic, and other personnel as he may require in order adequately to perform his functions."

[16] Former section 204 (b), Public Law 253, 80th Congress, July 26, 1947 (61 Stat. 495), as amended by section 6 (b), Public Law 216, 81st Congress, August 10, 1949 (63 Stat. 578).

quarters, forces, reserve components, installations, activities, and functions under the control or supervision of the Department of the Army.

(d) The Secretary of the Army shall cause a seal of office to be made for the Department of the Army, of such design, as the President may approve, and judicial notice shall be taken thereof. **Seal.**

(e) In general the United States Army, within the Department of the Army, shall include land combat and service forces and such aviation and water transport as may be organic therein. It shall be organized, trained, and equipped primarily for prompt and sustained combat incident to operations on land. It shall be responsible for the preparation of land forces necessary for the effective prosecution of war except as otherwise assigned and, in accordance with integrated joint mobilization plans, for the expansion of peacetime components of the Army to meet the needs of war.[17] **United States Army. Composition and organization.**

DEPARTMENT OF THE NAVY

SEC. 206. (a) The term "Department of the Navy" as used in this Act shall be construed to mean the Department of the Navy at the seat of government; the headquarters, United States Marine Corps; the entire operating forces of the United States Navy, including naval aviation, and of the United States Marine Corps, including the reserve components of such forces; all field activities, headquarters, forces, bases, installations, activities, and functions under the control or supervision of the Department of the Navy; and the United States Coast Guard when operating as a part of the Navy pursuant to law. **Department of the Navy. Definition.**

(b) In general the United States Navy, within the Department of the Navy, shall include naval combat and services forces and such aviation as may be organic therein. It shall be organized, trained, and equipped primarily for prompt and sustained combat incident to operations at sea. It shall be responsible for the preparation of naval forces necessary for the effective prosecution of war except as otherwise assigned, and, in accordance with integrated joint mobilization plans, for the expansion of the peacetime components of the Navy to meet the needs of war. **United States Navy. Composition and organization.**

All naval aviation shall be integrated with the naval service as part thereof within the Department of the Navy. Naval aviation shall consist of combat and service and training forces, and shall include land-based naval aviation, air transport essential for naval operations, all air weapons and air techniques involved in the operations

---

[17] Subsection (b) amended by section 12 (a), Public Law 216, 81st Congress, August 10, 1949 (63 Stat. 578) ; subsections (a), (c), (d) and (e) from section 205 Public Law 253, 80th Congress, July 26, 1947 (61 Stat. 495).

and activities of the United States Navy, and the entire remainder of the aeronautical organization of the United States Navy, together with the personnel necessary therefor.

The Navy shall be generally responsible for naval reconnaissance, antisubmarine warfare, and protection of shipping.

The Navy shall develop aircraft, weapons, tactics, technique, organization and equipment of naval combat and service elements; matters of joint concern as to these functions shall be coordinated between the Army, and Air Force, and the Navy.

United States Marine Corps. Composition and organization. (c) The United States Marine Corps, within the Department of the Navy, shall be so organized as to include not less than three combat divisions and three air wings, and such other land combat, aviation, and other services as may be organic therein, and except in time of war or national emergency hereafter declared by the Congress the personnel strength of the Regular Marine Corps shall be maintained at not more than four hundred thousand.[18] The Marine Corps shall be organized, trained, and equipped to provide fleet marine forces of combined arms, together with supporting air components, for service with the fleet in the seizure or defense of advanced naval bases and for the conduct of such land operations as may be essential to the prosecution of a naval campaign. It shall be the duty of the Marine Corps to develop, in coordination with the Army and the Air Force, those phases of amphibious operations which pertain to the tactics, technique, and equipment employed by landing forces. In addition, the Marine Corps shall provide detachments and organizations for service on armed vessels of the Navy, shall provide security detachments for the protection of naval property at naval stations and bases, and shall perform such other duties as the President may direct: *Provided*, That such additional duties shall not detract from or interfere with the operations for which the Marine Corps is primarily organized. The Marine Corps shall be responsible, in accordance with integrated joint mobilization plans, for the expansion of peacetime components of the Marine Corps to meet the needs of war.[19]

DEPARTMENT OF THE AIR FORCE

Department of the Air Force. Secretary, appointment of. SEC. 207. (a) Within the Department of Defense there is hereby established a military department to be known as the Department of the Air Force, and the Secretary of the Air Force who shall be the head thereof. The Secretary of the Air Force shall be appointed from civilian life by the President by and with the advice and consent of the Senate.

---

[18] As amended by Public Law 416, 82d Congress (61 Stat. 502).
[19] From section 206, Public Law 253, 80th Congress, July 26, 1947 (61 Stat. 495).

(b) Repealed.

(c) The term "Department of the Air Force" as used in this Act shall be construed to mean the Department of the Air Force at the seat of government and all field headquarters, forces, reserve components, installations, activities, and functions under the control or supervision of the Department of the Air Force.

Definition.

(d) There shall be in the Department of the Air Force an Under Secretary of the Air Force and two Assistant Secretaries of the Air Force, who shall be appointed from civilian life by the President by and with the advice and consent of the Senate.

Under Secretary and Assistant Secretary of the Air Force.

(e) The several officers of the Department of the Air Force shall perform such functions as the Secretary of the Air Force may prescribe.

Functions of officers.

(f) So much of the functions of the Secretary of the Army and of the Department of the Army, including those of any officer of such Department, as are assigned to or under the control of the Commanding General, Army Air Forces, or as are deemed by the Secretary of Defense to be necessary or desirable for the operations of the Department of the Air Force or the United States Air Force, shall be transferred to and vested in the Secretary of the Air Force and the Department of the Air Force: *Provided*, That the National Guard Bureau shall, in addition to the functions and duties performed by it for the Department of the Army, be charged with similar functions and duties for the Department of the Air Force, and shall be the channel of communication between the Department of the Air Force and the several States on all matters pertaining to the Air National Guard: *And provided further*, That, in order to permit an orderly transfer, the Secretary of Defense may, during the transfer period hereinafter prescribed, direct that the Department of the Army shall continue for appropriate periods to exercise any of such functions, insofar as they relate to the Department of the Air Force, or the United States Air Force or their property and personnel. Such of the property, personnel, and records of the Department of the Army used in the exercise of functions transferred under this subsection as the Secretary of Defense shall determine shall be transferred or assigned to the Department of the Air Force.

Transfer of functions from Army to Air Force.

National Guard Bureau, Air Force functions and duties of.

Continuance of functions by Department of the Army.

(g) The Secretary of the Air Force shall cause a seal of office to be made for the Department of the Air Force, of such device as the President shall approve, and judicial notice shall be taken thereof.[20]

Seal.

---

[20] Subsection (a) amended by section 12 (b), Public Law 216, 81st Congress, August 10, 1949 (63 Stat. 578).; subsection (b) repealed by section 12 (c), Public Law 216, 81st Congress, August 10, 1949 (63 Stat. 578); subsections (c), (d), (e), (f), and (g) from section 207, Public Law 253, 80th Congress, July 26, 1947 (61 Stat. 495).

SEC. 208. (a) The United States Air Force is hereby established within the Department of the Air Force. The Army Air Forces, the Air Corps, United States Army, and the General Headquarters Air Force (Air Force Combat Command), shall be transferred to the United States Air Force.

United States Air Force. Establishment.

(b) There shall be a Chief of Staff, United States Air Force, who shall be appointed by the President, by and with the advice and consent of the Senate, for a term of four years from among the officers of general rank who are assigned to or commissioned in the United States Air Force. Under the direction of the Secretary of the Air Force, the Chief of Staff, United States Air Force, shall exercise command over the air defense command, the strategic air command, the tactical air command, and such other major commands as may be established by the Secretary under section 308 (b) of the Air Force Organization Act of 1951, and shall have supervision over all other members and organizations of the Air Force, and shall be charged with the duty of carrying into execution all lawful orders and directions which may be transmitted to him. The functions of the Commanding General, General Headquarters Air Force (Air Force Combat Command), and of the Chief of the Air Corps and of the Commanding General, Army Air Forces, shall be transferred to the Chief of Staff, United States Air Force. When such transfer becomes effective, the offices of the Chief of the Air Corps, United States Army, and Assistants to the Chief of the Air Corps, United States Army, provided for by the Act of June 4, 1920, as amended (41 Stat. 768), and Commanding General, General Headquarters Air Force, provided for by section 5 of the Act of June 16, 1936 (49 Stat. 1525), shall cease to exist. While holding office as Chief of Staff, United States Air Force, the incumbent shall hold a grade and receive allowances equivalent to those prescribed by law for the Chief of Staff, United States Army. The Chief of Staff, United States Army, the Chief of Naval Operations, and the Chief of Staff, United States Air Force, shall take rank among themselves according to their relative dates of appointment as such, and shall each take rank above all other officers on the active list of the Army, Navy, and Air Force: *Provided,* That nothing in this Act shall have the effect of changing the relative rank of the present Chief of Staff, the United States Army, and the present Chief of Naval Operations.

Chief of Staff, Appointment of.

Duties.

Termination of functions.

Grade and rank.

(c) All commissioned officers, warrant officers, and enlisted men, commissioned, holding warrants, or enlisted, in the Air Corps, United States Army, or the Army Air Forces, shall be transferred in branch to the

Transfer of military personnel.

167

United States Air Force. All other commissioned officers, warrant officers, and enlisted men, who are commissioned, hold warrants, or are enlisted, in any component of the Army of the United States and who are under the authority or command of the Commanding General, Army Air Forces, shall be continued under the authority or command of the Chief of Staff, United States Air Force, and under the jurisdiction of the Department of the Air Force. Personnel whose status is affected by this subsection shall retain their existing commissions, warrants, or enlisted status in existing components of the armed forces unless otherwise altered or terminated in accordance with existing law; and they shall not be deemed to have been appointed to a new or different office or grade, or to have vacated their permanent or temporary appointments in an existing component of the armed forces, solely by virtue of any change in status under this subsection. No such change in status shall alter or prejudice the status of any individual so assigned, so as to deprive him of any right, benefit, or privilege to which he may be entitled under existing law.

(d) Except as otherwise directed by the Secretary of the Air Force, all property, records, installations, agencies, activities, projects, and civilian personnel under the jurisdiction, control, authority, or command of the Commanding General, Army Air Forces, shall be continued to the same extent under the jurisdiction, control, authority, or command, respectively, of the Chief of Staff, United States Air Force, in the Department of the Air Force.

[margin note: Transfer of property and records.]

(e) For a period of three years from the date of enactment of this Act, personnel (both military and civilian), property, records, installations, agencies, activities, and projects may be transferred between the Department of the Army and the Department of the Air Force by direction of the Secretary of Defense.

[margin note: Transfer of personnel, property and records between Army and Air Force.]

(f) In general the United States Air Force shall include aviation forces both combat and service not otherwise assigned. It shall be organized, trained, and equipped primarily for prompt and sustained offensive and defensive air operations. The Air Force shall be responsible for the preparation of the air forces necessary for the effective prosecution of war except as otherwise assigned and, in accordance with integrated joint mobilization plans, for the expansion of the peacetime components of the Air Force to meet the needs of war.[21]

[margin note: Composition and Organization.]

---

[21] Subsection (a) amended by section 12 (d), Public Law 216, 81st Congress, August 10, 1949 (63 Stat. 578) ; subsection (b) amended by section 402, Public Law 150, 82d Congress, September 19, 1951 ; subsection (e) amended by section 12 (h), Public Law 216, 81st Congress, August 10, 1949 (63 Stat. 578) ; subsections (c), (d), and (f) from section 208, Public Law 253, 80th Congress, July 26, 1947 (61 Stat. 495).

SEC. 209. Each transfer, assignment, or change in status under section 207 or section 208 shall take effect upon such date or dates as may be prescribed by the Secretary of Defense.[22]

ARMED FORCES POLICY COUNCIL

Armed Forces Policy Council. Composition.

SEC. 210. There shall be within the Department of Defense an Armed Forces Policy Council composed of the Secretary of Defense, as Chairman, who shall have power of decision; the Deputy Secretary of Defense; the Secretary of the Army; the Secretary of the Navy; the Secretary of the Air Force; the Chairman of the Joint Chiefs of Staff; the Chief of Staff, United States Army; the Chief of Naval Operations; and the Chief of Staff, United States Air Force. The Armed Forces Policy Council shall advise the Secretary of Defense on matters of broad policy relating to the armed forces and shall consider and report on such other matters as the Secretary of Defense may direct.[23]

Functions.

JOINT CHIEFS OF STAFF

Joint Chiefs of Staff. Establishment. Composition.

SEC. 211. (a) There is hereby established within the Department of Defense the Joint Chiefs of Staff, which shall consist of the Chairman, who shall be the presiding officer thereof but who shall have no vote; [24] the Chief of Staff, United States Army, the Chief of Naval Operations; and the Chief of Staff, United States Air Force. The Joint Chiefs of Staff shall be the principal military advisers to the President, the National Security Council, and the Secretary of Defense.

Commandant.

The Commandant of the Marine Corps shall indicate to the Chairman of the Joint Chiefs of Staff any matter scheduled for consideration by the Joint Chiefs of Staff which directly concerns the United States Marine Corps. Unless the Secretary of Defense, upon request from the Chairman of the Joint Chiefs of Staff for a determination, determines that such matter does not concern the United States Marine Corps, the Commandant of the Marine Corps shall meet with the Joint Chiefs of Staff when such matter is under consideration by them and on such occasion and with respect to such matter the Commandant of the Marine Corps shall have coequal status with the members of the Joint Chiefs of Staff.[25]

Duties.

(b) Subject to the authority and direction of the President and the Secretary of Defense, the Joint Chiefs of

---

[22] From Public Law 253, 80th Congress, July 26, 1947 (61 Stat. 495).
[23] Amended by section 7 (a), Public Law 216, 81st Congress, August 10, 1949 (63 Stat. 578).
[24] Reorganization Plan 6 of 1953 transferred the management functions of the Joint Chiefs of Staff to the Chairman. (See appendix II.)
[25] Amended by Public Law 416, 82d Congress (66 Stat. 283).

Staff shall perform the following duties, in addition to such other duties as the President or the Secretary of Defense may direct:

(1) preparation of strategic plans and provision for the strategic direction of the military forces;

(2) preparation of joint logistic plans and assignment to the military services of logistic responsibilities in accordance with such plans;

(3) establishment of unified commands in strategic areas;

(4) review of major material and personnel requirements of the military forces in accordance with strategic and logistic plans;

(5) formulation of policies for joint training of the military forces;

(6) formulation of policies for coordinating the military education of members of the military forces; and

(7) providing United States representation on the Military Staff Committee of the United Nations in accordance with the provisions of the Charter of the United Nations.

(c) The Chairman of the Joint Chiefs of Staff (hereinafter referred to as the "Chairman") shall be appointed by the President, by and with the advice and consent of the Senate, from among the Regular officers of the armed services to serve at the pleasure of the President for a term of two years and shall be eligible for one reappointment, by and with the advice and consent of the Senate, except in time of war hereafter declared by the Congress when there shall be no limitation on the number of such reappointments. The Chairman shall receive the basic pay and basic and personal money allowances prescribed by law for the Chief of Staff, United States Army, and such special pays and hazardous duty pays to which he may be entitled under other provisions of law.

Chairman, Appointment and qualifications of.

(d) The Chairman, if in the grade of general, shall be additional to the number of officers in the grade of general provided in the third proviso of section 504 (b) of the Officer Personnel Act of 1947 (Public Law 381, Eightieth Congress) or, if in the rank of admiral, shall be additional to the number of officers having the rank of admiral provided in section 413 (a) of such Act. While holding such office he shall take precedence over all other officers of the armed services: *Provided*, That the Chairman shall not exercise military command over the Joint Chiefs of Staff or over any of the military services.

(e) In addition to participating as a member of the Joint Chiefs of Staff in the performance of the duties assigned in subsection (b) of this section, the Chairman shall, subject to the authority and direction of the Presi-

Chairman, Additional duties of.

dent and the Secretary of Defense, perform the following duties:

> (1) serve as the presiding officer of the Joint Chiefs of Staff;
> (2) provide agenda for meetings of the Joint Chiefs of Staff and assist the Joint Chiefs of Staff to prosecute their business as promptly as practicable; and
> (3) inform the Secretary of Defense and, when appropriate as determined by the President or the Secretary of Defense, the President, of those issues upon which agreement among the Joint Chiefs of Staff has not been reached.[26]

JOINT STAFF

Joint Staff.
Composition.
Director.
Duties.

SEC. 212. There shall be, under the Joint Chiefs of Staff, a Joint Staff to consist of not to exceed two hundred and ten officers and to be composed of approximately equal numbers of officers appointed by the Joint Chiefs of Staff from each of the three armed services. The Joint Staff, operating under a Director thereof appointed by the Joint Chiefs of Staff, shall perform such duties as may be directed by the Joint Chiefs of Staff. The Director shall be an officer junior in grade to all members of the Joint Chiefs of Staff.[27]

MUNITIONS BOARD [28]

Munitions
Board.
Establishment.

SEC. 213. (a) There is hereby established in the Department of Defense a Munitions Board (hereinafter in this section referred to as the "Board").

Composition.

(b) The Board shall be composed of a Chairman, who shall be the head thereof and who shall, subject to the authority of the Secretary of Defense and in respect to such matters authorized by him, have the power of decision upon matters falling within the jurisdiction of the Board, and an Under Secretary or Assistant Secretary from each of the three military departments, to be designated in each case by the Secretaries of their respective departments. The Chairman shall be appointed from civilian life by the President, by and with the advice and consent of the Senate, and shall receive compensation at the rate of $14,000 a year.

Chairman, Appointment and compensation of.

Duties.

(c) Subject to the authority and direction of the Secretary of Defense, the Board shall perform the following duties in support of strategic and logistic plans and in consonance with guidance in those fields provided by the

---

[26] Subsections (a), (b), and (c) amended by section 7 (b), Public Law 216, 81st Congress, August 10, 1949 (63 Stat. 578); subsections (d) and (e) added by section 7 (b) above.
[27] Amended by section 7 (c), Public Law 216, 81st Congress, August 10, 1949 (63 Stat. 578).
[28] Reorganization Plan 6 of 1953 (section 2 (a)) abolished the Munitions Board and the Research and Development Board and transferred functions to the Secretary of Defense. (See appendix II for text of Reorganization Plan 6.) Section 2 (d) of Reorganization Plan 6 abolished the Munitions Board guidance functions which are set forth in section 213 (c).

Joint Chiefs of Staff, and such other duties as the Secretary of Defense may prescribe:

(1) coordination of the appropriate activities with regard to industrial matters, including the procurement, production, and distribution plans of the Department of Defense;

(2) planning for the military aspects of industrial mobilization;

(3) assignment of procurement responsibilities among the several military departments and planning for standardization of specifications and for greatest practicable allocation of purchase authority of technical equipment and common use items on the basis of single procurement;

(4) preparation of estimates of potential production, procurement, and personnel for use in evaluation of the logistic feasibility of strategic operations;

(5) determination of relative priorities of the various segments of the military procurement programs;

(6) supervision of such subordinate agencies as are or may be created to consider the subjects falling within the scope of the Board's responsibilities;

(7) regrouping, combining, or dissolving of existing interservice agencies operating in the fields of procurement, production, and distribution in such manner as to promote efficiency and economy;

(8) maintenance of liaison with other departments and agencies for the proper correlation of military requirements with the civilian economy, particularly in regard to the procurement or disposition of strategic and critical material and the maintenance of adequate reserves of such material, and making of recommendations as to policies in connection therewith; and

(9) assembly and review of material and personnel requirements presented by the Joint Chiefs of Staff and by the production, procurement, and distribution agencies assigned to meet military needs, and making of recommendations thereon to the Secretary of Defense.

(d) When the Chairman of the Board first appointed has taken office, the Joint Army and Navy Munitions Board shall cease to exist and all its records and personnel shall be transferred to the Munitions Board. *Joint Army and Navy Munitions Board, termination of.*

(e) The Secretary of Defense shall provide the Board with such personnel and facilities as the Secretary may determine to be required by the Board for the performance of its functions. *Personnel and facilities.*

Research and Development Board. Establishment. Composition.

SEC. 214. (a) There is hereby established in the Department of Defense a Research and Development Board (hereinafter in this section referred to as the "Board"). The Board shall be composed of a Chairman, who shall be the head thereof and who shall, subject to the authority of the Secretary of Defense and in respect to such matters authorized by him, have the power of decision on matters falling within the jurisdiction of the Board, and two representatives from each of the Departments of the Army, Navy, and Air Force, to be designated by the Secretaries of their respective Departments. The

Chairman, appointment and compensation of.

Chairman shall be appointed from civilian life by the President, by and with the advice and consent of the Senate, and shall receive compensation at the rate of

Purpose of Board.

$14,000 a year. The purpose of the Board shall be to advise the Secretary of Defense as to the status of scientific research relative to the national security, and to assist him in assuring adequate provision for research and development on scientific problems relating to the national security.

(b) Subject to the authority and direction of the Secretary of Defense, the Board shall perform the following

Duties.

duties and such other duties as the Secretary of Defense may prescribe:

(1) preparation of a complete and integrated program of research and development for military purposes;

(2) advising with regard to trends in scientific research relating to national security and the measures necessary to assure continued and increasing progress;

(3) coordination of research and development among the military departments, and allocation among them of responsibilities for specific programs;

(4) formulation of policy for the Department of Defense in connection with research and development matters involving agencies outside the Department of Defense; and

(5) consideration of the interaction of research and development and strategy, and advising the Joint Chiefs of Staff in connection therewith.

Joint Research and Development Board, termination of.

(c) When the Chairman of the Board first appointed has taken office, the Joint Research and Development Board shall cease to exist and all its records and personnel shall be transferred to the Research and Development Board.

Personnel and facilities.

(d) The Secretary of Defense shall provide the Board with such personnel and facilities as the Secretary may determine to be required by the Board for the performance of its functions.

---

*Abolished by Reorganization Plan 6 of 1953. See footnote 28 above.

A. REORGANIZATION PLAN NO. 6 OF 1953

Prepared by the President and transmitted to the Senate and the House of Representatives in Congress assembled, April 30, 1953, pursuant to the provisions of the Reorganization Act of 1949, approved June 20, 1949, as amended.

SECTION 1. *Transfers of functions.*—(a) All functions of the Munitions Board, the Research and Development Board, the Defense Supply Management Agency, and the Director of Installations are hereby transferred to the Secretary of Defense.

(b) The selection of the Director of the Joint Staff by the Joint Chiefs of Staff, and his tenure, shall be subject to the approval of the Secretary of Defense.

(c) The selection of the members of the Joint Staff by the Joint Chiefs of Staff, and their tenure, shall be subject to the approval of the Chairman of the Joint Chiefs of Staff.

(d) The functions of the Joint Chiefs of Staff with respect to managing the Joint Staff and the Director thereof are hereby transferred to the Chairman of the Joint Chiefs of Staff.

SEC. 2. *Abolition of agencies and functions.*—(a) There are hereby abolished the Munitions Board, the Research and Development Board, and the Defense Supply Management Agency.

(b) The offices of Chairman of the Munitions Board, Chairman of the Research and Development Board, Director of the Defense Management Agency, and Director of Installations are hereby abolished.

(c) The Secretary of Defense shall provide for winding up any outstanding affairs of the said abolished agency, boards, and offices, not otherwise provided for in this reorganization plan.

(d) The function of guidance to the Munitions Board in connection with strategic and logistic plans as required by section 213 (c) of of the National Security Act of 1947, as amended, is hereby abolished.

SEC. 3. *Assistant Secretaries of Defense.*—Six additional Assistant Secretaries of Defense may be appointed from civilian life by the President, by and with the advice and consent of the Senate. Each such Assistant Secretary shall perform such functions as the Secretary of Defense may from time to time prescribe and each shall receive compensation at the rate prescribed by law for assistant secretaries of executive departments.

SEC. 4. *General Counsel.*—The President may appoint from civilian life, by and with the advice and consent of the Senate, a General Counsel·of the Department of Defense, who shall be the chief legal officer of the Department, and who shall perform such functions as the Secretary of Defense may from time to time prescribe. He shall receive compensation at the rate prescribed by law for assistant secretaries of executive departments.

SEC. 5. *Performance of functions.*—The Secretary of Defense may from time to time make such provisions as he shall deem appropriate authorizing the performance by any other officer, or by any agency or employee, of the Department of Defense or any function of the Secretary, including any function transferred to the Secretary by the provisions of this reorganization plan.

SEC. 6. *Miscellaneous provisions.*—(a) The Secretary of Defense may from time to time effect such transfers within the Department of Defense of any of the records, property, and personnel affected by this reorganization plan, and such transfers of unexpended balances (available or to be made available for use in connection with any affected function or agency) of appropriations, allocations, and other funds of such Department, as he deems necessary to carry out the provisions of this reorganization plan.

(b) Nothing herein shall affect the compensation of the Chairman of the Military Liaison Committee (63 Stat. 762).

B. THE KEY WEST AGREEMENT

FUNCTIONS OF THE ARMED FORCES
AND THE JOINT CHIEFS OF STAFF*

1 October 1953

Introduction
Section I—Principles
Section II—Common Functions of the Armed Forces
Section III—Functions of the Joint Chiefs of Staff
Section IV—Functions of the United States Army
Section V—Functions of the United States Navy and Marine Corps
Section VI—Functions of the United States Air Force
Section VII—Glossary of Terms and Definitions

INTRODUCTION

Congress, in the National Security Act of 1947, has described the basic policy embodied in the Act in the following terms:

"In enacting this legislation, it is the intent of Congress to provide a comprehensive program for the future security of the United States; to provide for the establishment of integrated policies and procedures for the departments, agencies, and functions of the Government relating to the national security; to provide three military departments for the operation and administration of the Army, the Navy (including naval aviation and the United States Marine Corps), and the Air Force, with their assigned combat and service components; to provide for their authoritative coordination and unified direction under civilian control but not to merge them; to provide for the effective strategic direction of the armed forces and for their operation under unified control and for their integration into an efficient team of land, naval, and air forces."

In accordance with the policy declared by Congress, and in accordance with the provisions of the National Security Act of 1947, [as

* This document is the October 1, 1953, revision of the "Key West Agreement" promulgated as Secretary of Defense Memorandum, April 21, 1948. It is taken from DOD Directive No. 5100.1, March 16, 1954. Words or paragraphs enclosed in brackets [ ] were *added* to the original 1948 Agreements by the October 1, 1953, revision. Words *deleted* by this revision are given in the footnotes except for "National Military Establishment" which was changed to "Department of Defense" throughout.

176

amended, (including Reorganization Plan No. 6 of 1953)] and to provide guidance for the departments and the joint agencies of the [Department of Defense] the Secretary of Defense, by direction of the President, hereby promulgates the following statement of the functions of the armed forces and the Joint Chiefs of Staff.

SECTION I. — PRINCIPLES

[1.   No function in any part of the Department of Defense, or in any of its component agencies, shall be performed independent of the direction, authority, and control of the Secretary of Defense.]

2.   There shall be the maximum practicable integration of the policies and procedures of the departments and agencies of the [Department of Defense.] This does not imply a merging of armed forces, but does demand a consonance and correlation of policies and procedures throughout the [Department of Defense,] in order to produce an effective, economical, harmonious, and business-like organization which will insure the military security of the United States.

3.   The functions stated herein shall be carried out in such a manner as to achieve the following:

(a) Effective strategic direction of the armed forces.

(b) Operation of armed forces under unified command, wherever such unified command is in the best interest of national security.

(c) Integration of the armed forces into an efficient team of land, naval, and air forces.

(d) Prevention of unnecessary duplication or overlapping among the services, by utilization of the personnel, intelligence, facilities, equipment, supplies, and services of any or all services in all cases where military effectiveness and economy of resources will thereby be increased.

(e) Coordination of armed forces operations to promote efficiency and economy and to prevent gaps in responsibility.

4.   It is essential that there be full utilization and exploitation of the weapons, techniques, and intrinsic capabilities of each of the services in any military situation where this will contribute effectively to the attainment of over-all military objectives. In effecting this, collateral as well as primary functions will be assigned. It is recognized that assignment of collateral functions may establish further justification for stated force requirements, but such assignment shall not be used as the basis for establishing additional force requirements.

5.   Doctrines, procedures, and plans covering joint operations and joint exercises shall be jointly prepared. Primary responsibility for

development of certain doctrines and procedures is hereinafter assigned.

6.   Technological developments, variations in the availability of manpower and natural resources, changing economic conditions, and changes in the world politico-military situation may dictate the desirability of changes in the present assignment of specific functions and responsibilities to the individual services. This determination and the initiation of implementing action are the responsibility of the Secretary of Defense.

SECTION II.— COMMON FUNCTIONS OF THE ARMED FORCES

A.   *General.*—As prescribed by higher authority and under the[1] direction of the [Secretary of Defense with the advice of the] Joint Chiefs of Staff, the armed forces shall conduct operations wherever and whenever necessary for the following purposes:

1.   To support and defend the Constitution of the United States against all enemies, foreign or domestic.

2.   To maintain, by timely and effective military action the security of the United States, its possessions, and areas vital to its interest.

3.   To uphold and advance the national policies and interests of the United States.

4.   To safeguard the internal security of the United States.

B.   *Specific*

1.   In accordance with [continuous] guidance from the Joint Chiefs of Staff, to prepare forces and to establish reserves of equipment and supplies, for the effective prosecution of war and to plan for the expansion of peacetime components to meet the needs of war.

2.   To maintain in readiness mobile reserve forces, properly organized, trained, and equipped for employment in emergency.

3.   To provide adequate, timely, and reliable intelligence for use within the [Department of Defense.]

4.   To organize, train, and equip forces for joint operations.

5.   To conduct research, to develop tactics, techniques, and organization, and to develop and procure weapons, equipment, and supplies essential to the fulfillment of the functions hereinafter assigned, each Service coordinating with the others in all matters of joint concern.

6.   To develop, garrison, supply, equip, and maintain bases and other installations, to include lines of communication, and to provide administrative and logistical support of all forces and bases.

7.   To provide, as directed by proper authority, such forces, military missions, and detachments for service in foreign countries as may

be required to support the national interests of the United States.

8.   As directed by proper authority, to assist in training and equipping the military forces of foreign nations.

9.   Each service to assist the others in the accomplishment of their functions, including the provision of personnel, intelligence, training, facilities, equipment, supplies, and services as may be determined by proper authority.

10.   Each service to support operations of the others.

11.   Each service to coordinate operations (including administrative, logistical, training, and combat) with those of the other services as necessary in the best interests of the United States.

12.   Each service to determine and provide the means of communications by which command within the service is to be exercised.

13.   To refer all matters of strategic significance to the Joint Chiefs of Staff.

[14.   *Unified Commands*

(a)   The Secretary of Defense after consultation with the Joint Chiefs of Staff shall designate in each case one of the military departments to serve as the executive agency for unified commands and other matters requiring such designation.

(b)   Under the arrangements herein established, the channel of responsibility will be from the Secretary of Defense to the designated civilian Secretary of a military department.

(c)   For strategic direction and for the conduct of combat operations in emergency and wartime situations, the Secretary of the military department designated as executive agent shall forthwith authorize the military chief of such department in such situations to receive and transmit reports and orders and to act for such department in its executive agency capacity. The military chief will keep his Secretary, the Secretary of Defense, and the Joint Chiefs of Staff fully informed of decisions made and actions taken under such authority. The military chief will in such circumstances be acting in the name and under the direction of the Secretary of Defense. Promulgated orders will directly state that fact.]

SECTION III. — FUNCTIONS OF THE JOINT CHIEFS OF STAFF

A.   *General.*—The Joint Chiefs of Staff, consisting of [the Chairman;] the Chief of Staff, U. S. Army; the Chief of Naval Operations; and the Chief of Staff, U. S. Air Force [2] are the principal military advisers to the President, the [National Security Council] and the Secretary of Defense. [The Commandant of the U. S. Marine Corps has co-equal status with the members of the Joint Chiefs of Staff on matters which directly concern the Marine Corps.]

B. *Specific.*—Subject to the authority and direction of the President and the Secretary of Defense, it shall be the duty of the Joint Chiefs of Staff:

1. To prepare strategic plans and to provide for the strategic direction of the Armed Forces,[8] [including guidance for the operational control of forces and for the conduct of combat operations.]

2. To prepare joint logistic plans and to assign to the military services logistic responsibilities in accordance with such plans.

3. To prepare integrated joint plans for military mobilization, and to review major material requirements and personnel qualifications and requirements of the Armed Forces in the light of strategic and logistic plans.

4. To promulgate to the individual departments of the [Department of Defense] general policies and doctrines in order to provide guidance in the preparation of their respective detailed plans.

5. As directed by proper authority, to participate in the preparation of combined plans for military action in conjunction with the armed forces of other nations.

6. To establish unified commands in strategic areas when such unified commands are in the interest of national security.[4]

7.[5] To determine what means are required for the exercise of unified command, and to[6] [recommend to the Secretary of Defense the assignment] to individual[7] [military departments] the responsibility of providing such means.

8. To approve policies and doctrines for:

(a) Joint operations, including joint amphibious and airborne operations, and for joint training.

(b) Coordinating the educations of members of the Armed Forces.

9. To recommend to the Secretary of Defense the assignment of primary responsibility for any function of the Armed Forces requiring such determination.

10. To prepare and submit to the Secretary of Defense, for his information and consideration in furnishing guidance to the Departments for preparation of their annual budgetary estimates and in coordinating these budgets, a statement of military requirements which is based upon agreed strategic considerations, joint outline war plans, and current national security commitments. This statement of requirements shall include: tasks, priority of tasks, force requirements, and general strategic guidance concerning development of military

installations and bases, equipping and maintaining the military forces, and research and development and industrial mobilization program.

11.   To provide United States representation on the Military Staff Committee of the United Nations, in accordance with the provisions of the Charter of the United Nations and representation on other properly authorized military staffs, boards, councils, and missions.

SECTION IV.—FUNCTIONS OF THE UNITED STATES ARMY

The United States Army includes land combat and service forces and such aviation and water transport as may be organic therein. It is organized, trained, and equipped primarily for prompt and sustained combat operations on land. Of the three major services, the Army has primary interest in all operations on land, except in those operations otherwise assigned herein.

A.   Primary functions

1.   To organize, train, and equip Army forces for the conduct of prompt and sustained combat operations on land. Specifically:

(a) To defeat enemy land forces.

(b) To seize, occupy, and defend land areas.

2.   To organize, train, and equip Army antiaircraft artillery units.

3.   To organize and equip, in coordination with the other services, and to provide Army forces for joint amphibious and airborne operations, and to provide for the training of such forces in accordance with policies and doctrines of the Joint Chiefs of Staff.

4.   To develop, in coordination with the other services, tactics, technique, and equipment of interest to the Army for amphibious operations and not provided for in Section V, paragraph A 4 and paragraph A 11 (c).

5.   To provide an organization capable of furnishing adequate, timely, and reliable intelligence for the Army.

6.   To provide Army forces as required for the defense of the United States against air attack, in accordance with joint doctrines and procedures approved by the Joint Chiefs of Staff.

7.   To provide forces, as directed by proper authority, for occupation of territories abroad, to include initial establishment of military government pending transfer of this responsibility to other authority.

8.   To develop, in coordination with the Navy, the Air Force, and the Marine Corps, the doctrines, procedures, and equipment employed by Army and Marine forces in airborne operations. The Army shall have primary interest in the development of those airborne doctrines, procedures and equipment which are of common interest to the Army and the Marine Corps.

9.   To formulate doctrines and procedures for the organization, equipping, training, and employment of forces operating on land, at division level and above, including division, corps, army and general reserve troops, except that the formulation of doctrines and procedures for the organization, equipping, training, and employment of Marine Corps units for amphibious operations shall be a function of the Department of the Navy, coordinating as required by paragraph A 11 (c), Section V.

10.   To provide support, as directed by higher authority, for the following activities:

(a)   The administration and operation of the Panama Canal.

(b)   River and harbor projects in the United States, its territories, and possessions.

(c)   Certain other civil activities prescribed by law.

B.   *Collateral functions.* — The forces developed and trained to perform the primary functions set forth above shall be employed to support and supplement the other services in carrying out their primary functions, where and whenever such participation will result in increased effectiveness and will contribute to the accomplishment of the over-all military objectives. The Joint Chiefs of Staff member of the service having primary responsibility for a function shall be the agent of the Joint Chiefs of Staff to present to that body the requirements and plans for the employment of all forces to carry out the function. He shall also be responsible for presenting to the Joint Chiefs of Staff for final decision any disagreement within the field of his primary responsibility which has not been resolved. This shall not be construed to prevent any member of the Joint Chiefs of Staff from presenting unilaterally any issue of disagreement with another service. Certain specific collateral functions of the Army are listed below:

1.   To interdict enemy sea and air power and communications through operations on or from land.

Section V.—Functions of the Navy and Marine Corps

Within the Department of the Navy, assigned forces include the entire operating forces of the United States Navy, including naval aviation, and the United States Marine Corps. These forces are organized trained, and equipped primarily for prompt and sustained combat operations at sea, and for air and land operations incident thereto. Of the three major services, the Navy has primary interest in all operations at sea, except in those operations otherwise assigned herein.

A.   *Primary Functions*

1.   To organize, train, and equip Navy and Marine Forces for the

conduct of prompt and sustained combat operations at sea, including operations of sea-based aircraft and their land-based naval air components. Specifically:

(a) To seek out and destroy enemy naval forces and to suppress enemy sea commerce.

(b) To gain and maintain general sea supremacy.

(c) To control vital sea areas and to protect vital sea lines of communication.

(d) To establish and maintain local superiority (including air) in an area of naval operations.

(e) To seize and defend advanced naval bases and to conduct such land operations as may be essential to the prosecution of a naval campaign.

2. To conduct air operations as necessary for the accomplishment of objectives in a naval campaign.

3. To organize and equip, in coordination with the other services, and to provide naval forces, including naval close air-support forces, for the conduct of joint amphibious operations, and to be responsible for the amphibious training of all forces as assigned for joint amphibious operations in accordance with the policies and doctrines of the Joint Chiefs of Staff.

4. To develop, in coordination with the other services, the doctrines, procedures, and equipment of naval forces for amphibious operations, and the doctrines and procedures for joint amphibious operations.

5. To furnish adequate, timely and reliable intelligence for the Navy and Marine Corps.

6. To be responsible for naval reconnaissance, anti-submarine warfare, the protection of shipping, and for mine laying, including the air aspects thereof, and controlled mine field operations.

7. To provide air support essential for naval operations.

8. To provide sea-based air defense and the sea-based means for coordinating control for defense against air attack, coordinating with the other services in matters of joint concern.

9. To provide naval (including naval air) forces as required for the defense of the United States against air attack, in accordance with joint doctrines and procedures approved by the Joint Chiefs of Staff.

10. To furnish aerial photography as necessary for naval and Marine Corps operations.

11. To maintain the United States Marine Corps, which shall include land combat and service forces and such aviation as may be organic therein. Its specific functions are:

(a) To provide Fleet Marine Forces of combined arms, together with supporting air components, for service with the Fleet in the seizure or defense of advanced naval bases and for the conduct of such land operations as may be essential to the prosecution of a naval campaign. These functions do not contemplate the creation of a second land Army.

(b) To provide detachments and organizations for service on armed vessels of the Navy, and security detachments for the protection of naval property at naval stations and bases.

(c) To develop, in coordination with the Army, the Navy, and the Air Force, the tactics, technique, and equipment employed by landing forces in amphibious operations. The Marine Corps shall have primary interest in the development of those landing force tactics, technique, and equipment which are of common interest to the Army and the Marine Corps.

(d) To train and equip, as required, Marine Forces for airborne operations, in coordination with the Army, the Navy, and the Air Force in accordance with policies and doctrines of the Joint Chiefs of Staff.

(e) To develop, in coordination with the Army, the Navy, and the Air Force, doctrines, procedures, and equipment of interest to the Marine Corps for airborne operations and not provided for in Section IV, paragraph A8.

12. To provide forces, as directed by proper authority, for the establishment of military government, pending transfer of this responsibility to other authority.

B. *Collateral Functions.*—The forces developed and trained to form the primary functions set forth above shall be employed to support and supplement the other services in carrying out their primary functions, where and whenever such participation will result in increased effectiveness and will contribute to the accomplishment of the over-all military objectives. The Joint Chiefs of Staff member of the service having primary responsibility for a function shall be the agent of the Joint Chiefs of Staff to present to that body the requirements and plans for the employment of all forces to carry out the function. He shall also be responsible for presenting to the Joint Chiefs of Staff for final decision any disagreement within the field of his primary responsibility which has not been resolved. This shall not be construed to prevent any member of the Joint Chiefs of Staff from presenting unilaterally any issue of disagreement with another service. Certain specific collateral functions of the Navy and Marine Corps are listed below:

1. To interdict enemy land and air power and communications through operation at sea.

2. To conduct close air support for land operations.

3. To furnish aerial photography for cartographic purposes.

4. To be prepared to participate in the over-all air effort as directed by the Joint Chiefs of Staff.

SECTION VI. — FUNCTIONS OF THE UNITED STATES AIR FORCE

The United States Air Force includes air combat and service forces. It is organized, trained, and equipped primarily for prompt and sustained combat operations in the air. Of the three major services, the Air Force has primary interest in all operations in the air, except in those operations otherwise assigned herein.

A. *Primary Functions*

1. To organize, train and equip Air Force forces for the conduct of prompt and sustained combat operations in the air. Specifically:

(a) To be responsible for defense of the United States against air attack in accordance with the policies and procedures of the Joint Chiefs of Staff.

(b) To gain and maintain general air supremacy.

(c) To defeat enemy air forces.

(d) To control vital air areas.

(e) To establish local air superiority except as otherwise assigned herein.

2. To formulate joint doctrines and procedures, in coordination with the other services, for the defense of the United States against air attack, and to provide the Air Force units, facilities, and equipment required therefor.

3. To be responsible for strategic air warfare.

4. To organize and equip Air Force forces for joint amphibious and airborne operations, in coordination with the other services, and to provide for their training in accordance with policies and doctrines of the Joint Chiefs of Staff.

5. To furnish close combat and logistical air support to the Army, to include air lift, support, and resupply of air-borne operations, aerial photography, tactical reconnaissance, and interdiction of enemy land power and communications.

6. To provide air transport for the armed forces except as otherwise assigned.

7. To provide Air Force forces for land-based air defense, coordinating with the other services in matters of joint concern.

8. To develop, in coordination with the other services, doctrines,

procedures, and equipment for air defense from land areas, including the continental United States.

9. To provide an organization capable of furnishing adequate, timely, and reliable intelligence for the Air Force.

10. To furnish aerial photography for cartographic purposes.

11. To develop, in coordination with the other services, tactics, technique, and equipment of interest to the Air Force for amphibious operations and not provided for in Section V, paragraph A4 and paragraph A 11 (c).

12. To develop, in coordination with the other services, doctrines, procedures and equipment employed by Air Force forces in airborne operations.

B. *Collateral Functions.*—The forces developed and trained to perform the primary functions set forth above shall be employed to support and supplement the other services in carrying out their primary functions, where and whenever such participation will result in increased effectiveness and will contribute to the accomplishment of the over-all military objectives. The Joint Chiefs of Staff member of the service having primary responsibility for a function shall be the agent of the Joint Chiefs of Staff to present to that body the requirements and plans for the employment of all forces to carry out the function. He shall also be responsible for presenting to the Joint Chiefs of Staff for final decision any disagreement within the field of his primary responsibility which has not been resolved. This shall not be construed to prevent any member of the Joint Chiefs of Staff from presenting unilaterally any issue of disagreement with another service.. Certain specific collateral functions of the Air Force are listed below:

1. To interdict enemy sea power through air operations.

2. To conduct antisubmarine warfare and to protect shipping.

3. To conduct aerial mine-laying operations.

SECTION VII.—GLOSSARY OF TERMS AND DEFINITIONS

The usual and accepted definitions and interpretations of the English language, as contained in Webster's New International Dictionary (Unabridged), are applicable to this document, except that for purposes of clarity and to ensure a common understanding of its intent, certain words and phrases are defined specifically as follows:

Air Defense.—All measures designed to nullify or reduce the effectiveness of the attack of hostile aircraft or guided missiles after they are airborne.

Air Superiority.—That degree of capability (preponderance in morale and material) of one air force over another which permits the conduct of air operations by the former at a given time and place without prohibitive interference by the opposing air force.

Air Supremacy.—That degree of air superiority wherein the opposing air force is incapable of effective interference.

Amphibious Operation.—An attack launched from the sea by naval and landing forces embarked in ships or craft involving a landing on a hostile shore. An amphibious operation includes final preparation of the objective area for the landing and operations of naval, air, and ground elements in over-water movements, assault, and mutual support. An amphibious operation may precede a large-scale land operation, in which case it becomes the amphibious phase of a joint amphibious operation. After the troops are landed and firmly established ashore the operation becomes a land operation.

Antisubmarine Operations.—Operations contributing to the conduct of antisubmarine warfare.

Antisubmarine Warfare.—Operations conducted against submarines, their supporting forces and operating bases.

Base.—A locality from which operations are projected or supported. May be preceded by a descriptive word such as "air" or "submarine", which indicates primary purpose.

Close Air Support.—The attack by aircraft of hostile ground or naval targets which are so close to friendly forces as to require detailed integration of each air mission with the fire and movement of those forces.

Functions.—Responsibilities, missions, and tasks.

In coordination with.—In consultation with. This expression means that agencies "coordinated with" shall participate actively; that their concurrence shall be sought; and that if concurrence is not obtained, the disputed matter shall be referred to the next higher authority in which all participants have a voice.

Joint.—As used in this paper, and generally among the Armed Forces, connotes activities, operations, organizations, etc., in which elements of more than one service of the [Department of Defense] participate.

Military.—A term used in its broadest sense meaning of or pertaining to war or the affairs of war, whether Army, Navy, or Air Force.

Naval Campaign.—An operation or a connected series of operations conducted essentially by naval forces including all surface, subsurface, air, amphibious, and Marines, for the purpose of gaining, extending, or maintaining control of the sea.

Operation.—A military action, or the carrying out of a military mission, strategic, tactical, service, training, or administrative; the process of carrying on combat on land, on sea, or in the air, including movement, supply, attack, defense, and maneuvers needed to gain the objectives of any battle or campaign.

Strategic Air Operations.—Air operations contributing to the conduct of strategic air warfare.

Strategic Air Warfare.—Air combat and supporting operations designed to effect, through the systematic application of force to a selected series of vital targets, the progressive destruction and disintegration of the enemy's war-making capacity to a point where he no longer retains the ability or the will to wage war. Vital targets may include key manufacturing systems, sources of raw material, critical material, stock piles, power systems, transportation systems, communications facilities, concentration of uncommitted elements of enemy armed forces, key agricultural areas, and other such target systems.

/s/ C. E. WILSON
Secretary of Defense

[1] The word "general" was deleted.

[2] "and the Chief of Staff to the Commander in Chief, if there be one" was deleted.

[3] "to include the direction of all combat operations" was deleted.

[4] "and to authorize commanders thereof to establish such subordinate unified commands as may be necessary" was deleted.

[5] The former paragraph 7 was deleted. It read as follows: "7. To designate, as necessary, one of their members as their executive agent for: (a) A Unified Command; (b) Certain operations, and specified commands; (c) The development of special tactics, technique, and equipment, except as otherwise provided herein; and (d) The conduct of joint training, except as otherwise provided herein.

[6] The word "assign" was deleted.

[7] The word "members" was deleted.

BIBLIOGRAPHY

A. Selected Chronological List of Key Documents Hearings, and Reports, 1944-1955

This list does not purport to be comprehensive. The selections are based on the following criteria: (a) general accessibility; (b) usefulness as a source of information; and (c) influence on the development of the national security structure.

1944 *Proposal to Establish a Single Department of Armed Forces, Hearings,* House Select Committee on Postwar Military Policy, 78th Cong., 2d. Sess., 1944. (Woodrum Committee)

1945 *Department of Armed Forces, Department of Military Security, Hearings,* Senate Military Affairs Committee, 79th Cong., 1st Sess., 1945, including pp. 411-439: *Report of the Joint Chiefs of Staff Special Committee for Reorganization of National Defense,* April 1945. (The Richardson Committee)

1945 *Department of State Bulletin,* "The State-War-Navy Coordinating Committee", Vol. XIII, 1945, No. 333, p. 745.

1945 *Report to the Honorable James Forrestal on Unification of the War and Navy Departments and Postwar Organization for National Security, Senate Committee on Naval Affairs,* October 22, 1945. (The Eberstadt Report)

1945 Message from the President, December 19, 1945, H. Doc. No. 392, 79th Cong.

1946 *Hearings on S. 2044* Senate Committee on Naval Affairs, 79th Cong., 2d Sess., 1946.

1947 Communication from the President to Congress, H. Doc. No. 56, 80th Cong., 1947.

1947 *The National Security Act of 1947, Hearings on H. R. 2319,* House Committee on Expenditures in the Executive Departments, 80th Cong., 1st Sess., 1947.

1947 *The National Defense Establishment, Hearings on S. 758,* Senate Armed Forces Committee, 80th Cong., 1st Sess., 1947, including Executive Order 9877 (12 F.R. 147) on roles and missions.

1947 *Conference Report on the National Security Act of 1947,* H. Rep. No. 1051, 80th Cong., 1947.

1947 *The National Security Act of 1947* (P.L. 253, July 26, 1947, 80th Cong., 1947 61 Stat. 495, 50 U.S.C. 401). (See Appendix II, *supra.*)

1948 *First Report of the Secretary of Defense,* Washington 1948. (Subsequent Annual and Semi-Annual Reports of the Secretary of Defense—which include reports by the Secretaries of the Military Departments—are not listed hereafter.)

1948 "Functions of the Armed Forces and the Joint Chiefs of Staff," Secretary of Defense Memorandum, 21 April 1948. (The Key West Agreements; DOD Directive No. 5100.1 16 March 1954; See Appendix III *supra.*)

1949 *Report of the Commission on Organization of the Executive Branch of the Government,* 1949, (The Hoover Commission) including Appendices G (report of the Task Force on National Security Organization) and H (report of the Task Force on Foreign Affairs).

1949   *National Security Act Amendments of 1949*, Senate Committee on Armed Services, Report No. 366, 81st Cong., 1st Sess., 1949.

1949   *Reorganizing Fiscal Management in the National Military Establishment*, House Committee on Armed Services, H. Rep. No. 1064, 81st Cong., 1st Sess., 1949.

1949   The National Security Act Amendments of 1949 (P.L. 216, August 10, 1949, 81st Cong. (63 *Stat.* 578, 5 U.S.C. Supp. 171)

1949   *National Defense Program—Unification and Strategy, Hearings*, House Committee on Armed Services, 81st Cong., 1st Sess., 1949.

1950   *Unification and Strategy, Report*, House Committee on Armed Services, House Doc. No. 600, 81st Cong., 2nd Sess., 1950. (B-36 Investigation)

1951   *The Military Situation in the Far East, Hearings*, Senate Committees on Armed Services and Foreign Relations, 82nd Cong., 1st Sess., 1951. (The MacArthur Hearings)

1951   *Hearings on S. 677*, Senate Committee on Armed Services, 82nd Cong., 1st Sess., 1951. (Marine Corps Bill)

1951   *The Administration of Foreign Affairs and Overseas Operations*, Brookings Institution, U.S. Bureau of the Budget, Washington 1951.

1952   Letter, Secretary of Defense Lovett to President Truman, November 18, 1952. (*Army-Navy-Air Force Journal*, Vol. 90, p. 725.)

1953   *Report of the Rockefeller Committee on Department of Defense Organization*, April 11, 1953. (Committee Print, Senate Committee on Armed Services, 83d Cong., 1st Sess.)

1953   *Reorganization Plan No. 6 of 1953, Hearings on H. J. Res. 264*, House Committee on Government Operations, 83d Cong., 1st Sess., 1953, including The President's Message and the text of Reorganization Plan No. 6 of 1953. (See Appendix III, supra.)

1955   Commission on Organization of the Executive Branch of Government, (The Hoover Commission) *Report on Business Organization of the Department of Defense; Report on Overseas Economic Operations*, June 1955. (The *Final Report* of the Commission to Congress contains a list of the task force and committee reports, many of which were concerned with aspects of national security.)

B.   Selected List of Books and Articles by Subject.

POLITICO-MILITARY COORDINATION

Air War College: *White House Strategy Making Machinery* (Col. Wendell E. Little, USAF) Air University Press, Maxwell Air Force Base, Alabama, 1954.

Finletter, Thomas K.: *Power and Policy*, Harcourt Brace, New York, 1954.

Kingston-McCloughry, E. J.: *The Direction of War*, Jonathan Cape, London, 1955.

May, Ernest R.: "The Development of Political-Military Consultation in the United States," *Political Science Quarterly*, Vol. LXX, No. 2 June 1955, pp. 161-180.

Sapin, Burton, and Snyder, Richard: *The Role of the Military in American Foreign Policy*, Doubleday and Co., New York, 1954.

Souers, Sidney W.: "Policy Formulation for National Security," *American Political Science Review*, Vol. XLIII, No. 3, June 1949.

THE PRESIDENT AND THE EXECUTIVE OFFICE

Brownlow, Louis: *The President and the Presidency*, Public Administration Service, Chicago, 1949.

Corwin, Edward S.: *The President, Office and Powers*, 3d Edition, New York University Press, New York, 1948.

Donovan, Robert J.: *Eisenhower—The Inside Story*, Harper and Brothers, New York, 1956.

Hobbs, Edward H.: *Behind the President, A Study of Executive Office Agencies*, Public Affairs Press, Washington, 1954.

Koenig, Louis, Editor: *The Truman Administration*, New York University Press, New York, 1956. (Selected speeches and documents.)

Rovere, Richard H.: *Affairs of State: The Eisenhower Years*, Farrar, Straus, & Cudahy, New York, 1956.

Sherwood, Robert E.: *Roosevelt and Hopkins: An Intimate History*, Harper & Brothers, New York, 1948.

Truman, Harry S.: *The Truman Memoirs:* Volume I, *Year of Decisions*, 1955, Volume II, *Years of Trial and Hope*, 1956, Doubleday & Co., New York.

THE BUDGET

Huzar, Elias: *The Purse and the Sword*, Cornell University Press, Ithaca, 1950.

Knight, Charlotte: "Mystery Man of the Pentagon", *Colliers*, January 22, 1954, pp. 30-36. (About Wilfred J. McNeil, Defense Comptroller).

Smithies, Arthur: *The Budgetary Process in the United States*, Mc-Graw-Hill, New York, 1955.

INTELLIGENCE

Harkness, Richard and Gladys: "The Mysterious Doings of CIA", *Saturday Evening Post*, October 30, November 6 and 13, 1954.

Hillsman, Roger: *Strategic Intelligence and National Decisions*, The Free Press, 1956

Kent, Sherman: *Strategic Intelligence*, Princeton University Press, Princeton, 1951.

THE NATIONAL SECURITY COUNCIL

Anderson, Dillon: "The President and National Security", *Atlantic Monthly*, January, 1956, pp. 42-46.

Cutler, Robert: "The Development of the National Security Council", *Foreign Affairs*, April 1956, pp. 441-458.

Fischer, John: *Master Plan U.S.A.*, Harper & Brothers, New York, 1951, Chapter II.

Krock, Arthur: "The NSC's Development Under Cutler", The *New York Times* March 18, 1955.

Leviero, Anthony: " 'Untouchable, Unreachable, and Unquotable' That Sums up Robert Cutler, the President's Alter Ego on the National Security Council", *New York Times Magazine*, January 30, 1955.

Wyeth, George A., Jr.: "The National Security Council," *Journal of International Affairs*, Columbia University, Vol. VIII, No. 2, 1954, pp. 186-195.

FOREIGN POLICY AND FOREIGN AID

American Assembly: *The Representation of the United States Abroad*, Columbia University, Graduate School of Business, New York, 1956, especially Part 6.

Brookings Institution: *The Administration of Foreign Affairs and Overseas Operations*, Washington, Government Printing Office, 1951.

Brown, W. A., Jr., and Opie, Redvers: *American Foreign Assistance,* The Brookings Institution, Washington, 1953.

Cheever, D. S. and Haviland, H. F.: *American Foreign Policy and the Separation of Powers,* Harvard University Press, Cambridge, 1952.

Elliott, William Y., Ed., Report of a Study Group, Woodrow Wilson Foundation: *The Political Economy of American Foreign Policy,* Holt, New York, 1955; *U.S. Foreign Policy: Its Organization and Control,* Columbia University Press, New York, 1952.

McCamy, James L.: *The Administration of American Foreign Affairs,* Knopf, New York, 1950.

Macmahon, Arthur W.: *Administration in Foreign Affairs,* University of Alabama Press, Alabama, 1953.

Snyder, Richard C. and Furniss, Edgar S., Jr.: *American Foreign Policy,* Rinehart, New York, 1954.

UNIFICATION

Air University: *Unification of the Armed Forces* (R. Earl McClendon, Documentary Research Division) Maxwell Air Force Base, Alabama, 1952.

Arnold, H. H.: *Global Mission,* Hutchinson & Co., London, 1951.

Cline, Ray S. and Matloff, Maurice: "Development of War Department Views on Unification," *Military Affairs,* Vol. XIII (1950).

Forrestal James, *The Forrestal Diaries,* Walter Millis Ed., with E. S. Duffield, The Viking Press, New York, 1951.

Huie, William B.: *The Fight for Air Power,* L. B. Fischer, New York, 1942.

Knox, Dudley W.: "Development of Unification", *U.S. Naval Institute Proceedings,* LXXVI, pp. 1309-1315, December 1950.

Moran, Charles: "Security by Enactment," *U.S. Naval Institute Proceedings,* LXXIV, 1948.

Nelson, Otto L.: *National Security and the General Staff,* Infantry Journal Press, Washington, 1954.

Pitzer, J. M.: "The Nature of Command", *The Army Combat Forces Journal,* December 1955, p. 19.

Stimson, Henry L. and Bundy, McGeorge: *On Active Service in Peace and War,* Harper & Brothers, New York, 1947.

CIVIL-MILITARY RELATIONS

Committee on Civil-Military Relations Research, Social Science Research Council: *Civil Military Relations* (an annotated bibliography) Columbia University Press, New York, 1954.

Huntington, Samuel P.: *The Soldier and the State: The Theory and Politics of Civil-Military Relations,* to be published early in 1957 by Harvard University Press, Cambridge.

Katzenbach, Edward L., Jr.: *The Pentagon and the Hill: A Study of The Role of Congress in the Formulation of Military Policy,* to be published early in 1957.

Kerwin, Jerome G., Ed., *Civil-Military Relationships in American Life,* University of Chicago Press, Chicago, 1948.

Smith, Louis: *American Democracy and Military Power,* University of Chicago Press, Chicago, 1951.

Tansill, William R.: "The Concept of Civil Supremacy over the Military in the United States", *Public Affairs Bulletin* No. 94, The Legislative Reference Service, Library of Congress, Washington, 1951.

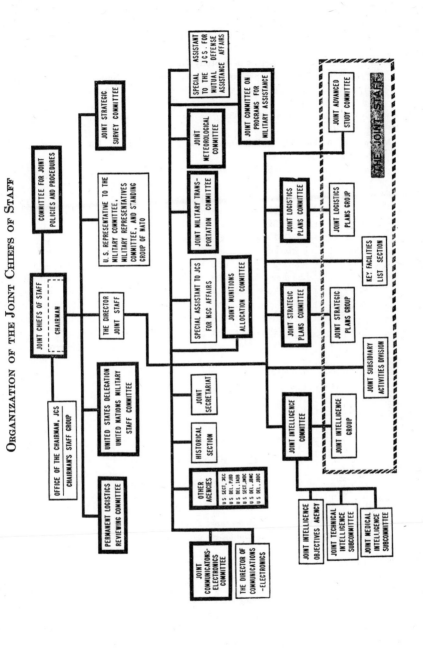

THE ORGANIZATION FOR NATIONAL SECURITY

EXECUTIVE OFFICE OF THE PRESIDENT

The President*
Vice President*

The White House | Office--Special Assistants

| Staff | NSC | PL.BD. | OCB | BOB** | ODM* | CEA |

CIA

Consultants

*Statutory NSC member
**Usually represented at NSC meetings

Secy State*
S T A T E
I C A

The Cabinet

8 other Executive Depts

Treasury**
Justice**
Post Office
Interior
Agriculture
Commerce
Labor
HE & W

36 other independent agencies

USIA**

AEC**

SECRETARY OF DEFENSE
DEPUTY SECRETARY OF DEFENSE

JOINT SECRETARIES

SPECIAL ASSISTANTS (as designated)

ARMED FORCES POLICY COUNCIL

GENERAL COUNSEL

ASSISTANT SECRETARY OF DEFENSE (Comptroller)

ASSISTANT SECRETARY OF DEFENSE (Manpower and Personnel)

DEFENSE FORCES POLICY BOARD

ASSISTANT SECRETARY OF DEFENSE (Research and Development)

ASSISTANT SECRETARY OF DEFENSE (Application Engineering)

ASSISTANT SECRETARY OF DEFENSE (Supply and Logistics)

JOINT CHIEFS OF STAFF

ASSISTANT SECRETARY OF DEFENSE (International Security Affairs)

ASSISTANT SECRETARY OF DEFENSE (Legislative and Public Affairs)

ASSISTANT SECRETARY OF DEFENSE (Properties and Installations)

ASSISTANT SECRETARY OF DEFENSE (Health and Medical)

ASSISTANT TO THE SECRETARY (Atomic Energy)

COMMAND
LINE

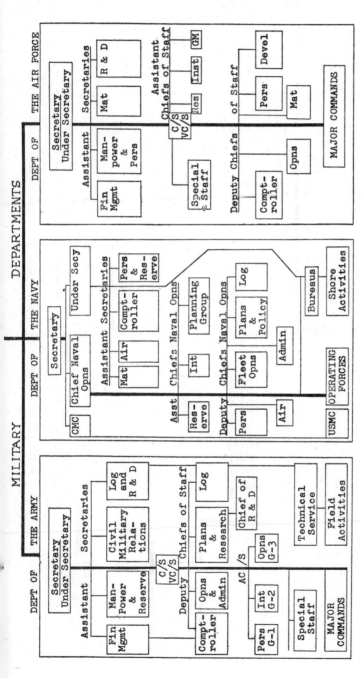

MILITARY DEPARTMENTS

Admin: Administration. AEC: Atomic Energy Commission. C/S: Chief of Staff; (VC/S—Vice). CEA: Council of Economic Advisers. CIA: Central Intelligence Agency. CMC: Commandant, U.S. Marine Corps. Devel: Development. Fin Mgmt: Financial Management. GM: Guided Missiles. HE&W: Health, Education and Welfare. ICA: International Cooperation Administration. Int: Intelligence. Log: Logistics. Mat: Material. NSC: National Security Council. OCB: Operations Coordinating Board. ODM: Office of Defense Mobilization. Pers: Personnel.

PL.BD: NSC Planning Board. R & D: Research and Development. Res: Reserve. USIA: United States Information Agency. USMC: United States Marine Corps. The Army portion of the chart does not reflect changes of recent months. The AC/SG-1 became ADC/S Personnel and the AC/S G-3 was eliminated. A Director of R & D now ranks with the Assistant Secretaries and the Chief of R & D with the DC/S. Special staff offices were regrouped to report through the appropriate DC/S.

INTERNATIONAL SECURITY AFFAIRS

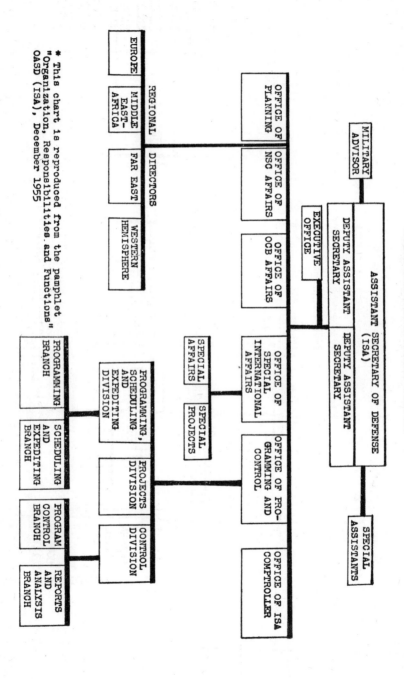

* This chart is reproduced from the pamphlet "Organization, Responsibilities and Functions" OASD (ISA), December 1955.

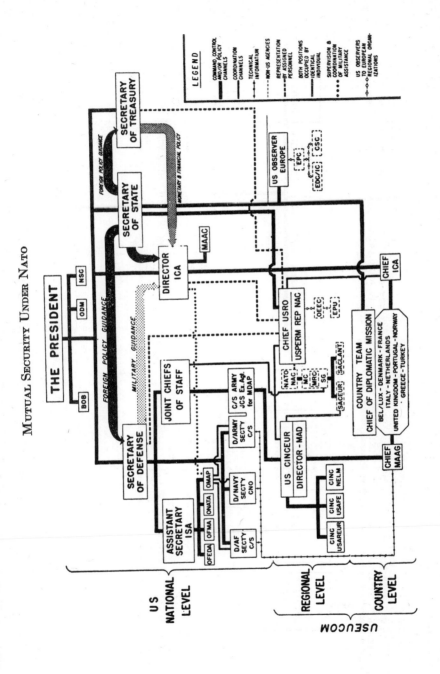

INDEX

ABDA *see* Unified command
Adams, Sherman, 18
Air Force, 11, 12, 68, 75, 76, 86, 97n; Assistant Secretary of, 52; and Key West Agreement, 88-89; organization chart of, 195.
Almond, Gen. Edward M., 4
Ambassador to U.N., 31
Ammunition shortages, Korea, 102
Anderson, Dillon, 31, 36n, 37n
Anderson, Robert, 53
ARCADIA Conference, 71
Arends, Rep. Leslie C., 105
Armed Forces Policy Council, 46, 57, 118
Armed Forces Reserve Act of 1955, 23, 25, 124n, 127
Army, 8, 11, 48, 67-68, 111; Chief of Staff, 54; in Key West Agreement, 88; organization chart of, 195; reorganization, 129; role in ISA, 51-54; unification plans, 73-75; "unity of command," 86
Army aviation, 96n
Arnold, Gen. H. H., 71
Atomic energy, 6, 116, 149. *See also* Joint Committee on Atomic Energy
Atomic Energy Commission, 22, 25, 36n, 89, 114, 116
Atomic warfare, 89, 95, 134
Austria, occupation of, 10

B-36 investigation, 85, 91, 94, 97n, 135
Berlin blockade, 60, 89
Board of National Estimates, 21
Bonesteel, Brig. Gen. Charles H., III, 60n
British defense organization, 143-52
British military organization, 65, 93
Brookings Institute, 38, 42
Budget, defense, 118-19, 144
Budget Bureau, 19-20, 78
Burke, Adm. Arleigh A., 134
Burns, Arthur, 19
Bush, Vannevar, 102
Business and Defense Services Administration, 24
Byrnes, James F., 38

Cabinet, 9, 17, 26n, 143, 151
"Carte Blanche," 6, 13n
Casablanca Conference, 9
Central Intelligence Agency (CIA), 12, 20-22, 35
Central Intelligency Agency Act, 20
Cheever, Daniel S., 43n
Chiefs of Staff *see* Joint Chiefs of Staff
Churchill, Winston, 3, 71, 146, 148
Civil affairs officers in Germany, 10

Civil Defense officials, 31
Civil Service Commission, 17
Civilian-military relations, 56, 66, 71-77; in OSD, 111, 127, 128, 129-30
Clark, Gen. Mark W., 10
Clay, Gen., Lucius D., 10
Coast Guard, U.S., 24, 111
Cold war, 7, 37n, 43, 58
Collins, Lt. Gen. J. Lawton, 74
Collins Plan, 74, 80, 137
Combined Chiefs of Staff, 9, 71, 152
Commander-in-Chief, 14-15
Commerce, U.S. Department of, 24.*See also* Maritime Commission
Commission on Organization of the Executive Branch, 1949, 38, 90
Committee on Administrative Management, 17
Committee on Government Organization, President's Advisory, 19
Committee of Imperial Defense, Great Britain, 11, 145, 148
Committee on International Information Activities, 33
Communist objectives, 7
Congress, U.S., criticizes defense, 101-03; establishes Hoover Commission, 28; and NSC, 33; and OSD, 113; and presidency, 15-16; and Rockefeller Report, 105-06; role in national security, 7; special agencies of, 17; and State Department, 39, 41
Congressional investigations, 39
Constitution, U.S., and the presidency, 14-15
Consultants of National Security Council, 31
Crommelin, Capt. John G., 98n
Council of Economic Advisors, 18-19
Council on Foreign Economic Policy, 26n
Council of Foreign Ministers, 10
Council of National Defense, 8
Country Plan *see* OCB
Cutler, Gen. Robert, 26n, 31, 34, 36n; as Special Assistant to the President, 30

Dawes, Charles G., 20
Defense, Department of (DOD), 17, 22, 33, 45 ff, 65, 89, 92, 99, 127, 137; comptrollers, 93; Directive, 121; Instruction, 121; organization chart, 194; political pressures on, 65-66. *See also* Munitions Board
Defense Cataloging and Standardization Act, 101
Defense Mobilization Board, 23, 24
Defense policy, U.S. and British, 143-45

198